FEARING THE BLACK BODY

Fearing the Black Body

The Racial Origins of Fat Phobia

Sabrina Strings

NEW YORK UNIVERSITY PRESS
New York

NEW YORK UNIVERSITY PRESS
New York
www.nyupress.org

References to Internet websites (URLs) were accurate at the time of writing. Neither the author nor New York University Press is responsible for URLs that may have expired or changed since the manuscript was prepared.

Library of Congress Cataloging-in-Publication Data
Names: Strings, Sabrina, author.
Title: Fearing the black body : the racial origins of fat phobia / Sabrina Strings.
Description: New York, NY : New York University Press, [2019] |
Includes bibliographical references and index.
Identifiers: LCCN 2018026988| ISBN 9781479819805 (cl : alk. paper) |
ISBN 9781479886753 (pb : alk. paper)
Subjects: LCSH: Feminine beauty (Aesthetics)—Social aspects—United States. |
African American women—Social conditions. | Overweight women—United States—
Social conditions. | Obesity—Social aspects—United States.
Classification: LCC HQ1220.U5 S77 2019 | DDC 305.48/896073—dc23
LC record available at https://lccn.loc.gov/2018026988

New York University Press books are printed on acid-free paper, and their binding materials are chosen for strength and durability. We strive to use environmentally responsible suppliers and materials to the greatest extent possible in publishing our books.

Manufactured in the United States of America

10 9 8 7 6 5 4 3 2 1

Also available as an ebook

For my grandmother Alma Jean Green

CONTENTS

Introduction

The Original Epidemic

"Actually Starving! A Prominent New York Man Dies in Sight of Food. Why Could This Be So!" This dramatic if slightly awkward headline appeared in the February 16, 1894, edition of the *New York Times*, atop an article that began, "Thousands of men and women in New York are starving, although they have plenty of money to buy the best food!"

The unnamed author of the article went on to quote what was described as a "prominent physician" on the state of the American diet and physique. According to the doctor, the situation was dire. "I say . . . that they are starving to death—slowly, but surely," he stated, adding that although many of those afflicted were members of the middle and upper classes, they nevertheless looked "emaciated [and] appear to be consumptives."[1]

This article underscored the deep anxiety felt by many in the nineteenth-century regarding the state of the American physique. Doctors in particular agonized over what they described as the "pale, thin, and puny" forms that were apparently proliferating around the country. Several described with horror the "narrow chests, and lank limbs, and flabby muscles, and tottering steps [that] meet us at every corner."[2] Thinness, it seems, was nothing short of an epidemic.

If in those years slenderness was considered a general American failing, the paleness, leanness, and malnutrition of women was particularly troubling. Prompted by the fragile state of their bodies, esteemed doctors wrote disquieting manifestos on the question of their frailty.

The writings of the prolific and well-regarded New Englander Dr. William Alcott, a distant relative of the novelist Louisa May Alcott, were typical. In his 1855 treatise *The Young Woman's Book of Health*, Alcott lamented the reality that "our children, females among the rest, are trained

Figure I.1. "Actually Starving," *New York Times*,
Feb. 16, 1894.

by a community which is thus destitute of a true appetite."[3] He warned
Americans to take heed of what he described as the "whole generation of
women trained as a whole to tenderness, delicacy, nervousness, feeble-
ness of muscle [and] want of appetite."[4] Being "tall, slender and delicate,"
he claimed, did not prepare a young woman for the vicissitudes of life.[5]

Dr. John Harvey Kellogg, the famed Seventh-day Adventist already
known for his sanitarium in Battle Creek, Michigan, but not yet known
as a purveyor of breakfast cereals, concluded in his *Ladies' Guide in
Health and Disease*, "Particularly in this country, and especially in the
cities and towns, girls as a rule are found to be decidedly lacking in
physical development."[6] What the fair sex in America needed, Kellogg
contended, was a nutritional revolution because their poor eating habits
produced bodies that were "scrawny" and "waspish."[7]

It was more than a simple question of health or even aesthetics. The
slenderness of American girls was regarded as nothing less than a threat
to the nation. An 1888 article from the *Washington Post* that appeared

under the headline "Are Girls Growing Smaller?" exclaimed, "The girl of the period ranges from 140 pounds down in some cases to 80 pounds or less. . . . In England and Germany the figures are higher. . . . Eighty pounds of femininity is of course, not much." And, the writer added, "our women will go on getting thinner and thinner until they disappear. It has happened in Boston already. The American stock . . . can't hold its own against the big-boned strong-built foreigner. The Irish have crowded the Yankee out of New England."[8]

The weight of American women represented, to many, a national black eye. But was it truly the case, as was often suggested, that these women were simply nutritionally uninformed? Given the right information, would they gain in flesh and, by proxy, in health, strength, and beauty?

The evidence suggests otherwise. Many well-to-do women it seems were trying to be slender at a moment when doctors routinely attacked slenderness as unhealthy.[9] The historian Adele Clarke noted that women of the fashionable classes were "wasting in style."[10] The svelte style, being contrary to conventional medical wisdom, had clearly been motivated by other factors.

Indeed, while many considered thinness an American shortcoming, for the adherents of the style, slenderness served as a marker of moral, racial, and national superiority. This attitude is on full dsiplay in an 1896 article from *Harper's Bazaar* titled "Are Our Women Scrawny?" It begins with a reflection on the slenderness of American women: "American women in general are still thought to be sallow and scrawny." The article's anonymous author contests this assertion, claiming that while poorer women may be malnourished, few women of the privileged classes are so slim as to look peaked, as may have been the case with their foremothers. Today, the author asserts, American women have a "wholesome glow in their cheek" and a bit more flesh on their bones, both of which are a testament to the "wholly unmeasured success" of the American experiment.[11]

Yet, while praising a new and laudable "roundness" to the figure of the modern girl, the author nevertheless betrays a preference for traditional American slenderness. Of the shifting outlines of the nation's women, the author wrote, "One cannot help noticing in every metropolitan assembly that the feminine litheness and flexibility for

Figure I.2. "Are Our Women Scrawny?," *Harper's Bazaar*, Nov. 1896.

which the republic has been famous is already on the wane, and that the opposite extreme is menacing."[12]

That fatness is described as "menacing" is telling. The author provides a sense of the foreboding associated with excess weight. Not only does stoutness supposedly sabotage the nation's aesthetic identity, it also evokes the poor eating habits and immorality of the European elite. Worse still, extreme or "gross" corpulence slides into an association with primitive Africans. The author spells this out for the reader: "Stoutness, corpulence, and surplusage of flesh" are never desirable "except among African savages."[13]

This raises several questions. First, what led some well-to-do Americans to believe that slenderness, especially among women, was both aesthetically preferable and a sign of national identity? How did fatness become a sign of immorality? How did fatness become linked to

"Africanity" or blackness? And finally, if the medical establishment just over a century ago feared the meagerness of the physiques of (elite white) women, when and how did they come to view fatness, especially among black women, as the greater threat to public health, as they would in the late twentieth and early twenty-first centuries with the "obesity epidemic"?

In this book, I examine the history and legacy of the preference for slimness and aversion to fatness, with attention to their racial, gender, class, and medical contours. This book enters a decades-long conversation about the preference for slenderness and the phobia about fatness in the United States. Much of this research describes the emphasis on slenderness for "women."[14] But while most authors show that an aversion to fatness and a preference for slenderness has been most evident among middle- and upper-class white women, few have addressed the role of race and class status in the development of these dispositions.

Relatedly, scholars have shown that the fear of fatness commonly targets low-income women of color, and especially black women.[15] These and other scholars, including Sander Gilman, Jennifer Morgan, and Janell Hobson, have shown that black women's bodies have long been treated as being in "excess."[16] Still, few have attempted to explain how, historically, fatness became linked to blackness. Amy Farrell's 2011 book *Fat Shame* stands out in that it underscores the entwined racial past of fat stigma and the thin ideal. The book does not explore, however, how these racial connotations developed, nor does it explain the centrality of anti-blackness within them.

We also learn little about the role of morality in much of the existing literature. R. Marie Griffith's landmark 2004 text *Born Again Bodies: Flesh and Spirit in American Christianity* shines in this respect, offering a compellingly deep dive into the admonitions against gluttony and fatness in Christianity. Nevertheless, though it reveals that during the nineteenth century the fit body was used to buttress claims of racial and ethnic superiority, questions remain about how these relationships developed and were popularized within the American mainstream.

This work departs from much of the existing scholarship in that it provides a historiography of the development of pro-thin, anti-fat biases. That is, while several studies have explored the historical antecedents of our contemporary size biases, none, to my knowledge, have endeavored a historical analysis that examines the key figures involved in their propagation, as well as the sociocultural and political factors contributing to their reinforcement. This book seeks to address this gap as possibly the first historical study of fat phobia and thin fetishism in the West, with an emphasis on the intertwined racial, gender, and moral issues involved in their advancement.

I argue that two critical historical developments contributed to a fetish for svelteness and a phobia about fatness: the rise of the transatlantic slave trade and the spread of Protestantism. Racial scientific rhetoric about slavery linked fatness to "greedy" Africans. And religious discourse suggested that overeating was ungodly.

These rationales for anti-fat bias had been circulating relatively independently in parts of western Europe for more than two centuries. Not until the early nineteenth century in the United States, in the context of slavery, religious revivals, and the massive immigration of persons deemed "part-Africanoid," did these notions come together under a coherent ideology. In the United States, fatness became stigmatized as both black and sinful. And by the early twentieth century, slenderness was increasingly promoted in the popular media as the correct embodiment for white Anglo-Saxon Protestant women. Not until after these associations were already in place did the medical establishment begin its concerted effort to combat "excess" fat tissue as a major public health initiative. In this way, the phobia about fatness and the preference for thinness have not, principally or historically, been about health. Instead, they have been one way the body has been used to craft and legitimate race, sex, and class hierarchies.

These findings further reveal that the slender ideal and fat phobia are not distinct developments—as they are often treated in the literature. The fear of the imagined "fat black woman" was created by racial and religious ideologies that have been used to both degrade black women *and* discipline white women. This is critical, since most analyses of race and aesthetics describe the experiences of either black people (and other people of color) or white people. This book reveals race to be a double agent. It entails the synchronized repression of "savage" blackness and the generation of disciplined whiteness. The discourse of fatness as "coarse," "immoral," and "black" worked to denigrate black women, and it concomitantly became the impetus for the promulgation of slender figures as the proper form of embodiment for elite white Christian women.

For my analysis, I draw on the work of two eminent social theorists, Pierre Bourdieu and Michel Foucault. According to Bourdieu, elites are constantly working to differentiate themselves from the lower classes. In so doing, they often distinguish themselves by cultivating tastes, diets, and physical appearances that are in opposition to those of the subordinated groups. These "social distinctions" serve to naturalize and normalize social hierarchies.[17]

Building on this work, I show how racial discourse was deployed by elite Europeans and white Americans to create social distinctions between themselves and so-called greedy and fat racial Others. Black people, as well as so-called degraded or hybrid whites (e.g., Celtic Irish, southern Italians, Russians), were primary targets of these arguments. Elite white people also used Protestant discourse to claim a moral superiority over these same poor, immigrant, and racial Others. I rely on the work of gender scholars to show that since women have long been evaluated based largely on their physical appearance, racial-moral social distinctions primarily targeted the women in each racial/ethnic group.[18]

If Bourdieu can help us understand the racial-moral dimension of the spread of fat aversion and thin preoccupation, Michel Foucault gives us insight into the centrality of medicine in the propagation of these dispositions. According to Foucault, medicine intervenes as a key institution of the twentieth century, providing information on "how to live" for health and longevity. Its dictates inform what Foucault calls the "biopolitics" of health management, which include disciplinary practices that one must perform to be considered a healthy and thereby good citizen. However, the medical disciplinary regime has not been objectively applied to all persons. Instead, it is treated as an imperative for dominant groups, to the exclusion of poor, racially Othered groups. This approach helps to maintain social and in many instances specifically racialized and gendered hierarchies.[19]

* * *

Researching the aesthetic, moral, and racial underpinnings of the American fear of fat required an eclectic approach. I began by reading the landmark texts by historians and feminist scholars on the history of fat phobia and the slender ideal.[20] In doing so, I discovered three points of agreement. First, there was a general consensus among historians and prominent feminist scholars that the fear of fat and glorification of thinness first gained widespread appeal in the United States. Second, these attitudes had more impact on elite and white women than on men, working-class persons, or people of color. Third, little is known about the factors contributing to the development of these attitudes.

In an effort to discover what led to the consolidation of these attitudes around the turn of the twentieth century, I used two comparative historical methods: process tracing and historical narrative. In process tracing, I used multiple sources of data to shed light on key individuals and events contributing to the growing anti-fat, pro-thin biases in the West. I used historical narrative to weave a tapestry illustrating the impact and interrelationship of these events.

I began with the Renaissance, a period in which, as sociologists and historians have shown, voluptuous physiques were in vogue throughout much of the Western world.[21] I traced developments in art and philosophy from the Renaissance through the Enlightenment in Europe, the period in which, scholars have shown, svelte aristocratic women and courtiers were commonly depicted by renowned artists and thinkers. I studied the writings of artists and philosophers in an effort to describe the sociohistorical and intellectual context for the association of race, weight, and beauty between the early fifteenth and late eighteenth centuries.

Questions concerning the purported racial origin of fatness appeared in many philosophical treatises, as did questions about its (im)morality. Therefore, I returned to explorations of the body and the oral appetite in the ascendant branch of Christianity: Protestantism. I examined key texts by prominent Protestant proselytizers, especially those who made public pronouncements against overfeeding and fatness.

To weave a historical narrative of these many related developments in art, philosophy, and religion, I needed to understand how they were being transmitted to the public. The eighteenth century marked the rise of newspapers and magazines in Europe, and so I examined influential early publications, such as *The Spectator*, to understand how ideas in high art and philosophy about body size, race, attractiveness, and morality were represented.

Scholars have identified the United States as the country in which the pro-thin, anti-fat bias was gaining strength among elite, morally upright white Americans (especially women) by the nineteenth century and crystallized into a mainstream position by the early twentieth century. Therefore, I also examined American magazines and newspapers published between 1830 and 1920, among them *Cosmopolitan* (originally a magazine designed to appeal to families), the *New York Times*, and the *Washington Post*, to look for evidence of these connections.

Finally, I discovered that many of the popular periodicals cited concerns about health and illness purportedly associated with corpulence. By the late nineteenth century, these publications relied increasingly on doctors' advice to make their claims. Therefore, I researched the depictions of overweight and obesity in the medical literature from 1880 to 1930. I chose materials that appeared in authoritative books or medical journals, such as the *Journal of the American Medical Association* (*JAMA*), or works written by recognized medical authorities.[22]

This book has three parts. Part 1, "The Beauty of the Robust," offers a retrospective view of the exaltation of plump feminine physiques that existed throughout much of Western history. I also note signs of a shift in the seventeenth century as European men of learning began to degrade fatness as evidence of insipidity. In chapter 1, "Being Venus," I describe Western aesthetic ideals of the sixteenth century and show that key artists and philosophers during the High Renaissance described "plump" and "proportionate" women as beautiful, following Christian and neoclassical conventions of beauty. I argue that contact with African women during the rise of the slave trade did not change these standards. Moreover, I show that black women were incorporated into the High Renaissance rhetoric and imagery of beauty as equally voluptuous, if socially inferior, counterparts to European women. In chapter 2, "Plump Women and Thin, Fine Men," I describe the rise of the robust "snow-white" female body as desirable. I also show that the fat male body became a sign of poor moral character and mental incapacity. That is, alongside the exaltation of fat and curvy (white) women, fat men were lambasted among intellectuals as being of "poor constitution." English philosophers claimed that a fat male body was indicative of a "dull mind." Thus, a philosopher's slim ideal was born.

Part 2, "Race, Weight, God, and Country," describes how body size became a sign of race, morality, and national identity during the eighteenth and nineteenth centuries. In chapter 3, "The Rise of the Big Black Woman," I detail how philosophers and race scientists made the case for intellectual and physical differences between whites and the "colored races." In this period we see some of the earliest examples of learned men denigrating a so-called "black" fatness. In chapter 4, "Birth of the Ascetic Aesthetic," I focus on the developing relationship between Protestant Christian identity and self-abnegation. I show that abstemiousness in England during the eighteenth century laid the groundwork for moralizing surrounding the oral appetites that would be seen in subsequent eras, particularly in the United States. I also show that some devout Protestants viewed fatness—the purported evidence of intemperate eating—as immoral. Slenderness, by contrast, was viewed as closer to godliness. In chapter 5, "American Beauty: The Reign of the Slender Aesthetic," I show that American Anglo-Saxon women adopted the ideals surrounding eating and embodiment that were popularized in eighteenth-century England. In the context of religious health reform movements and the massive immigration of Irish racial Others, Anglo-Saxon women used strict diets and slimness to convey religious enlightenment and racial uplift. In chapter 6, "Thinness as American Exceptionalism," I reveal how the presence of the next wave of immigrants—southern and eastern Europeans—contributed to the mainstream consolidation of the aesthetic of slenderness. Following the trail of race science, I show that a new eugenic discourse of racial amalgamation among northern and western Europeans circulated widely in the late nineteenth and early twentieth centuries. This rhetoric promoted the desirability of women from these racial groups. It also intimated that the American melting pot created exceptional svelte beauties drawn from these superior races.

Part 3, "Doctors Weigh In," examines how the American medical establishment viewed fatness and thinness from the late nineteenth to the late twentieth centuries. In chapter 7, "Good Health to Uplift the Race," I profile the life and works of the esteemed Dr. John Harvey Kellogg. I show that he, like many medical men of his day, regarded poor diet and excessive slimness, especially among elite American women, as a threat to the nation. Kellogg and others hoped to encourage women to gain weight to demonstrate the vigor of the nation. In chapter 8, "Fat,

Revisited," I explain the growth of anti-fat attitudes in the medical field. Due to the rise of actuarial tables that identified excess weight as a health risk, doctors became increasingly concerned about overweight. While the transition was slow at first, the standardization of "normal weight" and an intensified concern about "obesity," especially among women, were firmly established within the mainstream of medical science by the turn of the twenty-first century. In the book's epilogue, "The Obesity Epidemic," I highlight the swing from one epidemic, that of the too-thin American woman, to the other, that of the too-fat American woman, in the span of a century. And I underscore the role that race, aesthetics, morality, and medicine continue to play in the so-called obesity epidemic.

PART I

The Beauty of the Robust

1

Being Venus

I have seen some amongst them whose whole bodies have
been so well-built and handsome that I never beheld finer
figures, nor can I conceive how they might be bettered, so
excellent were their arms, and all their limbs.
—Albrecht Dürer on the African physique, 1528

Her name was Katharina. In her portrait, drawn in 1521, she wears a
simple headdress with a single jewel in the center. Her youth is skillfully
captured in the roundness and fullness of her cheeks. Her plump body
is covered by an unadorned V-neck shirt and a modest, high-collared
frock. The entire effect is one of demure and unassuming beauty. Katharina's eyes are downcast, giving the twenty-year-old an air of solemnity
and gravity that might have seemed out of place were she not a slave.[1]

Katharina lived in Antwerp, Belgium. She was one of two slaves
owned by João Brandão, the trade representative to the king of Portugal. Albrecht Dürer, the renowned Renaissance artist, happened to be
passing through Antwerp in 1521, creating sketches and woodcuts that
he sold around the city. On a brief visit with the Brandão family, he encountered Katharina, and was sufficiently moved by her comeliness to
immortalize her in silverpoint.

The artist's decision to draw the young African woman may have
seemed inconsequential at the time. Hers was one of many sketches of
Africans that Dürer completed during his lifetime. Nevertheless, his
depiction of Katharina was a momentous event. *Portrait of an African
Woman, Katharina* became the first known portrait of a black person
in Antwerp. And it was produced at a time in Dürer's illustrious career
during which, after years of studying the human form, he had come
to the conclusion that what made something beautiful could never be
fully comprehended or definitively laid out. For reasons he could not
describe, Katharina too was a beauty.[2]

Figure 1.1. Albrecht Dürer, *Portrait of an African Woman, Katharina*, 1521. Galleria degli Uffizi, Florence.

A great deal has been written about the aesthetic standards for women that prevailed during the Renaissance. While much of this literature shows that larger, fleshier physiques were prized, it also shows that what was considered attractive was not just about the size of the body, but also its shape. Proportionate and well-rounded physiques were revered, as they were believed to reveal something of the beauty and mystery of divinity. A woman might find herself being considered "too thin" or "too fat," given the prevailing preference for proportionate—often implying "medium"—physiques. But if a lady had to err on one side of the scale, a fat woman was generally preferred to one who might be derisively labeled "lean" or "bony."

Comparatively fewer works, however, have explored how the growing population of black women who came to Europe as part of the slave trade affected representations of female beauty during the High Renaissance (late fifteenth to mid-sixteenth centuries). This is not a minor oversight; the most famous artistic expressions of female beauty during this period derived from northern and western Italy and the Low Countries. The major cities in these regions simultaneously served as key ports of the expanding slave trade. Consequently, black women often appear in meditations on beauty by the era's most important artists.

The burgeoning population of African women as slaves and domestic servants in northern and western Europe between 1490 and 1590 frequently led to the incorporation of black women into the lexicon of what was defined as "perfect female beauty." The inclusion of black women as beautiful in both high art and aesthetic discourse was neither simple nor without problems. African women were described as well-proportioned and plump, and consequently viewed as physically appealing. Yet the burgeoning discourse about Africans suggested that their purported distinctive facial features made them facially unattractive. Black women were further denigrated due to their servile status. Therefore, despite black women's reputation as well-formed beauties, their purported African physiognomy and status as slaves became the early basis of "social distinctions" between low-status African women and their high-status European counterparts.[3]

What follows is a discussion of notions of perfect female beauty in three of the most trafficked centers of artistic ingenuity: western Italy, northern Italy, and the Low Countries. In all three, the correct model of female beauty was a central topic of conversation. Well-apportioned female figures were venerated throughout these areas. However, in two locations—Antwerp, Belgium, and Venice, Italy—the mushrooming population of black women led to their inclusion as beauties of low status and questionable facial allure, but having the right proportions and just enough *embonpoint* to titillate European sensibilities.

* * *

Katharina was known by Dürer simply as the "Mooress."[4] His journal tells us almost nothing about what motivated him to sketch the young African woman, nor do we learn about the duration or substance of their encounter. What we do learn from the journal is that Dürer regarded himself as an artist and philosopher of the human form. As such, he took an exceptional interest in the growing numbers of Africans arriving in northern Europe as part of the slave trade.[5]

By the mid-fifteenth century, African slaves were being shuttled to European ports by the hundreds. The Portuguese, who in the 1440s became the first European nation to enter the African slave trade, maintained a dominant position until 1492, when Columbus made contact with the Americas.[6] Although Spanish and Flemish traders mounted a challenge to the Portuguese slave-trading monopoly between the 1450s and 1470s, by the end of the century most of the Africans making their way into Europe did so in the holds of vessels manned by Portuguese traders. The Portuguese were thus largely responsible for introducing African slaves into northern Europe, and some of the earliest Africans to be seen in the Low Countries arrived as slaves to Portuguese merchants.[7] This appeared to be the case with Katharina and her owner, João Brandão. Antwerp, where they were settled, had been a key trading hub in the fifteenth century. By the sixteenth century, the city became "the center of a new global economy of luxury goods."[8] Slaves themselves were an important form of luxury commodity in the new economy and were common among wealthy merchants.

Dürer's interest in Katharina within this sociocultural milieu was galvanized by his long-professed desire to understand the contours of human beauty. By the time he visited Antwerp in the early sixteenth century, Dürer had abandoned the idea of locating a singular ideal, concluding that beauty was found in the differences between the various peoples of the world. This conception of beauty-in-difference was inspired, in part, by the gospel. In Dürer's reading of the scripture, God had made all of mankind equal. And yet the Creator produced a tremendous amount of human biodiversity. The task of the portraitist, Dürer believed, was to identify the "big differences" between the various nations of mankind. Doing this would help the artist grasp the beauty of humanity in all its fullness and richness. According to Dürer, "The Creator fashioned men once and for all as they *must* [*sic*] be, and I hold that the perfection of form and beauty is contained in the sum of all men."[9]

These sentiments were articulated about the time that Dürer wrote what was titled an "Aesthetic Excursus" detailing the major difference between Africans and Europeans. This document, written sometime between 1512 and 1515, was eventually tacked on to the end of the third book of his *Four Books on Human Proportion,* published posthumously in 1528. At that time, the artist claimed that the major difference between blacks and whites was to be found in the features and attractiveness of the face.

> Thus thou findest two families of mankind, white and black; and a difference between them is to be marked. . . . Negro faces are seldom beautiful because of their very flat noses and thick lips.[10]

This tract was written before Dürer's encounter with Katharina in Antwerp. It is likely that the artist relied on stereotypical accounts of "African physiognomy" that were in circulation during the sixteenth and seventeenth centuries.[11] These accounts served to underscore the African's inferior social position as the slave trade expanded.[12]

Indeed, there is reason to believe that Dürer's disdain for African features in the "Aesthetic Excursus" was at least partly motivated by the general tone of European high art and philosophy at the time. In another of his sketches, the *Berlin Study Sheet,* made during the same period, Dürer drafted a row of humanity that shows "prototypical" faces of the various nations of mankind. The artist placed his version of the "ideal" or "normative" European face at the forefront of humanity.[13] The final "African" visage with its exaggerated features, which some scholars argue represented a cross between a Negro and an ape, looks back warily at the rest of humanity. Historians suggest that Dürer was likely inspired by Leonardo's and other artists' haunting renderings of grotesque wild men.[14]

After his visit to Antwerp, however, Dürer appeared to revise this position. In his *Portrait of Katharina* and his sketch of Rodrigo, a black man and another of João Brandão's slaves, the artist portrayed the models' faces with dignity and solemnity. They also held a type of beauty that the artist suggested he couldn't quite specify.[15]

If Dürer wavered on the question of the black face, he was resolute when it came to the beauty of the black body. Like many artists, Dürer believed that God had bestowed upon Africans a bevy of physical blessings. The limbs of Africans, he claimed, were shapely and well formed. And there was an elegance to be found in their

Figure 1.2. Albrecht Dürer, *Berlin Study Sheet*, 1513. Staatliche Museen zu Berlin.

well-apportioned physiques. In the "Aesthetic Excursus," alongside his derision of the African face, the artist intoned,

> Howbeit I have seen some amongst them whose whole bodies have been so well-built and handsome that I never beheld finer figures, nor can I conceive how they might be bettered, so excellent were their arms, and all their limbs.[16]

His views on the excellence of the black physique and the disfigurement of the black face were based on the reigning definitions of attractiveness. In other words, rather than reflecting any reality about black people, they reflected what Bourdieu called a "judgment of tastes."[17] This is an aesthetic value system crafted by elites that places qualities symbolizing refinement (and a remove from the vulgar, the common, and the low) atop the aesthetic hierarchy. Within the aesthetic system of the High Renaissance, pointed noses and fine lips were typically associated with a refined facial beauty. At the same time, well-formed, proportionate figures represented the height of bodily beauty. This aesthetic pairing led to the degradation of the African face and the exaltation of the African body. It also contributed to Dürer's uncertainty, by the time he rendered the lovely Katharina, about the precise contours of true beauty.

* * *

Dürer did not simply inherit the value system that placed black people in aesthetic limbo. He had, in fact, been one of the key architects of this system, which, by the time he met Katharina, he himself had come to view as insufficient. Nevertheless, that reassessment came toward the end of his career. As a young man in the 1490s, Dürer had made the quest for true beauty his holy grail. He had left his native Germany in the 1490s and settled in Venice, the artistic heart of the Renaissance. It was there that he met the well-known painter and draftsman Jacopo de Barbari. Barbari's exact year and place of birth are unknown, but it is believed that he was born around 1470, making the two artists fairly close in age. They met therefore as peers, rather than as artist and acolyte. But Barbari's techniques in painting the human form inspired and bedeviled the German artist. As a result, Dürer would chase what he considered to be their perfection for the next two decades.

To Dürer, the genius of Barbari's work was that he drew male and female physiques using measurements calibrated to produce "perfect" human proportions. Dürer was in awe. Barbari's approach to beauty had generated images of men and women that were, in Dürer's opinion, stunning, and they quickly eclipsed his preexisting singular ideal of beauty.[18] Bodily beauty, like facial beauty, had a variety of manifestations. But the running theme, the one thing that must be present, Dürer believed, was perfect proportionality.

Dürer's wide-eyed zeal might have been something of a tip-off for Barbari. The Italian artist, wary that his secret might get out, kept his method closely guarded. He refused to reveal his process to Dürer despite their continued contact and a visit with Dürer in his hometown. Rebuffed, Dürer set himself to developing his own canon of proportions beginning in 1512, and continuing for the next decade.

Following what was standard procedure during that era, Dürer searched for clues to perfect proportions among the ancients. He took to studying the work of the celebrated Roman architect Vitruvius, and from his studies he arrived at the following conclusion: "The head of a man is

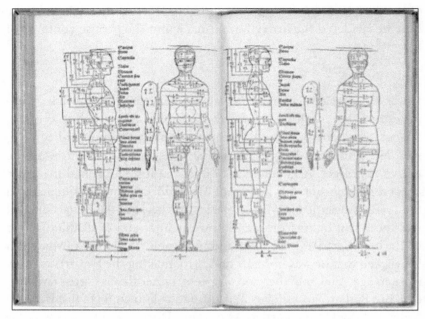

Figure 1.3. Albrecht Dürer, image of "normal" man and woman, *Four Books on Human Proportion*, 1528.

an eighth part of him." Further, "one also finds a square from the feet to the crown of the head . . . the span (of the outstretched arms) is equal to the height (of the body)."[19] Using these calculations, he believed, Vitruvius had rendered human perfection: "He has brought human limbs together in a perfect proportion in so satisfactory a manner that neither the ancients nor the moderns are able to overthrow it."[20] Dürer used his adapted Vitruvian standard to create his idea of a "normal" male and female form, as would be described in his *Four Books on Human Proportion*.

The intense attention to detail in the precise calculation of the idealized length and breadth of each body part drew the respect of his contemporaries. Dürer, moreover, added something to the equation that Vitruvius had not: variety. After drawing a "normal" man and woman, he sketched several men and women with the necessary and proper proportions but of different body sizes. Among these sketches there were a disproportionate number of images of plump women.

It is unclear from the manuscripts why there was a preponderance of fleshy, rounded women among the artist's sketches in *Four Books on Human Proportion*. Surviving reports suggest that Dürer worked with two hundred to three hundred live models in the formulation of his canon of proportions.[21] Therefore, it could have been simply that more voluptuous women had made themselves available as models. But that interpretation belies his dedication to the project of empirically fleshing out the parameters of perfect proportionality and thereby beauty. Because he worked on this project for over a decade, a more likely reason was a personal predilection for rounded women. Many of the women he drew, including Katharina and his own wife, Agnes, were fleshy and curvaceous.

Dürer anticipated that his canon of proportions would offer new insights that would separate his work from the canon of perspective current in Italy.[22] As it applied to feminine loveliness, this difference was

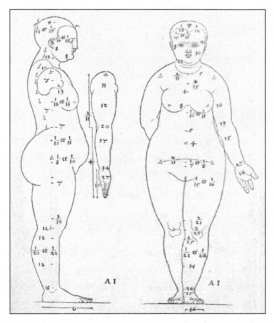

Figure 1.4. Albrecht Dürer, image of "normal" woman (front and profile), *Four Books on Human Proportion*, 1528.

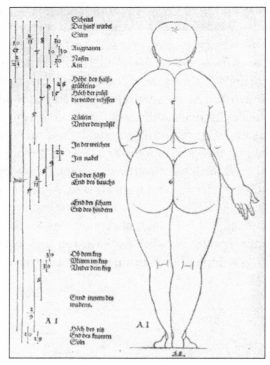

Figure 1.5. Albrecht Dürer, image of "normal" woman
(back), *Four Books on Human Proportion*, 1528.

found largely in the means, not the ends. For if Dürer's mathematical
theorizing led him to calculations about perfect proportionality with a
seeming predilection for plumpness, a similar standard was in fashion
in the most important centers of Renaissance Italy.

Urbino is a case in point. A thriving center of the Italian Renaissance,
Urbino was distinct from other centers of the Renaissance such as Antwerp and Venice in one critical respect: its involvement in the slave
trade was minimal. For this reason, the question of black aesthetics was
not a topic that many artists or philosophers considered, and Africans
were less commonly represented in art from the region. Urbino was,
however, an important place for the discussion and dissemination of
ideas about female beauty. It was also the birthplace of Raphael, one of
the most influential painters of the High Renaissance. Raphael devoted

less energy than did Dürer to waxing intellectual about method. Nevertheless, as an artist, he remained deeply invested in the craft of representing true beauty.

In 1514 Raphael drafted a letter on the topic to his friend Conte Baldassare Castiglione. The letter served as one of the few instances in which the artist delineated, in writing, his approach to portraying feminine loveliness. In it, Raphael confided to Castiglione that "in order to paint one beautiful woman, I'd have to see several beautiful women."[23] The statement was reminiscent of Dürer's claim that God dispersed beauty over the whole world and that an artist needed a diversity of models to comprehend beauty in all its richness. Indeed, the two artists were colleagues; while the German artist was older and already celebrated by the time of Raphael's rise to fame, by 1514 the two were part of something of a mutual admiration society, exchanging prints and praising one another's work.[24]

To Raphael, as to Dürer, no one woman could have it all. In order to comprehend and later represent beauty in a woman, he needed to work with as many women as possible who were judged to be attractive by the casual male observer. Sadly, due to what Raphael described as a shortage of both beautiful women and competent male judges, he explained that instead he usually relied on his own best judgment: "I make use of a certain idea which comes to my mind."[25] This may have been something of a half-truth. The Renaissance represented a rebirth of ancient Greek and Roman art and philosophy. Italian high society at the time was saturated by a rediscovery of the art and ideas of classical antiquity. Urbino itself was teeming with neoclassicists, many of whom were members of the Florentine Academy, a center for the discussion and dissemination of neoclassical, and especially Neoplatonic, ideas.

The "idea" that came to Raphael's mind was at least partially inspired by current neoclassical theories about true beauty, which described beauty as requiring symmetry, harmony, and perfect proportionality.[26] His own work is extolled in part for its achievements in enlivening these classical ideals, even if he was perhaps unwilling to articulate the extent to which he was conversant with them.

The friend to whom he divulged his process of depicting female beauty, Castiglione, was by contrast an open and ardent Neoplatonist. Nearly fifteen years after Raphael sent him a letter with his mini-treatise on beauty,

Castiglione's tome, *The Book of the Courtier*, appeared in print. In it, he used fictionalized versions of what he claimed were real conversations to reveal the aristocratic ideal of feminine loveliness at the court of Urbino.

In one conversation, a man by the name of Giuliano de Medici is urged to explain exactly what qualified as "beauty." Giuliano offers the generally well-respected neoclassical view shot through with Christian idioms, stating that "there are divers [*sic*] sorts of beauty."[27] When this definition proves unsatisfying, he becomes more specific. Differing from the likes of Dürer, Giuliano betrayed a decided preference for a lady who is neither "too fat" nor "too thin":

> Since women may and ought to take more care for beauty than men—and there are divers sorts of beauty—this Lady ought to have the good sense to discern what those garments are that enhance her grace. . . . Thus, if she is a little more stout or thin than the medium, or fair or dark, let her seek help from dress, but as covertly as possible.[28]

Giuliano's preference for women he describes as "medium," a term that was seemingly self-evident and yet maddeningly unspecific, was part of the Italian neoclassicists' understanding of beauty. As with Dürer, harmony and proportionality were integral, a point Giuliano under-scores when he states, "If the form of the whole body is fair and well proportioned, it attracts and allures anyone who looks upon it."[29] But whereas Dürer calculated proportionate physiques in a manner that sep-arated the concepts of "proportion" and "size," the Italian humanists of the Florentine Academy had a slightly more exacting standard of female beauty, one derived from the ancients. Their model was a Roman god-dess, resurrected in the Florentine Academy in the late fifteenth century. Her name was Venus.[30]

Giuliano did not use the name "Venus" in *The Book of the Courtier*. He didn't need to. Giuliano de Medici carried the family name that was synonymous with the goddess's return to glory. His father was Lorenzo de Medici, celebrated fifteenth-century Florentine ruler, patron of the arts, and sponsor of the Florentine Academy. In the 1460s, Lorenzo be-came friends with a young artist whom his own father (Piero di Cosimo de Medici) had taken in shortly before his death, the famed Alessandro Botticelli.

Figure 1.6. Sandro Botticelli, *The Birth of Venus*, c. 1482–1485. Image courtesy of Art Resource, New York.

Botticelli's achievements were sundry, but the artist was best known for his images of Venus, the goddess of love. His first Venus, *La Primavera*, painted around 1482, shows the goddess standing in a mythically dark forest, surrounded by enticing globes of fruit. She is flanked by gods and nymphs, dancing joyously and reveling in the love inspired by nature's beauty and bounty. Botticelli's next Venus was his most iconic painting. *The Birth of Venus* depicts the goddess naked atop a shell that is gliding into shore. Zephyrs from the left blow her golden hair as she gathers it in her right hand and uses it to conceal her pelvic area. With her left hand she half-heartedly attempts to cover her breasts, coyly leaving one available for the viewer's gaze. From the right, her handmaiden approaches to provide her with the garments that would be needed to clothe the demure goddess in such a realm.

Botticelli, who was Lorenzo de Medici's friend and confidant, was a member of the Florentine Academy. He was thus inspired by the poetic works and philosophical tête-à-têtes to which he was privy. *The Birth of Venus* is often regarded as the earliest Renaissance painting to reimagine a style known as "Venus Pudica," in which the modest Venus reaches to cover her pubis and often her breasts.[31]

Figure 1.7. Raphael, *La Fornarina*, 1518–1520. Image
courtesy of Art Resource, New York.

Botticelli would not have been the only artist inspired by the Medicis
to paint the goddess of love. Raphael knew the Medicis well, having been
commissioned more than once to paint portraits of members of the family. He might not have mentioned a neoclassical influence for his portraits of beautiful women in his letters to Castiglione, a but he painted
several Venuses in his lifetime. One of the most mystifying and controversial was a portrait of a nude woman, her hands modestly covering
her private parts—said to be his mistress and muse, Margherita Luti.[32]

The character Giuliano de Medici mentions none of this in his exege-
sis on beauty in *The Book of the Courtier*. His family history and their
eminence in molding Renaissance aesthetic ideals were left unstated.
His contemporaries, however, would have been well aware of the family's influence on feminine aesthetic standards. This may have been why

Castiglione chose to make Giuliano his mouthpiece on the question of feminine loveliness.

Giuliano's stated preference for women who were both "medium" and "proportionate" was representative of the Italian canon of perspective, as it was embodied by Venus. It is relevant, of course, that this preference was not so rigidly codified that women who were stout or spindly might not be able to make themselves attractive, according to Giuliano, through fashion. If "medium" women were preferred, fat and thin women were not summarily dismissed.

It is equally intriguing that in the same breath in which Giuliano mentions body size, he muses on skin color, suggesting that women who were "fair or dark" might too improve upon their shortcomings through dress. This nod to those of different skin tones may have contained a subtle reference to Africans. Although slavery was not a booming enterprise in

Figure 1.8. *Alessandro de Medici, Duke of Florence*, 1535 or later. Image courtesy of Art Resource, New York.

Urbino at the time, Africans were not an unknown presence. Giuliano's own blood relation, Alessandro de Medici, the later Duke of Florence, was also known as *il moro*—the moor—since his mother was black.[33]

Castiglione's *Book of the Courtier* is regarded as a seminal text. An etiquette book of sorts, the work reveals the new rules of conduct at the very moment they were being restated and refined by the Italian upper class. Castiglione's characters even assume an uncomfortable coyness when it comes to plain speaking about *les regoles di bellezza*, or the rules of beauty. They tread lightly on topics that the lowly commoner might otherwise pursue with abandon.

Scarcely a whiff of this high-minded affectation is found in Agnolo Firenzuola's 1541 retort to Castiglione's work, tellingly titled *On the Beauty of Women*. Firenzuola was born in Florence in 1493. He traveled to Siena, where he studied law, before heading off to Rome to take holy orders in 1518. In Rome he took vows as a Vallambrosian monk before realizing that the life of the monastic and its attendant celibacy did not really suit him. In 1526, according to contemporary accounts, he was "dispensed from his vows."[34]

Firenzuola stayed in Rome, where he entered the shimmering circle of literati that included the distinguished Pietro Bembo. A Catholic cardinal, aristocrat, and student of the works of Plato and Petrarch, Bembo, then in his fifties, had lived in Urbino and was well acquainted with the ruling Medici clan. Along with being known for his own neoclassical poetry, Bembo had famously appeared as an interlocutor in *The Book of the Courtier*, sparring with Giuliano de Medici on the definition of true beauty.

Inspired by present company, Firenzuola decided to compose his own discourse on beauty. His treatise, like *The Book of the Courtier,* was written in dialogue form. Firenzuola, however, switched the sexual composition of his group, having four women converse with one man about what precisely constitutes perfect female beauty. In a Christian/neoclassical view that invoked Raphael, he claimed that no one woman had been endowed with all the necessary elements of beauty, but rather that nature had dispersed the good bits here and there. Thus, to animate his vision of perfect female beauty, Firenzuola crafted a montage of body parts taken from the four female conversants in his treatise.[35]

The first element of true beauty was, of course, proportionality. Clearly inspired by the Neoplatonists such as Bembo, with whom he dined, Celso, the lone male character among his conversants, describes this proportion as "mysterious" and claims that it is "a measure that is not in our books, which we do not know, nor can even imagine."[36] This limitation did not prevent him from trying. For while beauty's specifications and precise measurements could not be detailed, their intellectual forebears had left them with a vision of feminine perfection: "The Ancients consecrated them to the beautiful Venus."[37] In which case, an important part of Firenzuola's project is enabling his male mouthpiece, Celso, to sift through the many women he knows, including those present in the dialogues, to identify who has features that approach the exquisite proportions of Venus.

In a nod to both the ancients and Castiglione, Firenzuola writes of his well-proportioned Venus as being medium-sized, but still shapely. Firenzuola conveys this through Celso, who states that the ideal woman is "somewhere between lean and fat, plump and juicy, of the right proportions."[38] That this woman should still remain "plump and juicy" is telling. Evoking others in the Renaissance pantheon, Firenzuola reminds us that even as proportionality is sought, so too is fleshiness. In fact, if one is to drift to one side of the scale, it should be in the direction of voluptuousness, not slimness. Quoting Aristotle, Celso claims, "If the good habits of the body are evident in the firmness and thickness of the flesh, *the bad habits must then be evident in its flabbiness and thinness.*"[39] In other words, "thickness" was a sign of good health, whereas thinness was a signal of poor health and hygiene. In a point-by-point analysis of the figure, Celso informs the women that cleavage should be "plump, so that no sign of bones can be seen," the hips should be "wide" and "pronounced," and the arms should be "fleshy and muscular, but with a certain softness."[40]

Though thickness had been deemed superior to thinness, the question nevertheless remained: Was it possible that a woman could be considered too fat to be beautiful? When asked this, Celso equivocated momentarily, before responding that even "quite fat" women could achieve the heights of beauty:

> CELSO: One likes a robust body, with nimble, capable limbs, well placed and well proportioned. But, I would not want my ideal beauty to be too big or very fat.

SELVAGGIA: Yet, even though Iblea Soporella is quite fat, she is still a very beautiful young lady who carries herself well. . . .

CELSO: . . . This young lady has such a majesty in her body, a beauty in her eyes . . . it seems her fatness has granted her a beauty, that agility. . . . I judge her to be one of the most beautiful women in these parts of town.[41]

On the Beauty of Women illustrates the value placed on fleshy feminine forms in Rome, an artistic and intellectual hub of the Renaissance. Its professed preference for plump and proportionate figures echoed the sentiments expressed in *The Book of the Courtier*. Yet, unlike Castiglione's masterwork, *On the Beauty of Women* included a declared preference for fat over thin women. This declaration simultaneously harkened back to Dürer and presaged the growing praise for voluptuous figures that was to come in the world of art and feminine aesthetics.

Though Firenzuola himself mingled with many of the important figures of his time, he never attained the recognition for his work that Castiglione or Raphael had. Still, many twentieth- and twenty-first-century scholars have returned to his work for its insights into sixteenth-century aesthetics.[42]

Firenzuola shared much with the literati of Rome. While there, he contracted syphilis, the same illness many contemporary scholars believed felled Raphael. His contraction of syphilis had the seeming effect of restoring his devotion to God. He returned to the monastery in 1538, becoming an abbot at the San Salvatore monastery in Prato, where he remained until his death in 1543.

Firenzuola did not make any mention of dark-skinned women in his book. In contrast to the Low Countries (where Dürer had encountered Katharina), African slaves were a minimal presence in Rome and many other major Italian centers. This was not the case, however, in Venice. Dark-skinned captives had been brought to the region since the Crusades.[43] The slave-trading enterprise in this way expanded, rather than introduced, the population of forced black laborers in the region.

By 1490, when the trade in captured Africans became a bona fide industry, there was already a visible population of Africans in Italy. Venice, a vital center of the Italian Renaissance, was also a key trading destination. By the late fifteenth century, ships bearing African captives were a common sight in this seaport. And whereas many earlier waves of Africans arriving in the region were largely male, by 1490 a sizeable number of black women could be seen among the newly imported vassals.[44]

The introduction of a significant population of black women and girls in the city made them in many respects a hot commodity. Their presence signaled both the exotic lands beyond the sea and the European conquest of said lands. For these reasons, black women and girls retained as maidservants became a fashionable accessory for aristocratic Italian women.[45] This much was evident in a letter composed by Isabella d'Este in 1491. Isabella, the new Marquise of Mantua, was a respected cultural and political figure. She was also a patron of the arts and a lady of fashion. In her letter, written in May of that year, she badgered her agent in Venice to acquire "una moreta," a young black girl to serve as her maidservant, emphasizing that the girl should be "as black as possible."[46] A month later, Isabella wrote to her sister-in-law Anna Sforza, revealing that this was to be her second black maidservant. Of her original, slightly older maidservant, she writes, "We couldn't be more pleased with our black girl, even if she were blacker, because from being at first a little disdainful she has now become pleasing in words and acts, and we think she'll make the best buffoon in the world."[47]

With the growing presence of black girls and women in Italy came a new interest in their artistic portrayal. Black men had been represented in frescoes exalting biblical scenes since the thirteenth century, a black man having been venerated as one of the Three Kings in the Black Magus tradition.[48] But representations of black women in religious images had been far fewer. The rise of the slave trade in Venice led to the rapid incorporation of black women into a variety of religious, domestic, and mythological scenes. They were typically rendered as the physically alluring social inferiors to white women, a representation that reified social distinctions.

This was the artistic and cultural milieu into which Titian landed as an adolescent in the early sixteenth century. The actual date of Titian's birth is unknown. However, scholars believe that he was nearly twelve when he was sent from his hometown in Cadore to the city of Venice to apprentice as a painter.[49] From then until 1510, Titian apprenticed with the Bellini family, the city's best-known painters. Some critics argued that his talent outstripped that of the Bellinis even upon his arrival. But by the time the two most acclaimed painters of the Bellini family, Giorgione and Giovanni, had died, Titian had become the undisputed master of the Venetian school, a title he took with him to his death sixty years later.[50]

Titian was not to remain untouched by the conspicuous presence of Africans as servants in the region. One of his earliest representations of an African was found in his 1523 portrait *Laura Dianti and Her Page*. Laura Dianti was known by many as the mistress of Alfonso d'Este, Isabella's brother.[51] Her humble origins and uncertain status in the court made the painting controversial. Yet the work also suggests her evolving social status, as she is shown next to her small black pageboy, who looks up at her admiringly.[52] (Even as the growing fashion in the region was to procure black female servants, black male servants were still commonly used to represent black servitude in art.) *Laura Dianti and Her Page* was one of the earliest paintings to exemplify the domestic intimacy and social distance between Africans and Europeans.

Black women also appeared in Titian's vast portfolio. Titian pulled these women into the iconography of proportionate and fleshy feminine beauties, making them the aesthetic equals of European women. This was the case in what is considered one of the artist's greatest works, *Diana and Actaeon*. In this 1559 painting, Titian reimagines a tale from the Roman poet Ovid's *Metamorphoses*. In the myth, Actaeon, a young hunter fresh from the day's kill, wanders aimlessly through the woods with his hunting dogs. He happens upon the sacred cave of the goddess and virgin huntress Diana while she is bathing. His presence sparks a flurry of activity as nymphs beat their breasts, warning Diana of Actaeon's violent entry into their hallowed dwelling. Suspicious of his intent and believing that he has penetrated the cave for the express purpose of seeing her undressed, Diana curses him by turning him into a deer. Later, his own dogs devour him, ensuring that he will tell no one what he saw.[53]

While the tale itself was a well-rehearsed ancient myth, Titian adds a bit of colonial-era titillation by introducing a black female attendant into the story. The attendant is at Diana's back, helping the goddess lift the cloth that would cover her nude body. The attendant is the only woman who is clothed, her inelegant striped frock an artistic device signaling not her modesty but her status as Other.

Figure 1.9. Titian, *Diana and Actaeon*, 1556–1559. Image courtesy of Art Resource, New York.

Yet, along with his depiction of the servant's social status as inferior, Titian depicted her physique as no less alluring than that of the goddess. The attendant's plain smock slides off one shoulder as she reaches to assist Diana, revealing her own shapely form. The attendant's toned arm matches those of the nymphs bathing nearby. Indeed, there is a similarity in the silhouettes of the many women present. The forms of the many women drawn—reminiscent of Dürer's plump, proportionate women, as well as the fleshy Venus of the late Florentine Republic—reveal a congruity in their voluptuousness. Each serves as a representation of the beauty of the female body that apparently transcended both color and social status.[54]

Titian may have been in a class by himself as an artist. But he had many peers among the Italian Renaissance notables when it came to the convention of reimagining tales from antiquity, and inserting a black woman as the social subordinate and yet physical analog to voluptuous and comely white women. Andrea Mantegna, court artist of Isabella d'Este, reimagined Judith in what many believe to be the first biblical allegory to incorporate a black woman. Judith was a widow depicted in the Old Testament as beautiful and chaste. She uses her considerable womanly charms to gain entrée into the tent of Holofernes, the enemy Assyrian general. When he falls asleep drunk, she beheads him with the aid of her handmaiden.

Betraying the tension over the questionable attractiveness of the African face during the High Renaissance, Mantegna's first drawing of this biblical narrative, circa 1490, shows Judith grasping the general's heavy and lolling decapitated head by the hair as an older, wizened black woman stoops down with an empty sack to collect the head. In a second portrayal of this scene, the maidservant is young, perhaps younger than Judith. In this portrait the servant's facial features are presumptively African, and yet like Katharina, also attractive. In both paintings, the servant is as voluptuous and well-built as Judith.

Mantegna's use of a black woman as a handmaiden in an iconic Christian story was telling. At once evocative and firmly rooted in the late fifteenth-century cultural scene in which it was drawn, Mantegna's work reconstituted aristocratic white women's servants as having always been black.[55] But black women's subjectivity and subordination did not diminish their bodily beauty.

After Mantegna, many other artists reproduced the scene of Judith and Holofernes featuring a winsome black handmaiden. Paolo Veronese produced late sixteenth-century paintings of Judith that evoked Mantegna. One, painted between 1582 and 1585, shows a young, contemplative, and buxom Judith being assisted by her seemingly black servant. The servant's face is careworn, which may be an indication of her age, or alternatively an attempt to illustrate African physiognomy in a way that bespoke a harshness or unattractiveness. The servant in Veronese's portrait is nevertheless sexually alluring in build. Her toned, largely bare upper torso extends toward the viewer. Her cleavage, like Judith's, sits on display in the center of the frame, commanding an erotic attention.

Figure 1.10. Paolo Veronese, *Judith with the Head of Holofernes*,
1580. Image courtesy of Art Resource, New York.

The viewer's gaze is drawn more to the sensuality of the women than the triumphant act of decapitation, which, in the biblical tale, saves Judith's city from enemy plunder.

Veronese's version of Judith was composed only a few years before his death in 1588. By this time, he had lived in Venice for thirty-five years. And if Titian was in the estimation of many the unrivaled master of Venetian art, Veronese was esteemed for his beautiful, if often controversial, renditions of biblical tales and classical myths. In these works he was fond of including Africans in scenes in which they had previously been absent. No painter, in fact, during the two-hundred-year span between the late fifteenth and late seventeenth centuries that marked the simultaneous rise of both the slave trade and the Renaissance throughout Europe, painted more scenes featuring black figures.[56] His frequent incorporation of black people into his work did more than raise a few

Figure 1.11. School of Paolo Veronese, *Portrait of a
Moorish Woman*, 1550s. Image courtesy of Bridgeman
Images.

eyebrows; he was at one point subject to a trial for what was described as
his "misrepresentations" of the good book. His sentence? To correct the
offending piece so that it accurately reflected the scripture.[57]

Most of Veronese's figures were of black men and children. But an
unidentified student of his style and purported member of the school
of Paolo Veronese presented a portrait of a young black woman that
remains a significant contribution to the collection of black women in
Renaissance art. The painting, *Portrait of a Moorish Woman*, is a bust of
a bejeweled African woman in simple garb that recalls Dürer's *Katharina*. This painting, which was completed around 1550, shows none of
the melancholy that was evident in Dürer's portrait. The unidentified
"Moorish woman" is marked through her skin color, facial features, and
dazzling jewels as "African."[58] Her plain vestments are arranged in a bit

of peekaboo pageantry that conveys the influence of Veronese. They also remind viewers of her Otherness and her social station, even as her womanly charms are on full display.

Each of the three major centers of sixteenth-century Renaissance artistic production had a distinctive identity. Despite differences in method and execution, when it came to considerations of feminine attractiveness, Dürer's mathematical calculations, the Florentine Academy's neoclassicism, and the Venetian voluptuousness were all united by the notion that beauty was found in proportionality and that fleshiness was pleasing to the eye.

Such similarities are not surprising. The artists did not live in creative silos. Surviving reports reveal that artists like Dürer traveled throughout Italy, Belgium, and the Netherlands to finish commissioned pieces. They also uncover the creative love affair between artists in the various regions. Raphael and Dürer apparently exchanged prints of their works; each was known to admire the work of the other. In Venice, Titian's crush on Dürer bordered on infatuation, and Dürer noted his concern that the artist was simply copying his work. This concern, it seems, was not unfounded.[59] But it was also not without a hint of irony, given his own dogged attempt to pinch the secrets of execution of the Venetian artist Barbari.

It is perhaps because of the shared influences and similarities across regions that for centuries no one knew who sculpted the first African Venus. The statue was originally ascribed to Danese Cattaneo, an Italian sculptor who produced much of his work in Venice.[60] This view was later discredited, and the sculpture was attributed to other artists in Florence, northern Italy, and even France. In recent years, a Netherlander named Johan Gregor van der Schardt, who studied in Italy before being employed by the Holy Roman Emperor Maximilian II, has been credited with its creation.

The *African Venus* has many of the same attributes as the classical and neoclassical paintings and statues of Venus, including the famed Venus de Medici statue that was known to be part of the Medici family collection by the late sixteenth century.[61] Like the Venus de Medici, the *African Venus* was of a similarly proportionate, medium build, and fleshy. The blackness of the *African Venus* is marked by more than just her bronze coloring. The features of the face are also paradigmatically

Figure 1.12. *African Venus*, 1581 or later. Attributed to
Johan Gregor van der Schardt.

African. Her curly hair is covered by a nondecorative headdress, a detail
unique to African Venus statues. Also unique to these statues, in one
hand she holds a cloth presumably used to polish the mirror held in the
other, into which she gazes longingly.

The *African Venus* represents a curious play on the Venus iconography. On the one hand, the sculpture fits within the prevailing idiom of
beauty, representing the "refined tastes of the ruling elite of Europe" circulating during the Renaissance.[62] Her rounded, elongated limbs speak
to the influence of the Mannerist period, which extended approximately
from the 1520s to the 1580s. But because she is black, the sculptor also
used some markers to indicate her low social status. The African Venus
carries a cloth rag and wears a headdress that may signify that she is
a domestic servant. Black female servants were often fitted with simple headdresses, as was the case in Dürer's *Katharina*, Titian's *Diana*,
and Veronese's *Judith*. The African Venus is, moreover, immodest. In a

prelude to ideas about Africans that would be developed over the next several centuries, the African Venus is lacking in shame; whereas the Europeanized Venus Pudica covers her pubis and breasts, the African Venus is mesmerized by her own beauty as she gazes wistfully at her own reflection.[63]

There are thirteen known African Venus statues, each of a similar design as that purportedly crafted by van der Schardt in the 1580s. It is possible that van der Schardt's African Venus is one manifestation of a "profane" or lowly Venus, neither exalted nor heavenly. Her earthly beauty and its wholly physical manifestation would inspire lust, but not, as with the Venus Pudica, love.[64]

But a change was coming. In sixteenth-century Italian masterworks, low-status black women had been prized for their figures. But by the turn of the seventeenth century, black women were shifting from the aesthetic counterparts of European women to their aesthetic *counterpoints*. Their novelty having worn off in areas where the slave trade had been going on the longest, black women's figures too were being described as inferior. In the new "proto-racist" order,[65] black women were increasingly deemed little, low, and foul. The plump aesthetic became more and more frequently associated with white women.

At the same time in England, a country that arrived relatively late to the transatlantic slave trade, a new trend was taking off among refined men: thinness. In English high society, philosophers had started to rethink the meaning of the fat male body. Voluptuousness in women was all well and good; women were but the objects of men's fancies. Fatness in men signaled a lack of self-control, or dimness. For elite men, slenderness became bodily proof of rationality and intelligence.

2

Plump Women and Thin, Fine Men

Peter Paul Rubens was a dapper sort. Tall and good-looking, he was known by many women as *il fiammingo*, or the Fleming. The nickname was less a testament to the figure cut by Flemish men in general than to Rubens's preeminence among them. He dressed like a gentleman and had a certain grace and ease when he galloped about town, a stallion on his steed. His own good looks aside, Rubens was revered for his ability to turn any woman into a "Venus." His sumptuous paintings of full-bodied nudes were taken as a celebration of real women's curves, and they made the name Rubens synonymous with the voluptuous aesthetic of the late Renaissance. Even today a full-figured woman is often described as "Rubenesque." Yet what scholars have often failed to note is that not just any robust woman could fit this description. Along with Rubens's attraction to fleshiness was a predilection for whiteness. As the artist was to state in his own treatise on beauty, he preferred women whose skin was, as he put it, as "white as snow."

Rubens's story helps us to understand the unfolding preference for full-bodied white women in art and literature from the late sixteenth to the late seventeenth centuries, particularly in the Dutch Republic and England. The seventeenth century represented a seminal period for each of these states. Each experienced a Golden Age during the era, which coincided with, and was supported by, their emergence as the world's most powerful slave-trading countries.

Herein, I show that as the slave trade expanded to areas where Africans had been largely absent, the sudden and proliferating presence of black people sparked a simmering and often vocal discomfort. The germinating anti-black sentiment had ramifications for the way black people were represented in art and literature. That is, in the seventeenth century, a "proto-racist" discourse emerged that marked black women and men as unattractive, hypersexual, and diminutive in both size and social status.[1] White women were idealized as pure, chaste, and stately.

Figure 2.1. Peter Paul Rubens, *The Honeysuckle Bower*, 1609. Image courtesy of Art Resource, New York.

Curiously, at the same time that full-figured white women were ascending to the pinnacle of beauty, a visible cadre of well-to-do Englishmen were starting to openly abhor fleshiness in men. Fatness, for English intellectuals, was progressively linked to irrationality. Thinness was seen as more befitting the intelligent, self-possessed white male.

* * *

Rubens was the sixth of seven children. He was born in Siegen, Germany, in 1577. At that time, his father, Jan Rubens, was under house arrest. An avowed Calvinist, Jan had once been an alderman for the city of Antwerp. But nine years earlier, he had fled Antwerp under the threat of religious persecution, landing in Cologne, Germany, in 1568. There he became the chief counselor for Anna of Saxony, a Lutheran princess and wife of governor William of Orange.[2] The close relationship between Jan and Anna first drew suspicion, then later charges of sexual indiscretion. Jan was found guilt of adultery and imprisoned in a fortress under royal watch before being released to live in confinement, and under supervision, with his family in 1573.[3] He died in 1587, and his long-suffering Catholic wife returned to Antwerp with her four surviving children.[4] By the time they arrived, the once vibrant city was a shell of its former self. Jan Rubens's fear of persecution was apparently warranted: a year before Peter Paul's birth, the city had suffered a siege. Soldiers working for the Spanish crown had started a riot, setting homes ablaze and massacring tens of thousands of residents.[5] A decree reminiscent of those common during the Spanish Inquisition less than a century earlier demanded that those who remained either renounce Protestantism or pick up and leave.

It was in the midst of this social upheaval that the young Peter Paul Rubens found his calling. In Antwerp he was introduced to the Mannerist style, which still maintained its grip on the art world. In 1600 he took his budding talents to Italy, and upon his arrival in Mantua he was promptly retained by the Duke, Vincenzo Gonzaga (great-grandson of Isabella d'Este), and his wife, Eleanor de Medici, as their court painter. But this was not the Mantua of Isabella d'Este's day. When she was a young woman in the 1490s looking for a young girl "as black as possible," black people were a novel sight.[6] Now, a hundred more years into the African slave trade, they were much more commonplace.[7]

Rubens had little time to reflect on the African presence in Italy. Shortly after taking up the post of court painter for the Gonzagas, he was sent on a mission by Vincenzo to deliver copies of Raphael's masterworks to Philip II, king of Spain.[8] The stated aim was to put the Mantuan court in the good graces of the fickle young Spanish king. But there was a furtive little side project that made Vincenzo giddily await the artist's return.

Before his appointment as court painter for the Gonzagas, Rubens had been largely known for his altarpieces, expansive religious mise-en-scènes that were majestic in their depiction of tragedy. Vincenzo was no doubt pleased to have Rubens's services to animate biblical allegories or dignify members of the court. But the duke was also interested in having Rubens help him round out what was known as his "Gallery of Beauties."[9] The duke had filled his gallery with portraits of young women who had been anointed the best-looking ladies of the court. Part of Rubens's mission on his circuitous route through Madrid and Paris was to find and set to canvas additional pretty young ladies for the duke's private collection.[10] Rubens did not disappoint on his primary mission, and it is doubtful that he failed to complete his secret side assignment.

That his considerable talent would be devoted to painting handsome young ladies did not deter Rubens from reveling in his new appointment. Lacking the pedigree of the average court official, the artist was pleased to have been given the position, not to mention its attendant salary. Over time, however, his role as one of the many contributors to the duke's collection of what some deemed "high-end soft-core pornography" would come to distress him.[11] In the end, fatigued by his missions and commissions, and dissatisfied with his life in Mantua, Rubens successfully petitioned the duke to be relocated to Rome. There, disillusioned with Vincenzo's prurient whims, he returned to painting the altarpieces that were the launching pad for his early career.[12]

Despite his expressed disdain for the duke's libidinous interest in painted lovelies, it may have been his time in Mantua that led Pietro Paolo Rubens—for his time in Rome led him to Italianize his name—to become fixated with feminine beauty. After his return to Antwerp in 1608, he became more invested in its articulation and portrayal. Arguably, the performance of his duties at Mantua triggered a latent desire to celebrate (or objectify) women's bodies. And while Rubens was becoming publicly recognized as a gentleman and a scholar, his side commissions contributed to local speculation that he could turn any dowdy duchess into a "Venus" with just a few strokes of his brush.[13]

Sometime after 1609, when he officially terminated his service in Mantua and became court painter for the Archduke Albert of Brussels, Rubens returned to painting beautiful women. These portraits, however, had the cultural sanction of being elevated. Instead of painting the young maidens he came across at court, he now, like the masters of the High Renaissance, painted ancient goddesses and biblical queens. *This* was the sort of high art that inspired an admiration of one's talent.

One work he painted upon his return to Antwerp was *The Four Rivers of Paradise* (1615). The portrait features four male river gods peacefully relaxing with water nymphs, as nearby children make merry with earthly creatures.[14] There is also clear biblical symbolism, as the gods and nymphs recline harmoniously at the intersection of four rivers named in the Bible: the Nile, the Ganges, the Tigris, and the Euphrates.[15] Rubens created this work during the twelve-year truce between the Spanish Netherlands and Flanders. The painting celebrated the peace between the two sides and offered an allegory of the abundance made possible through unification. It also contained the artist's none-too-veiled hope that his own river town of Antwerp might, in these tenuous times of peace, return to its prewar glory.[16]

The Four Rivers of Paradise, inspired by Rubens's return to Antwerp, was one of two portraits he painted that year to feature an African woman. The woman in *The Four Rivers of Paradise* is an Ethiopian nymph, the consort for the river god of the Nile. Her body is largely obscured by the deep blue cloth adorning her frame. But what is visible of her upper torso indicates that she has the same enviable undulating curves as the fair-skinned nymphs.

Rubens's portrayal of an African woman in *The Four Rivers of Paradise* reveals the influence of Renaissance masters a century earlier. But unlike many earlier artists, Rubens portrayed an African woman who bears no marking of an inferior social status. On her head she wears not the simple headdress that would have been given her by Titian or Dürer but a tiara with glistening jewels. She is not wearing bedraggled clothes nor clutching a humbling dustcloth. Instead, she is covered with a luxurious blanket and held lovingly by the (white) god of the river Nile. In all these respects, this African woman is the physical and social equivalent of the white women depicted.[17]

The Four Rivers of Paradise in many ways represented a typical artistic portrayal of African women in the Low Countries at the time. During the late sixteenth and early seventeenth centuries, artists from the region typically lacked access to live models and had taken to making black women appear simply as dark-skinned Europeans.[18] In this respect, the

Figure 2.2. Peter Paul Rubens, *The Four Rivers of Paradise*, 1615. Image courtesy of Art Resource, New York.

portrait did reflect the era and environs, but it was not representative of Rubens's overall take on black women.

A very different treatment of black femininity can be seen in another work depicting a black woman, *Venus in Front of the Mirror*. Produced during the same year as *The Four Rivers of Paradise, Venus in Front of the Mirror* is one of his most iconic works. In the portrait, a voluptuous Venus sits in a garden with her back to the viewer. The dimpled flesh of her ample backside is partially covered by a shimmering white cloth. On her left is an impish winged cupid, who holds up a mirror so that Venus might admire her own beauty. In looking at herself, she meets the viewer's gaze in an unabashed recognition of our presumed approbation. On her right is her black maidservant. Her kinky hair is visible under a white cap. A single braid from the left side of her head barely stretches over the cap to connect with the other braid from the right. Her short curly hair is contrasted with Venus's long, straight blonde hair, which the maidservant holds in apparent admiration. And, while caressing Venus's

Figure 2.3. Peter Paul Rubens, *Venus in Front of the Mirror*, 1615. Image courtesy of Art Resource, New York.

sleek locks, the handmaiden lifts the flaxen hair to give the audience a better view of Venus's hindquarters.

The message of *Venus in Front of the Mirror* and that of *Bathsheba,* completed in 1635, are in striking contrast to that of *The Four Rivers of Paradise.* In the former two, black women serve as a mirror for white women's beauty. Their small, lean frames and short, coiled hair are used to communicate not just difference but destitution, a sense of something wanting. By contrast, the well-apportioned physiques and abundant locks of the white Venus communicated plenitude and blessedness.

Rubens's depictions of black women in *Venus in Front of the Mirror* and *Bathsheba* signal a clear shift from the status-based social distinction that was common during the High Renaissance. These renderings were indicative of the growing aesthetic distinctions being imposed between black and white women. Black women were no longer deemed the bodily equals but social inferiors of white women. Now, black women's very being was intended to evoke inferiority. In other words, whiteness stood not just for social supremacy, but general superiority.[19]

Rubens's changing representations of black women might be better understood if we examine the context in which these works were created. Antwerp, his adopted home, had been a cultural and economic powerhouse and a key port for the lucrative slave-trading industry since 1490.[20] But the fall of Antwerp in 1585 destroyed the city's position as a center of trade activity, slave or otherwise. Throughout the late fifteenth and early sixteenth centuries, the majority of slave traders were from Portugal. Once on amiable terms with the residents of Antwerp,

Figure 2.4. Peter Paul Rubens, *Bathsheba*, 1635. Image courtesy of Art Resource, New York.

Portuguese merchants cut a wide arc around the city during the war, cutting the port off from valuable resources.[21]

There is little surviving evidence to indicate the number of Africans in the city after the siege. Although many other major port cities were seeing an increase in their African populations, it is very likely that the black population in Antwerp would have plummeted. Fewer slaves were coming in. In addition, in an Inquisition-style decree, the Spanish mandated that Antwerp's Jewish and Protestant populations convert to Catholicism or vacate the city. Tens of thousands fled, heading north to Amsterdam, the pulsing new hub of the Low Countries. At the time, many of the city's Africans were slaves or domestic servants to the city's large population of Sephardic Jews.[22] Perhaps owing to the diminishing populations of black people in Antwerp, Rubens did not appear to have worked with black female models. His eclectic approach of representing black women as dark-skinned Europeans and small young servant girls to goddesses and high-born women appears to be a result of the lack of live models to work with.[23]

Regardless, Rubens did appear to have his mind made up about one thing: white women were the most beautiful women in the world. Rubens wrote a treatise on beauty and proportionality, one that contained an entire chapter devoted to the specific good looks of women. The manuscript, *Theory of the Human Figure,* was reminiscent of the late Renaissance master Albrecht Dürer's *Four Books on Human Proportion* in its studious return to classical theories of art and beauty. Indeed, while Rubens never took to mathematical calculations of perfect proportions, he wrote a statement on female beauty that could have easily been borrowed from the Renaissance master, claiming that "the body must not be too thin or too skinny, nor too large or too fat, but with a moderate embonpoint, following the model of the antique statues."[24] Moreover, like Dürer and other masters of the prior century, he paid homage to Venus and the classical ideal while also describing in detail the value of added padding in the proper places.[25] According to Rubens, "The hip, or the tops of the thighs, and thighs themselves should be large and ample, . . . the buttocks should be round and fleshy, . . . the knees should be fleshy and round."[26]

Where Rubens differed from Dürer was in his admiration of a peculiarly "white" kind of beauty. In his descriptions of the proper amount of flesh and fat that should be present on a woman's body, he also states, "The skin should be solid, firm and white, with a hint of a pale red, like the color of milk tinged with blood, or a mix of lilies and roses." Of the voluptuous backsides he fetishizes, he prefers that they remain "white as snow."[27]

Rubens made only one reference to a black woman in the text. In a section titled "How the Ancients Represented Their Goddesses," he notes that "Venus was represented by the Lacedaemonians being armed for battle. In Arcadia, she was black. In Cyprus she had a spike, a masculine air, and feminine garb. In Egypt, the goddess of love was represented with wings."[28] The point of mentioning the legend of the black Venus in Arcadia, it seems, was to diminish its stature or perhaps even discount it. Rubens effectively relegates the black Venus of Arcadia to a footnote in the history of Venus statues, a cultural curiosity, comparable to a winged goddess or one wielding a spike. He makes this position clear when he claims that "there are 100 other statues" he could mention, "but suffice it to say that each one represents the region it comes from."[29]

There is scant evidence from surviving texts to suggest that Rubens actively harbored a disdain for black women. Rather, he was working during a period of profound cultural change, a shift in the way Europeans saw Africans. Artists in the Dutch and English Golden Ages were less likely to gush about the beauty of Africans and more likely to note their social—and now also *embodied*—distinctions from whites.[30] Importantly, Rubens's work throws into relief the historical moment in which distinctions between African and European women came to increasingly rely on the physical body. For Rubens, and a growing number of artists and philosophers, white skin was necessary to elevate a woman to the height of bodily beauty.

It is not for nothing that the Netherlands would have been one of the earliest places to witness this evolution in the relationship between skin color and beauty. In the early seventeenth century, Dutch provinces were still embroiled in a costly war with Spain. What they desired, in addition to their independence, was a viable presence in the lucrative market of international trade. To that end the enslavement of Africans, while inhumane, was to prove intensely profitable. In 1602 the

Dutch government decided to throw its support behind homegrown merchants determined to enter the trade. Established in Amsterdam, a mere hundred miles from Antwerp, the Dutch East India Company (also known as the VOC) was made up of local merchants and investors.[31] It was backed by the States General of the Netherlands, which offered the chartered company a trade monopoly in trade routes between parts of Asia, South America, and South Africa. It became, by many accounts, the world's first multinational corporation.[32] Gaining a foothold in the spice industry after Antwerp had been cut off may have been one of the VOC's key directives, but it did more than dabble in the slave trade. Scholars have shown that by the 1650s, envoys with the VOC set down roots in the Cape of Good Hope, enslaving innumerable members of the indigenous Khoikhoi, or as they became known to the Dutch, the "Hottentot."[33]

If the VOC made slavery only one of the tools in its trading arsenal, the Dutch West India Company (WIC) made the traffic in human commodities its main directive. Founded only a few years after the VOC, the WIC had as one of its primary objectives what has been euphemistically described as establishing "direct relations with indigenous people in African coastal regions."[34] While the VOC operated largely on the Indian Ocean, the States General granted the WIC a trade monopoly on the Atlantic between Africa and the Americas. Between the 1630s and the 1650s, the WIC became the dominant force in the African slave trade.[35]

While these developments may seem tangential to the question of aesthetics, they were, in fact, integral to the issue. As Simon Gikandi has noted, the slave trade was fundamental to the development of the bourgeoning "culture of taste."[36] Within this culture, the objectification of black bodies and labor through the slave trade turned black people themselves into the shadow figures of modernity, appearing to exist outside of and in opposition to it.[37] Black people thus increasingly came to represent *différance,* or a perverse primitivity and backwardness, a "polemical otherness."[38] Black people became, in other words, aesthetic counterpoints within the budding culture of taste. This had a visible impact on the representations of black women, given the centrality of appearance to the assessment of a woman's worth.[39] Once accorded a measure of dignity and desirability, black women were progressively represented as small, low, and foul. White women dominated the landscape of statuesque beauties.

* * *

England had been a relative latecomer to the traffic in Africans in both art and commerce. The country had not participated in the slave trade during its entire first century. But in the late sixteenth century, England was transformed from underdog to dominant global power. As a nation, England appeared to have skipped the honeymoon phase of infatuation with African slaves witnessed elsewhere on the Continent during the early years of the slave trade. The first slaves had appeared in England in 1555.[40] That same year, damning representations of Africans cropped up. In one book from 1555, the authors described Africans as "animals . . . [who] would fall upon their women." Moreover, Africans were described as "utterly free from care because they are always sure to have plenty of food."[41]

The stereotype that black people were sexually and orally indulgent quickly gained traction.[42] By the early seventeenth century, the perception that Africans freely gratified their animal appetites was expressed by some of the most elite members of English high society.[43] The celebrated statesman and author Francis Bacon issued a two-part condemnation of African appearance and character that incorporated these two stereotypes, among others. In it, Bacon parroted the view, also popular in the Low Countries, that "Ethiopians," as he called them, were "little, foul, and ugly." He added to this the now familiar English view that black people were libidinous, writing that they embodied the very "Spirit of Fornication."[44]

Perhaps it will come as no surprise, then, that in seventeenth-century England, as in the Low Countries, as blackness was linked to unattractiveness so was whiteness increasingly linked to beauty. Turn-of-the-century England, known as the Golden Age of English art, philosophy, and culture, was distinct in the tenacity of these color-based associations. For starters, while whiteness had long been associated with purity, goodness, and beauty in the country, the reign of the virgin queen, praised for her glowing alabaster skin, codified the association for the citizenry.[45] Poets produced song and verse in homage to their Christian ruler, such as the following:

> Her hand as white as whale's bone
> Her finger tipt with Cassidone
> Her bosom, sleek as Paris plaster
> Held up two bowls of Alabaster.[46]

If the queen's skin was indeed "white as whale's bone," it wasn't attributable so much to God as to the milk-colored lead paint she was known to be fond of applying to her face and arms.[47] Nevertheless, the whiteness of her skin, even if owing to cosmetics, elicited positive feelings among her countrymen. The praise surrounding her eventually reached cult status. Historians have shown that her whiteness was a focus for her subjects' sentiments.[48]

There was a second reason that the fetish for whiteness reached a fever pitch in seventeenth-century England. Artistic representations had been severely restricted in the country as a result of the Protestant Reformation a century earlier. As a result, images that did not appear to accurately reproduce biblical lore, including those featuring black people, were forbidden and in some instances destroyed.[49] The pigeonholing of visual imagery effectively stunted the growth of British painting until the Restoration of Charles II in 1660.[50] For this reason, representations of black people by domestic painters were nearly nonexistent for the country's first century of involvement in the slave trade. When they did make appearances prior to 1660, it was less in the visual arts than in official court records, poetry, literature, and court masques.[51] The first black women in the court record, for example, arrived as maids in the retinue of Catherine of Aragon in 1501. Catherine appeared on official business, an arranged marriage to the English Prince Arthur. Very little information survives about her cortege, but we do know that her black female servants were ridiculed by Sir Thomas More, key counselor to Elizabeth's father, King Henry VIII, as "hunchbacked, undersized, and barefoot Pygmies of Ethiopia."[52]

Sir Thomas More's evaluation of black women as small and deformed was a prelude to the linking of black femininity and the grotesque in Elizabethan art and literature. William Shakespeare often featured tortured black characters in his plays. In *Othello*, the title character despaired over being treated as a "lascivious Moor."[53] Less frequently, however, have scholars commented on Shakespeare's dismissal of black femininity, as appears in his famed *Midsummer Night's Dream*.[54] In the play, Hermia is spurned by her suitor, Lysander, who rejects her in favor of the fair Helena. In the aftermath, Helena and Lysander attack Hermia. Lysander demands that she take her leave, yelling, "Away you Ethiope!" and "Out tawny, tartar, Out!" When Hermia still refuses to leave, the trio have the following exchange:

HELENA

O, when she's angry, she is keen and shrewd!
She was a vixen when she went to school;
And though she be but little, she is fierce.

HERMIA

"Little" again! nothing but "low" and "little"!
Why will you suffer her to flout me thus?
Let me come to her.

LYSANDER

Get you gone, you dwarf;
You minimus, of hindering knot-grass made;
You bead, you acorn.[55]

In a neat jumble, Shakespeare makes Hermia at once a "vixen," capable since a young age of luring men with her sexual charms, as well as a grotesque and "low" dwarf. For her sexual and physical transgressions, she is discarded. Helena, Lysander's newly chosen lover, is by contrast depicted as tall, white, and slim, like a "painted maypole."

English ladies weren't only painting themselves white to enhance their beauty. They were also painting themselves black to reveal, through contrast, the alleged hideousness of black women. In 1605, shortly after the death of Elizabeth, an infamous court masque known as *The Masque of Blackness* was presented by Jacob I's queen, Anne of Denmark, and her court. *The Masque of Blackness*, by Ben Jonson, presented the tale of King Niger and his twelve daughters. While the king tries to convince his daughters that they are beautiful, they despise their black skin. An oracle (Aethiope) tells the girls that if they wish to remove their blackness, they should go to the land with the name ending in -*TANIA* (that is, Britannia), also known as "Albion the Fair."

The twelve daughters were played by Queen Anne and her ladies in blackface. Their faces and their arms up to the elbows were painted black, leading the English art collector Sir Carleton, who once sat for a portrait by Rubens, to cringe, claiming the "lean-cheeked Moors" they invented to be a "loathsome sight" indeed.[56] Neither Sir Carleton nor the twelve painted black ladies were to find any relief until Ben Jonson finished the sequel, which was performed in 1608. At that time, they arrive at the Throne of Beauty in Britannia, where they bask in the sun's (less scorching) glow while chanting, "Yield night, then to the light, as blackness hath to beauty."[57]

Such was the double signification of fairness in sixteenth- and seventeenth-century English literature. After the Restoration, black women were seldom represented in painting, and when they did appear, they were not miraculously re-christened in England as the beauties they had been in other places at other times. Being commonly retained as pages and sexual conveniences for men from the rising world powers, they remained in the popular imagination as little, base, and licentious.

* * *

The rise of the slave trade also had a direct impact on changing ideas about the good qualities associated with being fat among the English people. Perishable goods reaped from slave labor began arriving from the colonies that would forever change the English way of life, one of which would go on to have a curious impact on the English diet and body size: sugar. Sugar production had been developing at breakneck speed in late sixteenth-century Brazil, then a colony of Portugal. In the 1620s the Dutch Republic attempted a hostile takeover of the northernmost Brazilian territories. The war that ensued was fought in a series of skirmishes in which the Dutch captured a key port in 1630, only to lose it again in 1654.[58] In the meantime, sugar production in Brazil dropped precipitously, a shift that allowed the British and their colony of Barbados to step into the void.[59]

The mind-boggling profits the English reaped from sugar plantations were one obvious benefit of this trade. Another was the widespread availability of a commodity once deemed so rare and enticing that it was dubbed "white gold." In 1660 England imported 1,200 barrels of sugar from Barbados and other key West Indian holdings. By 1700, that amount had jumped to 50,000 barrels. When it came to the sheer volume of sugar sent to the mother country, the British were rivaled only by the Dutch.[60] As sugar imports soared, prices plummeted, making what was formerly a luxury item readily available to the average citizen of England and Holland.[61] Teahouses and coffeehouses sprang up on fashionable London thoroughfares. Sugar was creating whole new industries in centers of European social life and culture, along with delicious new opportunities for daily delight.

But with the improved standard of living came the dissipations of the high life. While malnutrition remained the prevailing concern for most of the population, a mounting number of the moderately well-off were growing fat. Doctors in England eyed the swelling number of fat people with consternation. In 1620, for example, the Oxford-trained English physician Tobias Venner lamented the rising rates of corpulence among the English.[62] Using for the first time the word "obesus" to describe excess fat, Venner argued that "obesity" had adverse health consequences. He offered a treatment "to make slender such bodies as are too grosse."[63]

The changes in the English diet enabled by sugar plantations in the colonies also led to rising rates of a purportedly related illness: gout. With the introduction of sugar and sugar-sweetened alcoholic beverages such as sack (a sugar-sweetened wine), gout was becoming an epidemic in England, particularly among men, who are more susceptible to the illness. Known previously as the disease of kings and the king of diseases, by 1683 the sweeping problem of gout prompted Dr. Thomas Sydenham to write *A Treatise of the Gout and Dropsy* in an effort to detail the etiology of the disease and offer practical advice to its sufferers.[64]

In Sydenham's estimation, gout overwhelmingly struck those "who happen to be of a robust habit, who lead an indolent life, and are used to live very full."[65] The "robust habit" referred to a rich diet paired frequently with wine and beer. This behavior, he claimed, was particularly common among the male sex, since women rarely exhibited such a "voracious appetite" and "immoderate" drinking behavior.[66] And, believing that overindulgence was the cause, Sydenham added that gout typically beset the "gross and corpulent," although it occasionally befell lean and slender folk as well.[67] Sydenham was himself a gout sufferer. He believed himself to be speaking both as a medical authority and as a fellow, fat, gout-afflicted man. Interestingly, while Sydenham and Venner pointed to diet as causes of corpulence and illness, neither recognized sugar as a potential cause. Sydenham, in the denial typical of a sugar addict, actually suggested that a concoction using brown sugar and the syrup of marshmallows be used as a cure.[68]

Sugar was rarely if ever recognized by seventeenth-century English physicians as the culprit driving both gout and what was described as "gross" corpulence. But this was largely because many doctors didn't quite understand how along with the quantity, the quality of the food consumed, affected a person's weight. This situation was to change in the coming century. Still, in Holland, the other country where sugar consumption, corpulence, and gout were on the rise, at least one seventeenth-century physician was making the connection among the three. In the same year that Sydenham published his *Treatise*, the Dutch doctor Stephen Blankaart wrote that the ubiquity of sugar in Amsterdam was associated with the marked increase of cavities, corpulence, and gout.[69]

Fatness was becoming more common, but it remained a condition common among the relatively well-off. Regardless, Western doctors were making nascent arguments about the link between fatness and ill health.[70] Still, concerns about the physical health of the fat man as he partook of white gold and port wine was not the foremost concern of the high-minded Englishman. For the English intellectual, fat bodies had a different, pernicious association.

* * *

In Shakespeare's *Love's Labour's Lost*, the king of Navarre and three of his oldest friends swear an oath of austerity. As part of the oath, they promise to remain celibate, fast one day each week, and eat only one meal per day the remaining days of the week. The pact was to last for three years.[71] The character Longaville explains,

> I am resolved: 'tis but a three years' fast.
> The mind shall banquet though the body pine.

> Fat paunches have lean pates, and dainty bits
> Make rich the ribs, but bankrupt quite the wits.[72]

Longaville here describes a mind and body in conflict. When a man plies his body with food and drink, developing "fat paunches" and "rich ribs," he is also bankrupting his wits. But when a man fasts, starves his body, makes it "pine," now he is offering his mind a "banquet," one that makes possible higher intellectual pursuits.

This quote, particularly the couplet that begins, "Fat paunches have lean pates," was widely circulated in seventeenth-century England. Many believe it was originally penned by Shakespeare, but there is also evidence that he cribbed the idea from Saint Jerome, the fourth-century Roman priest. Jerome himself was thought to have translated the Greek expression "A fat belly does not produce fine senses."[73]

Even if Shakespeare is not the ultimate source of the expression, it is consequential that several of his works propagated the view that slim men had sharp wits, whereas fat men were insipid. This was to be found, for example, in *The Tragedy of Julius Caesar,* when Caesar states,

> Let me have men about me that are fat;
> Sleek-headed men and such as sleep o' nights:
> Yond Cassius has a lean and hungry look;
> He thinks too much: such men are dangerous.[74]

The view of fat men as too self-indulgent to be particularly intelligent was embodied in the character of Sir John Falstaff. Falstaff, who appears in several of Shakespeare's plays, was creative and resourceful in some respects, but too much of a gluttonous, drunken, braggart and a thief to be taken as a thoughtful nobleman. He cops to this in *Henry IV* when he cries, "If I do grow great, I'll grow less; for I'll purge, and leave sack, and live cleanly as a nobleman should do."[75]

Coming from one of the most important artist-intellectuals of the English Golden Age, these and other works by Shakespeare make a broad cultural statement. They suggest that greater than concerns about the potential relationship between fat and health during this era was the dread of fatness as indicative of weak character and dullness of mind. Indeed, it was not only artists and poets who made such connections.

Figure 2.5. Eduard von Grützner, *Falstaff*, 1910.

Many important scientists and natural philosophers shared the perception that full stomachs were correlated to empty heads.

The writings of René Descartes are a case in point. Though he was not an Englishman, Descartes's ideas were incredibly influential among English intellectuals. He too claimed that base sensual desires, especially for food and drink, could stand in the way of higher pursuits. Condemning the animal appetites, Descartes offered counsel to those who might otherwise be prone to overindulgence in food and drink. In a series of letters on the topic to his friend Princess Elisabeth of Bohemia, the granddaughter of King James I, he advised Elisabeth to regulate her food intake so as to ensure the best exercise of her mental faculties, urging "a good diet, taking only food and drink that refreshes the blood and purges without any effort."[76] Elisabeth countered: "As for the remedies against excessive passions: I agree that they are hard to practise, and indeed that they aren't sufficient to prevent bodily disorders; but they may suffice to prevent the soul from being troubled and losing its capacity for free judgment."[77] These correspondences underscore the belief that eating too much stymied rational thought. Freeing oneself from the whims of sensual desire created space for intelligent thought and action.

Elisabeth was not the only English person privy to Descartes's discourses on the appetites.[78] His ideas about the relationship between appetites and intellect spread like wildfire in England. Those who did not identify as Cartesians respected his import, even reproducing similar notions, particularly when it came to questions of overfeeding.[79] Walter Charleton, a natural philosopher and court physician to Elisabeth's uncle, Charles I, was one such intellectual. Charleton published his own treatise on the perils of overindulgence. The "finest wits," Charleton wrote, were not "the custody of gross and robust bodies; but for the most part [are lodged] in delicate and tender constitutions."[80] As a physician, Charleton was likely aware of the growing medical concern regarding portliness among English men. But, in keeping with many intellectuals at the time, Charleton's own concern seems to have been less about the effects of excess fat on the body than about what corpulence indicated about the mind. When he wrote about the ill effects of fatness, he was concerned with what obesity revealed about the character and mental capacity of the man who might so openly flaunt his rotund body.

Other English intellectuals were more directly influenced by Descartes. And in terms of the presumed relationship between fat and intellect, they resolved to practice what they preached. Robert Boyle, for example, a contemporary of Charleton and a follower of Descartes's life and work, was nearly as well known for his abstemious diet and delicate physique as for his theories. His body was believed to be a demonstration of his mental fortitude, as he was praised for his "depth of knowledge" and his refusal to allow the vagaries of appetite to derail him: "he neither ate, nor drank to gratify the varieties of appetite, but merely to support nature"; for these reasons, he was deemed "thin and fine"—with the latter term here serving as a synonym of refined—like a typical "hard student."[81]

English philosophers, several of whom were influenced by Descartes, treated fatness as evidence of vapidity. Such was the case with the philosopher Henry More. More's lean physique lent credibility to his intellectual pursuits. Early in his career, More maintained an avid love affair with Cartesianism, which came to an abrupt halt as he matured. But he never escaped the swirling cultural influence articulated perhaps most

Figure 2.6. Peter Lely, *Portrait of the Honorable Robert Boyle*, 1689. Image courtesy of Bridgeman Images.

notably by Descartes on the relationship between sensuality and intellect. More was known to have "reduc'd himself . . . to almost Skin and Bones."[82] He was praised by his own biographer for his temperance and his "ethereal sort of body," which served as evidence of his mastery over the animal nature within.[83]

This is where, unexpectedly, the artist and diplomat Peter Paul Rubens comes back into frame. Rubens never knew Charleton, who took the post as court physician one year after the artist's death, but he had frequent dealings with the English. In the early 1620s, Rubens could count King Charles I among his high-class art patrons and protégés. An amateur painter and art collector, Charles I had pestered Rubens for a self-portrait, which the artist reluctantly provided.[84]

Rubens died before Cartesianism took off. But it is worth noting that Descartes was only an important proponent, and not the progenitor, of the relationship between abstemiousness and intellect. Renaissance artists and intellectuals in England and the Low Countries often harbored a romance for Neoplatonic austerity. Rubens was, surprisingly perhaps, counted in this number. For though he is remembered for painting round and fleshy women with skin "white as snow," he himself observed a strict diet. Writing to his nephew, Rubens lamented the fatness of so-called modern men:

> The chief cause of the difference between the ancients and men of our age is our laziness. . . . [We are] always eating, drinking and [have] no care to exercise our bodies. Therefore, our lower bellies, ever filled by a ceaseless voracity, bulge out overloaded, our legs are nerveless, and our arms show the signs.[85]

The strapping Peter Paul would have none of this "flabbiness" for himself. He was known to rise at 4:00 a.m. and eat little throughout the day so that his stomach and its digestion would not get in the way of his intellectual and artistic endeavors.

The affectations of these artists, philosophers, and scientists may not have represented those of the average seventeenth-century man, but they slowly came to represent those of the typical intellectual. By the mid-eighteenth century, the archetype of the thin and refined male student and thinker was widespread, particularly in England. Still, sentiments about male slimness were divided. While some people continued to believe that a lean physique was a laudable display of a man's ambition and dedication to higher pursuits, others claimed that it represented a moribund seriousness and a complete abandonment of healthy living.[86] Thus, during the seventeenth century, when fatness began its slow decline into disrepute, it was concerns over *ascetics* and not aesthetics that drove the distaste for fat male bodies.

* * *

At the tail end of the seventeenth century came another important innovation by a French intellectual: racial categorization. François Bernier developed the first racial classification scheme in the Western world.

Like the ideas of Descartes, the ideas of Bernier were taken up swiftly and with relish among English intellectuals.

The creation of a racial classification system had a palpable impact on conceptions of whiteness and blackness. For while intellectual men had reserved for themselves the vaunted capacity of reason, the new and rapidly spreading ideas about race suggested that rationality was, in fact, an inherent quality of white persons. This rationality was now to apply to all aspects of life, including aesthetic ideals.

As we will see, it was from the late seventeenth century through the early nineteenth century that the inception and specification of ideas about white and black "races" changed yet again the understanding of the relative appearance of white and black women. For if black women were transformed from voluptuous bodily exemplars in the sixteenth century to little, low, and foul in the seventeenth century, in the eighteenth century their presumed racial proclivities (including that of irrational and unrestrained eating) would transform them into the unsightly—even "monstrously"—fat.

PART II

Race, Weight, God, and Country

3

The Rise of the Big Black Woman

François Bernier was the salt of the earth. His parents were tillers of the soil in a small farming town in northwestern France. From these humble origins, he would go on to make a significant contribution to Western intellectual history. He would be the first person in the world to create a system of human classification based on "race."

The field of what is today known as "race science" took off during the long eighteenth century, a period that encompasses the High Enlightenment and the peak of the transatlantic slave trade.[1] France and England were cultural and colonial powerhouses during the era. Learned men from these two nations generated a significant portion of the racial scientific theories.

Though Bernier was first to market, scholars have typically overlooked or diminished the significance of his racial theories. But Bernier's intervention in the field of race science was consequential. His work reveals the centrality of concerns about feminine aesthetics to race-making projects since their inception. That is, integral to Bernier's and many subsequent racial classification systems was the attempt to pin down fundamental physical differences between Europeans and non-Europeans, with an intense focus on the women in various categories. These differences were to serve as proof of European superiority. In this way, whereas women's physicality had been largely outside the social distinctions that were made between Europeans and Africans in the Renaissance, by the eighteenth century it was treated as foundational to them. The racialized female body became legible, a form of "text"[2] from which racial superiority and inferiority were read.

Bernier was born in 1625 in a small town in Anjou, France. Upon the death of his parents he came under the guardianship of his uncle, a priest.[3] At the age of fifteen, he moved to Paris to attend the Collège de Clermont, and it was there that this son of a farmer encountered the high gloss of the French elite, inhabiting the same adolescent social world as the celebrated French playwright Molière. At the Collège, Bernier became most closely acquainted with the notorious opponent of Descartes, the priest and philosopher Pierre Gassendi.[4] In the throbbing Parisian metropolis, Bernier trained under Gassendi in philosophy and physiology. Together, the two traveled to the south of France, where Bernier earned a medical degree from the University of Montpellier in just three months. The degree, however, carried the somewhat suspect stipulation that his fast-tracked medical knowledge was not to be exercised in the French commonwealth.

Bernier then set out for different pastures. In late 1658, by then in his early thirties, he landed in India, where he would remain for the next twelve years, serving as the private physician first for Prince Dara Shikoh and then for Dara's brother and rival for the throne, Aurangzeb. The intimate details of these events and his role as a foreign witness are described in Bernier's book *Travels in the Mogul Empire*.[5] His travelogue mirrors the narratives written by earlier Europeans on their treks beyond the continent. What distinguished Bernier's account, however, was that he chose not just to describe men and women from various locales in India but to sort them based on their skin color. According to Bernier, for example, "To be a Mogol it is enough that a foreigner have a white face and profess Mahometanism." This group was compared to the Franguis, or white Christians from Europe, and to the Indous, "whose complexion is brown."[6]

Bernier did not see himself as having invented these distinctions. In fact, he imagines himself an astute interpreter of existing social categories in India, in which he sees skin color as integral. In a letter to Jean-Baptiste Colbert, Louis XIV's finance minister, he marvels at the supposed Indian and Mogul fixation on biological purity and color, using the term "race" to mark distinctions between the various subgroups.[7]

Bernier had not invented the term "race," which had been in use since the Middle Ages.[8] But he was using it in a decidedly different fashion from those who came before. Bernier used the word to designate the clusters of people he encountered who varied by religion, region, and especially hue. The centrality of skin color in his early conception of race signaled a divergence from the ideas of theorists who preceded him. Still, in terms of Bernier's racial theorizing, this was only the beginning.

In the 1670s Bernier left India and returned to Paris, finding himself in a city embroiled in debates and demonstrations about one of the most pressing issues of his day: slavery. France had entered the transatlantic slave trade nearly a century after England, due in large part to religious infighting between the Catholic establishment and the Protestant Huguenots. The French slave trade was formally authorized by the monarchy in 1648. In 1664 Louis XIV granted Jean-Baptiste Colbert, along with his French West India Company, the sole rights to the transport of slaves from Africa to the French colonies in the Americas.[9]

The French slave trade was only a few years old by the time Bernier returned to his homeland, and it was experiencing considerable growing pains. Since 1315, the country had maintained what was known as a Freedom Principle, which stipulated that no person could be held as a forced laborer on French soil. This decree, however, said nothing about the practice of slavery in the French colonies, which the monarchy willingly allowed. The king thus found himself in the dubious position of denouncing slavery in the kingdom while issuing royal decrees sanctioning its practice in his colonies. The Janus-faced nature of these polices proved untenable. By the late seventeenth century, a smattering of African slaves were already making their way to French shores, sometimes as servants to colonial administrators, other times as stowaways. Many petitioned for their freedom the instant they set foot in the country. The king's position was to set free slaves seeking freedom within the country throughout the seventeenth century. This practice collided with the 1685 royal decree known as the Code Noir (Black Code), a law that regulated slavery in the colonies and served as a resounding renewal of colonial policies that condemned Africans to a lifetime of servitude. This inevitably led to ever more Africans seeking a taste of the vaunted but elusive French freedom that was being denied them in the overseas territories.[10]

Bernier was well aware of the tenuous political situation that slavery posed. He had a personal relationship with Colbert. Moreover, since his return to Paris, Bernier had become a member of Madame de la Sablière's salon, which was peopled with Louis XIV's courtiers and other nobles. One of the topics commonly up for debate was whether some groups of mankind were a different species than Europeans and thus

natural slaves.[11] This was not the first time Bernier would have encountered the question of whether "natural slaves" existed. These claims can
be traced to the origin story crafted by Isaac la Peyrère, who in the 1650s
conjectured that Gentiles were pre-Adamites, born before and somehow
superior to the Jews, who descended from the biblical Adam. Peyrère's
theory was deemed heretical by many in the 1650s, but in the context of
the rising slave trade and the profits it generated, many Frenchmen were
to soften on this position.

Scholars disagree as to whether Bernier himself was a polygenist,
a believer that the human races are of different origins.[12] But what is
evident is that his travels made him appear to others on the intellectual circuit as an expert on the topic of "alien" peoples. These attitudes,
along with Bernier's studies in physiology, ignited an idea. He resolved
to develop his own theory of humanity, one that could encompass and
explain the tremendous biodiversity he had encountered on his travels.
And in line with his medical training, his theory would be the first to
achieve this goal by identifying fundamental *physiological* differences
among swatches of humankind.

In 1684 Bernier sketched out his theory in a letter to Madame de la
Sablière that bore the rather grand title "A New Division of the Earth."
In this three-page manifesto, he explained his rationale for developing
this new model of humankind: "Hitherto, geographers have divided
the Earth only into different countries or regions therein; but my own
observations . . . have given me the idea of dividing it another way."[13]
The problem with the traditional, geographic dissection of the globe,
he concluded, was that it failed to acknowledge the tremendous physical distinctions found between peoples living in diverse parts of the
world. In Bernier's estimation, "Men are almost all distinct from one
another as far as the external form of their bodies is concerned, especially their faces, according to the different areas of the world they live
in."[14] And while globe-trotting men such as himself could "often distinguish unerringly one nation from another," he nevertheless found
that common unities of physical form across national boundaries
warranted a new system for classifying mankind, a system he called
"Types of Race."[15]

As noted, Bernier had not coined the term "race." But with his "New
Division of the Earth," he had fundamentally changed what it meant.

In his reimagination of the term, race did not apply only to the lowly "Jewish" or "Moorish" subjects of the crown or to the high-borns within the kingdom. Rather, all of the world's peoples had a race, one that could be identified both by where they lived and their external physical features.

Curiously, despite Bernier's certainty that everyone had a physically identifiable race, he nonetheless wavered on how many races there were in all, stating that there were "four or five."[16] The first race included people from three different continents, comprising "the whole of Europe in general except for part of Muscovy, . . . Africa, namely that between the kingdoms of Fez and Morocco, Algiers, Tunis and Tripoli, . . . and likewise a large part of Asia."[17] Into the second race he placed nearly the entire continent of Africa, excluding the northern coastal areas already ascribed to the first race.

The third race, covering the nations of China, Japan, and much of east Asia, also included "Usbekistan [sic], . . . a small part of Muscovy, the little Tartars, and the Turkomans."[18] In the fourth race, standing conspicuously alone, were the Lapps, or the indigenous people of Scandinavia. The almost-fifth race would have been reserved for the indigenous people of the Americas. But upon further consideration, he placed them too into the first type.[19]

Skin color was the major consideration used to sort people into racial groups. In Bernier's view, the first race had "white" or sun-tinged "olive skin." By contrast, black Africans, the so-called second race, had black skin that was the result of their "sperm and blood."[20] This simple one-liner, stated almost as if in passing, was of critical importance. Madame de la Sablière, hostess of his salon, had been an active participant in debates about the role of men's semen and women's eggs in the physical features of their offspring.[21] She therefore would likely have been invested in questions about the role of sperm in physical appearance. More to the point, this statement revealed Bernier's position on the biological basis of the physical distinctions among the so-called races. While it is unclear whether he was a proponent of the polygenetic argument, he nevertheless believed that white people were innately and physiologically distinct from black people. This fundamental biological divergence was, he suggested, the basis of the observed external physical differences.[22]

In his modest treatise, Bernier did not come out in favor of African chattel slavery. Yet, in the context of debates about the appropriateness of enslaving black persons, his assertion that white skin placed one in a biologically distinct "first race" while black skin placed a person in a "second race" carried the connotation of a social ladder of humanity with whites justifiably at the top. These ideas were to be read and expanded upon by subsequent scientists and philosophers, several of whom were deeply invested in maintaining or extending the slave trade.

If Bernier created racial categories for the express purpose of segregating groups of humanity based on their physical appearance, an important part of his project was to detail the particular aesthetic charms (or lack thereof) of the women of each race. Previous scholars have dismissed this aspect of Bernier's text as some form of bizarre fluff, evidence of his prurient fascination with women's looks.[23] But Bernier was building on a practice of learned men waxing intellectual about women's beauty that had existed since the Renaissance. Moreover, the section on female charms takes up nearly half of Bernier's brief manifesto. Under the circumstances, Bernier's estimation of women was not off-color, nor was it novel.[24] It simply used a new language, that of "race," to make judgments about feminine loveliness.

Bernier entered the discussion about race-specific female attractiveness with a note about the so-called Hottentot.[25] "Hottentot" was a derogatory name created by Dutch settlers. In theory, it applied to the Khoikhoi living in the area encompassing the Cape of Good Hope and extending to Cape Town in South Africa. In practice, however, it was often applied to all Khoisan, meaning both the Khoikhoi and the Bushmen of South Africa.[26] "Blacks of the Cape of Good Hope," Bernier wrote, "seem to constitute a different type from those of the rest of Africa. They are usually smaller, thinner, with uglier faces."[27] His estimation of the Hottentot is noticeably similar to the common view of Africans in England and Holland during the period as "little, low, and foul." Bernier was, in fact, attuned to existing stereotypes of the Hottentot, which he exposes by stating, "Some Dutchmen say they speak Turkey-Cock."[28]

What distinguished Bernier from the Dutch and English, however, was his assessment that the small, thin, and unappealing Hottentot were an aberration among blacks, a "different type," albeit relegated to the same race. The Hottentot, in his view, may have been short, meager, and unattractive, but this said nothing of the appearance of blacks generally, and especially black women. On the contrary, Bernier wrote, he had encountered black women who were among the most beautiful in the world:

> What I have observed as regards the beauty of women is no less differenti-
> ated. Certainly, there are lovely ones, ugly ones to be found everywhere.
> I have seen some real beauties in Egypt, which put me in mind of the fair
> and famed Cleopatra. Among the Blacks of Africa I have also seen some
> very beautiful women who did not have thick lips and snub noses. I have
> encountered seven or eight in various places who were of such an astonish-
> ing beauty that they put in the shade the Venus of the Palazzo Farnese in
> Rome—with aquiline nose, small mouth, coral lips, ivory teeth, large bright
> eyes, gentle features and a bosom and everything else of utter perfection. At
> Moka, I saw several of them completely naked, waiting to be sold, and I can
> tell you, there could be nothing lovelier in the world to see.[29]

Bernier affirms racial differences in beauty by claiming that, like physical features in general, "the beauty of women is no less differenti-ated."[30] Nevertheless, he certifies black women's attractiveness by using the existing standard for white women: "aquiline nose, small mouth, coral lips, ivory teeth, large bright eyes, gentle features."[31] In this way, the black women who were good-looking could lay claim to that title only because of their similarity to the neoclassical ideal of Venus. Indeed, these women appear to be beating the Venus at her own game. Although Bernier was influenced by the trail of black denigration left by the Dutch and the English, he did not let their perspective of black women contra-dict what he had seen with his own eyes.

His discussion of the attractiveness of (some) black women was only the starting point of his extended treatment of racially specific entice-ments. Bernier also included sections on the women he encountered in India, Turkey, and Persia. His work reveals the centrality of concerns about aesthetics, especially women's appearance, in the articulation of racial theories. That is, to the extent that "sperm and blood" determined race and appearance, beautiful women could serve as proof of a certain type of inherent racial superiority, or inferiority.

The long-term impact of Bernier's theories has been debated.[32] But as a progenitor of racial theories, Bernier was often cited by subsequent race theorists. Later race theorists would routinely use race as a justification for the colonial condition, and as a way to determine the attractiveness of women around the world. In the mid-eighteenth and early nineteenth centuries in the context of the Enlightenment and the peak of the slave trade, the science of race-making took flight. Then, as at its inception, philosophers underscored the purported racial distinctions in facial features, body type, and attractiveness between black women and white women.

Bernier's notion of race had touched a nerve. His letter to Madame de la Sablière was eventually published in the esteemed *Journal des Scavans* for the broader scientific community to mull over. Still, the evidence of its impact was not to be witnessed for another sixty years. As it turned out, many French scientists and philosophers at the time of his writing were preoccupied with either toeing the intellectual line or fleeing the country in the face of renewed religious persecution.

* * *

A variety of freedoms were restricted by Louis XIV in the 1680s. The king had long been begrudging at best when it came to the rights of Protestants. But in the watershed year of 1685, alongside the Code Noir, the king also issued the Edict of Fontainebleau. This order unraveled the Edict of Nantes, which had offered Protestant Huguenots a modicum of freedom in a Catholic nation, thereby effectively outlawing Protestantism in the territory. At the outset, rather than fight another bloody religious war, many Protestants chose to flee, repairing to various parts of England, the Dutch Republic, and Prussia.[33] But by the turn of the eighteenth century, many of the remaining Protestants, calling themselves the Camisards, took up arms in a new war. The reinvigorated religious battle competed with the war of Spanish succession for the king's attention and the crown's resources until Louis XIV's death in 1715.

The king's death had a ripple effect, triggering several important developments that would allow the national intelligentsia to return to honing their ideas of race. For one, Louis XIV's policies had prevented widespread slavery in the French territories. His passing gave functionaries an opportunity to push for new legislation enabling slave owners to safely travel to their homeland with their human assets in tow, without fear of these assets being liberated on arrival.

The Edict of October, issued in 1716, intended to quell these fears by introducing new regulations that would allow slave holders to keep their slaves as long as the slaves were registered at the courthouse; unregistered slaves could be set free. Louis XV himself issued the next key piece of legislation, the Declaration of 1738, stipulating that unregistered slaves, rather than being freed, would be seized and sent back to the colonies, where they would presumably find themselves slaves to a new master.[34] Importantly, these codes were to be specifically applied to *nègres*, or African slaves. This meant that persons coming before the court demanding their freedom could be set free if they could successfully prove that they were not African. Such "proof" was generally found in their physical traits, those having been elaborated by Bernier and a host of non-French European authors since the fifteenth century. Beginning in the 1740s, the intensely controversial nature of these laws and their requisite practice prompted a variety of intellectuals to revisit the question of potential fundamental differences within humankind.

In addition, the late king's death created the space for intellectual liberty that would allow the Enlightenment to flourish in France. The Enlightenment was a European intellectual movement that had actually begun in the mid-seventeenth century. Kindled by Descartes's 1637 *Discourse on Method* and its infamous postulate, "I think, therefore I am," a whole new era of inquiry developed in which reason was regarded as the primary source and arbiter of knowledge. These new adventures in what was called "rationalism" had been taking place largely outside the French commonwealth—in England, Scotland, and the Dutch Republic—since, in Descartes's home country, his ideas been deemed heretical by the monarchy. The death of Louis XIV loosened the monarchy's stranglehold on the dissemination of nontraditional ideas, officially launching the French Age of Reason. It was within this cultural and political environment that many of the most renowned thinkers of the French Enlightenment felt compelled to return their attention to the judiciously applied "fundamental differences" that exist within humanity. And quite promptly, Enlightenment luminaries like Georges-Louis Leclerc picked up where Bernier had left off.

* * *

Georges-Louis Leclerc was a prodigal son. His father was the lord of Buffon, a small township in eastern France. Born into a family of landed wealth, the teenage Georges-Louis bounced around colleges at his leisure before arriving in Angers in 1728. Shortly thereafter, his middling academic achievements were brought to an abrupt halt when, having been challenged to and subsequently losing a duel, he was forced to flee the city. Leclerc landed first in Nantes. From there, he set off for Italy and England with his comrade, a comparably well-off young English duke. Three years later, when Leclerc's mother died, he returned to take control of the family estate in Buffon, claiming his title, Comte de Buffon.

Back in his home country, he finally settled into a habit of serious intellectual inquiry. Within a few years, he had translated several key scientific works, including one by Sir Isaac Newton. In 1739 he was offered the privilege of serving as the keeper of the Jardin du Roi, or royal botanical garden in Paris, where he was assigned the task of cataloguing the royal holdings in natural history.[35] This activity culminated in Buffon's most significant work, *Histoire naturelle, générale et particulière* (*Natural History: General and Particular*), published in 1749.[36]

Buffon devoted a seminal chapter of the book, titled "Of the Varieties in the Human Species," to inquiries into the origin of presumed "natural" difference between the diverse peoples populating the earth. A staunch believer in the theory that all races descended from a common source, Buffon nevertheless believed in racial differences. He declared that individuals within a species who were capable of procreating, and whose offspring shared a set of traits that mirrored those of their progenitors, constituted members of a "race."[37] Echoing Bernier, Buffon avowed that the critical traits marking a race were physical, repeating the late doctor's point that "the first and most remarkable [difference] is the colour."[38]

After skin color, according to Buffon, the size and shape of the body were the next most important markers of physical distinction between the races. He had been aware of the stereotype of Africans as being "black, meager . . . and very small," which he attributed to the English seafarer Sir Francis Drake.[39] This stereotype, he claimed, was inaccurate. He countered by noting that there was considerable diversity among the peoples of Africa and that not all of them were diminutive in size. In Buffon's assessment, some Africans were meager and small, but they were not black Africans. Moors, he claimed, were "short, meagre, of a disagreeable aspect, but ingenious and subtle." Like Bernier, he claimed that they belong "to the race of whites."[40] Black Africans, or *les nègres* (the Negroes), by contrast, were "tall, plump . . . but simple and stupid."[41]

This distinction between Moors and blacks in size and stature, with blacks being labeled "plump," represented an important innovation in the elaboration of racial differences, or what Barbara and Karen Fields have called "racecraft."[42] This differentiation had been largely absent in England and Holland during the previous century, as evident in Buffon's criticism of Francis Drake's account of Africans. In this way, Buffon was able to speak authoritatively without having to wholly abandon the stereotype of "Africans" as short and slight, a stereotype already lodged in the European imagination. Rather, Buffon articulated a new physical identity for *black* Africans, who he claimed could be defined by both their dark skin and their enormity.[43]

According to Buffon, the "plumpness" of black Africans was evidence of their ease of circumstance and their idleness. The land "inhabited by the Negroes," he claimed, was "rich, abounding in pasturage, in millet, and in trees always green."[44] For this reason, black Africans were able to stay well nourished with little or no effort, which made them "well fed" but also "simple and stupid."[45] Buffon's linking of corpulence to laziness and slow-wittedness was in harmony with the ideas of the thin, fine, serious intellectuals of England of a century earlier, as well it should have been. Upon departing for England, Buffon found himself well received by the English intelligentsia. While there, he was elected a member of the Royal Society, one of Europe's first national scientific societies, whose founders included none other than the waifish Cambridge Platonist, Robert Boyle.

Buffon never met Boyle, who died before he was born. But Buffon would have been privy to the writings of Boyle and the Royal Society's other founders, as well as those of subsequent members represented in the Society's official journal, *Philosophical Transactions*. The journal was crammed with essays by scientists and physicians, several of whom shared Boyle's perspective that overindulgence and corpulence were signs of mental torpor. One entry, written in 1733 by a Dr. Alexander Stuart, is typical. Stuart was responding to a question about the cause of sleepiness after a meal. In his reply, Stuart conflated sleepiness with laziness, and claimed that this predicament was caused by overeating and a general lack of reasoned self-management, since it was usually "gross feeders, drunkards, corpulent, short neck'd by constitution" who felt sluggish after a meal. This lazy sleepiness, he argued, which routinely besets the robust and overindulgent, "never attends" those with the force of mind to be "temperate persons."[46] Stuart further added that the problem of post-meal lethargy was endemic in hot climates, which "makes the inhabitants generally lazy and inactive."[47]

Clearly, ideas linking insipidness, greediness, and corpulence had long been in circulation in the Royal Society. Beginning in the eighteenth century, these three traits were also being linked to hot climates. In this way, Buffon's theories connecting stupidity, plumpness or "bulk," and blackness were by no means fringe. His *Natural History* was intended to be the synthesis of decades' worth of great tomes and minor works that were part of the royal collection in France, as he still had an appointment in the Jardin du Roi. His connection with the Royal Society meant that his interpretation of the texts would likely reflect the Society's influence as well. Moreover, given the constant intellectual exchange between the English and the French during the Enlightenment, it is likely that many of the ideas, if not the critical texts themselves, would have been similar.

Buffon never traveled to the more remote regions of Africa that he expounded upon. More of an armchair cartographer, he used his significant talents for classification to make claims about the nature of the races.[48] And, as with Bernier, within his treatment of race he focused a great deal of his energy on the appearance of women. Buffon was the first celebrated scientist to assert that black Africans were plump, idle, and insipid. Yet, significantly, he did not find their figures unattractive. On the contrary. Buffon enthused about the "tall, plump" physique of *le nègre*, describing it as "well-made."[49] The term *le nègre* is itself gender-neutral, but when the topic turned to beauty, the language quickly became feminized.

Buffon appeared to find inspiration from a generation of race theorists as he slid seamlessly from the assertion that blacks were robust and well-made into a several-page dissertation on the beauty of shapely black women of select nations. In describing the women of Senegal, for example, whom he believed to be the most attractive of all black women, he stated,

> They are tall, very black, well proportioned, and their features are less harsh than those of the other Negroes. . . . [The Senegalese] have the same ideas of beauty as the Europeans, considering fine eyes, a well-formed nose, small mouth, and thin lips, as essential ingredients. . . . Their skin is soft and delicate, and, colour alone excepted, we find among them, women as handsome as in any other country of the world.[50]

In terms that echo the ideals of the High Renaissance, Buffon lauds the fine, "well-proportioned" figures of an entire nation of black women. In the midst of the Enlightenment's dismissal of corpulence as a sign of indolence and ignorance, particularly among men, he nevertheless continued to praise plumpness as an element of beauty in women. As with Bernier, it is significant that the presumed beauty of black African women is found not in their departure from European standards of face and physique, but in their adherence to those standards.

This may seem peculiar, given that the racial project was one of demarcation, of making and refining distinctions based on physical appearance. Instead, it reveals that the goal for many early theorists was to comprehend and make sense of the world's diversity. According to these theorists, women the world over may in some critical respects have been racially distinct, but this did not place all of them beyond the pale of sexual desirability. Evidently, some non-European women were measuring up, quite literally. In this way, early classification schemas may have been hierarchical, as we see with Bernier's "first race" theory and Buffon's estimation of the beauty of black women, "colour alone excepted." But the overarching project at the time was not necessarily to condemn black people to inferiority in every category.

Still, while such condemnation was not the original intent, the project of race making evolved. In the context of mushrooming French and British slave trade enterprises, presumed innate racial differences in mental capacity, industry, and sensual appetite came to be used as sound evidence of inherent inferiority. The body too became "legible" through racial discourse, as body size was increasingly linked to racial category.[51] This transformation built on the work of Buffon.

Discussions of race in *Natural History* represented little more than a review of the existing literature on the subject, and yet the work's influence was undeniable. *Natural History* was widely disseminated and often quoted among French intellectuals during the Enlightenment.[52] It found particular favor among radical rationalists such as Denis Diderot, whose own philosophical treatises on the use of reason (and not religion) for the attainment of moral excellence were winning him praise from the cognoscenti and heat from the Catholic clergy.

In 1749, as *Natural History* was being published, so was Diderot's *Letters on the Blind,* the most recent of his dissident discourses on Christianity. This work earned him a short stint in prison. When he was released, he lowered the volume of his atheistic rhetoric. He turned his attention instead to the development of a compendium that would rock the authority of the church in a more covert fashion, revealing the vast universe of knowledge being generated by rational scientific inquiry.[53] Diderot set to work on what would be his most celebrated and influential publication, the *Encyclopédie, ou Dictionnaire raisonné des sciences, des arts et des métiers (Encyclopaedia, or A Systematic Dictionary of the Sciences, Arts, and Crafts)*. In the first draft, he set himself the painstaking task of merging the most significant scientific and philosophical interventions of the time, which included skimpy characterizations of "Africa," "Africans," and "race." Explorations of the latter term were handpicked from his close friend Buffon's *Natural History,* from which he reportedly reproduced ideas as he saw fit.[54]

The first iteration of the *Encyclopaedia* offered only a terse summation of "Africans" suitable for use by those invested in commercial trade. But French investment in the slave trade was burgeoning, as was the number of black Africans making their way back to the French metropolis. The growing presence of blacks in the territories, along with the political dialogues swirling around them, may have encouraged Diderot to expand on the topic of blacks in subsequent editions of the *Encyclopaedia*. To do this, he tapped his friend and fellow philosopher Jean-Baptiste-Pierre Le Romain. Le Romain, who had lived in the Caribbean, was a self-styled expert on French colonies and sugar plantations.[55] He included in the *Encyclopaedia* the following description of *nègres* in the colonies:

> The [slaves] of Cap Verd . . . or Senegalese, are regarded as the most attractive in all of Africa. . . . The coast of Angola, the kingdoms of Loango and the Congo produce an abundance of attractive nègres. . . . Their penchant for pleasure makes them fairly unfit for hard labor, since they are generally lazy, cowardly, and very fond of gluttony. The least esteemed of all the nègres are the Bambaras; their uncleanliness, as well as the large scars that they give themselves across their cheeks from the nose to the ears, make them hideous. They are lazy, drunken, gluttonous, and apt to steal.[56]

Le Romain's judgment of the Senegalese as "the most attractive" of the black Africans seems to have been lifted directly from Buffon's text. Given not only the eminence of *Natural History* but also Diderot's personal ties to Buffon, this was probably no coincidence. But Le Romain dramatically shifted the tenor of his assessment from that of Buffon. In a neat few paragraphs he pulled together several defamatory generalizations about the blacks of Africa: that they were lazy and thieving, with a "penchant for pleasure" and a fondness of gluttony. Le Romain's use of the word "gluttony" had not been lifted from Buffon. In Buffon's opinion, the bulky frames of blacks were due to the ready availability of food, combined with their lack of the mental capacity needed to devote themselves to activities other than eating. Le Romain's use of the term "gluttony" implied something else, a willful greediness that ironically, given Diderot's atheism, evoked the seven deadly sins.

The *Encyclopaedia* seems to have been one of the earliest prominent publications to make the claim that blacks were "fond of gluttony." But it was not the first ever to do so, nor would it be the last. Reports had been making their way to Europe from the colonies describing the ritual practice of overfeeding in Africa for over a century. In the 1580s, for instance, the Italian botanist Prospero Alpini pronounced himself awestruck by what he called the "art of fattening" in Egypt. The women there, he claimed, ingested drugs and a cornucopia of food laden with animal fat in order to make themselves as rotund as possible. Alpini found this gluttonous indulgence a deeply disturbing "vice of the flesh," a sterling example of the immorality of the Egyptians:

> Can one desire anything more shameful than an obesity acquired through the infamous vice of the flesh and of unchecked sensuality? . . . This vice is so widespread down there that one sees most women flopped down on the ground like fat sows.[57]

Alpini was not alone in this assessment. In 1625 the Englishman Samuel Purchas published a four-volume set of stories pertaining to the inhabitants of distant lands, based partially on travel narratives left behind by his late countryman, Richard Hakluyt. In Purchas's *Hakluytus Posthumus, or Purchas His Pilgrimes*, he too expressed his disdain for the unbridled sensuality of blacks in Guinea, denouncing them as orally and sexually insatiable heathens:

> They have no knowledge of God. . . . They are very greedie eaters, and no lesse drinkers, and very lecherous, and theevish, and much addicted to uncleanenesse: one man hath as many wives as hee is able to keepe and maintaine.[58]

Accounts of black Africans eating to excess were clearly not unknown before the eighteenth century. But whereas earlier accounts fell into the category of outlandish tales of sensational cultural practices, by mid-century such narratives were becoming a type of gospel. Diderot's *Encyclopaedia* played no small part in this shift. The text was widely read and disseminated among intellectuals and those with commercial ties in Africa right up until the French Revolution.

The *Encyclopaedia* served as an important text in the new science of race. It lent credibility to the idea that it was not idle eating (as per Buffon) but the vice of gluttony that was inherent to the black African's sumptuous way of life. Given that such indulgence was intrinsic to the black way, it was not discouraged among the dark-skinned people but, according to scientists and philosophers in the new field of race science, positively encouraged.

If French intellectuals such as Buffon and Diderot detailed in their massive and influential oeuvres the so-called nature of the races, and within this the black African proclivity for overfeeding and fleshiness, British writers too were growing ever more scornful of the purported African gourmand.[59] The agreement among French and British authors on the question of excessive appetites among blacks is evident in the writings of the colonial transplant Edward Long. In 1774 Long wrote the influential *History of Jamaica*, in which he cast a wide net around the "Negroe race [*sic*]," suggesting that blacks in the Americas were no different from their brethren in Africa.[60] In a text rife with contradictions,[61] Long suggests that those persons from "Negro-land" in general "have no moral sensations, no taste but for women, gourmandizing and drinking to excess, but wish to be idle."[62]

If the statements labeling blacks as idle gourmands appear Buffonian, this is not a coincidence. Edward Long idolized Buffon, peppering his book with citations from the French thinker. It is not surprising, therefore, that Long, like Buffon, claims that many blacks were "large, fat, and well-proportioned," and not a few of the women were particularly "well-shaped" and worthy of praise.[63] This was owing not just to the "gourmandizing" predilection of blacks, but also the hot climates that contributed to their "corpulent and muscular" bodies.[64]

The major difference between Long and Buffon was that Long was a polygenist. He was convinced that the idle avarice of blacks, as well as their size and stature, proved that they were of a wholly different origin. In a mishmash of evidence used to reveal the absurdity of claims of human unity, Long cites not only Buffon but also a Shakespearean sonnet:

> "IN THE CATALOGUE THEY GO FOR *MEN*,
>   As hounds, and greyhounds, mongrels, spaniels . . .
>   *All* by the *name of dogs* . . .
>   That writes them all alike;—*And so of men*—"

says that faithful observer of nature our immortal Shakespear [*sic*]; and with him so far agrees the truly learned and sagacious naturalist Mons. Buffon, who investigates the marks of variation among mankind in the following manner: "Men differ from white to black, from compound to simple, by the height of stature, size . . . and other bodily characteristics; and from the genius to the dolt."[65]

Buffon and Shakespeare may seem like strange bedfellows. But Long's text shows how French and British literati could be randomly cited in service of claims about fundamental black-white distinctions.

It is not surprising that the French and British were at the helm of eighteenth-century racial scientific discourse marking black people as "gluttonous." The growing codification of black people as greedy eaters developed against the backdrop of the accelerating slave trade among these two colonial powers of the eighteenth century. This, together with the exigencies of reasoned self-management in the context of the High Enlightenment, transformed the act of eating from personal to political. Indulging in food, once deemed by philosophers to be a lowbrow predilection of slow-witted persons, became evidence of actual low breeding. It bespoke an inborn, race-specific propensity for laziness and ease, an unbridled desire to meet the demands of the flesh at the expense of cultivating higher pursuits. Such behavior was deemed wholly uncharacteristic of the rational thinkers sitting atop the new racial hierarchy.

And yet, up to this point, the large and robust feminine forms that such eating presumably engendered were still prized. The tail end of the eighteenth century would mark the dawn of a new era. In an attempt to rationalize even aesthetic values, the beauty of the plump feminine form was reconsidered.

* * *

Julien-Joseph Virey, the French anthropologist and naturalist, made no attempts to hide his admiration of Buffon. Virey had entered the military in the 1790s, his stint in the service being spent largely as a pharmacist at Val-de-Grâce hospital in Paris. It was likely in the armed service that Virey encountered Charles-Nicolas-Sigisbert Sonnini de Manoncourt. Sonnini de Manoncourt was a recognized naturalist and traveler who had himself been a member of the navy. He had also been a former secretary of Buffon, spending six months with the famed naturalist in the 1770s translating his texts. A shared fascination with natural history, and in particular the works of Buffon, led Virey and Sonnini de Manoncourt to collaborate on a reissue of Buffon's *Natural History* in 1799.[66]

For Virey, this was only the beginning. Two years later, he published his massive tome *Histoire naturelle du genre humain* (*Natural History of Mankind*), in which he provided his own anthropological insights into the nature and variety of humankind.

Virey, like his intellectual forebears, was captivated by the question of race, with a special interest in the character and physical traits of Africans.[67] In *Natural History of the Negro Race,* an excerpt from his *Natural History of Mankind* published as its own book in 1837, Virey asserts that Negroes were "of a mild disposition, robust, but slow and very lazy."[68] The Foulahs, a people inhabiting the region from Senegal to Northern Cameroon, he described as a "very handsome" people.[69]

With these observations, Virey appears to be simply retreading ground that had already been covered by Buffon and Diderot. Yet despite his admiration of Buffon, who had been a proponent of the environmental theory of racial difference, Virey had also been inspired by the creeping re-biologization of race that was taking place in his homeland. In the mid-eighteenth century in France, novel biological theories of racial difference—which were distinct from the early "sperm and blood" theories of Bernier—were gaining traction alongside the environmental theory of Buffon. Although Buffon had rejected claims of biological difference, during the eighteenth century they were revitalized.[70] By the nineteenth century they would be used to fill out and buttress Buffonian theories. Part of their appeal was that they provided a convenient explanation for both black skin and corpulence. According to the revitalized humoral theory, black skin was caused by a superabundance of black bile beneath the skin.[71] Moreover, an overflow of black bile could cause gastrointestinal disorders and weight gain.[72]

Virey was a voracious reader of bile theories, and he would make his own claims about black skin, gluttony, and weight. Black people, he claimed, were mindless, self-gratifying automatons who were "given up to the pleasures of the table, those great eaters, intemperate epicures who seem to live only to eat, have a stupid look . . . always digesting, they become incapable of thinking."[73] In this way, they were distinct from whites. He elaborated,

> In our white species, the forehead is projecting and the mouth retreating, as if we were rather designed to think than to eat; in the negro species,

the forehead is retreating and the mouth projecting, as if he were made to eat rather than to think.[74]

Virey further used the language of bile theory to claim that fatness was directly correlated with skin color: "[Those] who are darker than others of the same race are also more robust, active, and stout."[75] The reason for this, he asserted, was that "the hot sun causes the body to hold onto this excess liquid fat, allowing it to accumulate in the breast and belly."[76] In this way, those who live with greater exposure to the sun, are thus more likely to be darker-skinned, and are also going to experience an unsightly "excess" of liquid fat accruing on the body.

This was Virey's general view of the relationship between skin color and superfluous fat when he (inexplicably) chose the tawny-hued so-called Hottentot peoples as his example of dark-skinned greed and corpulence. His reason for doing so remains elusive. But, since Virey was yet another desk-bound French scholar, it is likely that he chose the Hottentot based largely on the proliferation of texts that had been written about them since the sixteenth century. It is also likely that his potential role in the dissection of one famous Hottentot played a part.[77]

Virey treated the Hottentot as exemplary, and yet also representative of "negresses."[78] In *Natural History of Mankind*, Virey notes that while Hottentot men have a robust but "firm" constitution, the women, particularly as they age, develop big bottoms and bellies that push out. In addition to living in a climate that causes the body to retain excess liquid fat, the women, he claims, are often sedentary or pregnant. This leads the superabundant fatty liquid to collect in their abdomen and long, pendulous breasts, and to wrap around their hips and buttocks.[79] The derrieres of Hottentot women, he added, resembled those of four-legged creatures, at times growing so large that they could be supported with a small cart, like a domesticated animal.[80]

It is questionable whether Virey ever encountered any of the living, breathing, "negresses" of which he speaks so authoritatively. Like Buffon, Virey seems to have gleaned his intimate knowledge of African people by reading the secondhand accounts of diverse European travelers. And many Europeans had written about the so-called Hottentot.

"Hottentot" was a name given the Khoikhoi by Dutch colonists, after the Dutch East India Company (VOC) settled the Cape of Good Hope

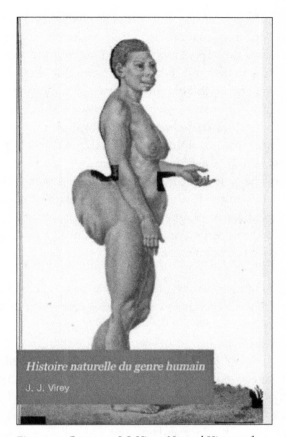

Figure 3.1. Cover art, J. J. Virey, *Natural History of Mankind*, 1824.

in the seventeenth century. Since that time, reports had made their way back to various European city centers depicting the unique physiology of their women. One of the earliest such reports came from Wilhelm ten Rhyne, a medical doctor with the VOC. In 1686 the doctor wrote of the elongated labia of the women, which was thought to resemble fingers that were protruding from their private parts, which he believed to be unique to the Hottentot.[81]

Reports of the peculiarity of the Hottentots were reproduced by travelers and self-styled anthropologists for the next century. A notable text by Dr. Anders Sparrman, a Swedish physician and naturalist and a student of Buffon's rival Carolus Linnaeus, saw several reprints in both British and American magazines.[82] In it, Sparrman expressed his consternation about the representation of Hottentot women, proclaiming that the world had been misled into believing that they were "monsters by nature." According to Sparrman, since the only difference between the Hottentot women and other women the world over, regardless of color, was their elongated clitoris and nymphae, they were not monstrous. To him, this physiological anomaly was simply proof of their "slothfulness and the warmth of the climate."[83]

Sparrman made no mention of the size or shape of the buttocks, breasts, or bellies of the Hottentot women. But had he done so, he likely would not have been as repulsed by their purported fatty nature as Virey had been. To the contrary, Sparrman introduced his discussion of the Hottentots with the following assertion:

> With regard to their persons, they are as tall as most Europeans; and as for their being in general *more slender*, this proceeds from their being more stinted and curtailed in their food.[84]

In describing the Hottentot as naturally slender, Sparrman offered a starkly different perspective from that of Virey. In fact, it mirrored the general description offered by Bernier some hundred years earlier. One reason for their different perspectives could be the fact that Sparrman, unlike Virey, actually traveled to the Cape and encountered real women there.[85]

There is another reason why their views may have been so disparate. With the arrival of the British came the proliferation of a new discourse about the Hottentot being overindulgent.[86] In 1777, for instance, a British woman named Jemima Kindersley published letters from her travels around the Cape of Good Hope, one of which included this observation about the Hottentot:

> Drunkenness and gluttony are the vices to which they are most addicted; having no moderation in either eating or drinking, but whenever it is in their power, indulge themselves in either to the greatest excess.[87]

Tales of the gluttonous Hottentot were uncommon among the Dutch or even in the British narratives of the sixteenth century. But in the context of the Enlightenment, the British preoccupation with the ills of excess feeding were folded into the racial discourse. This helped to make overindulgence evidence of not only slow wit but also barbarism.

Yet the increasingly widespread depiction of the Hottentot as gluttonous among British authors during the Enlightenment, like the depiction of black Africans generally, did not instantly change their representation from that of a slender to a fat people. In 1773 the London-born writer John Hawkesworth was credited with writing the first British portrayal of the Hottentot. Based on the travelogue of Captain James Cook, he said of them, "These are in general of a slim make, and rather lean than plump."[88]

In the 1790s two events collided to slowly shift the view of the Hottentot from thin to fat. First was the growing conflation of "Hottentot" with "Negro." This was shown in the work of the Swiss founder of physiognomy and Protestant pastor Johann Caspar Lavater. Lavater's work, in which he uses the terms as if interchangeably, was widely read and praised in Britain. After the 1795 British conquest of Cape Town, British reports of the Hottentot size and shape described them as remarkably similar to the "Negroes" that had been written about by English and French authors in the mid-eighteenth century. *An Account of Travels into the Interior of Southern Africa*, an 1804 book by an Englishman named John Barrow, details the Dutch Boers' mistreatment of the Hottentot, and explores how the inhumane conditions of the old colonizers had made them greedy and fat:

> Unwilling to work and unable to think; with a mind disengaged from every sort of care and reflection, indulging to excess in the gratification of every sensual appetite, the African peasant grows to an unwieldy size.[89]

But perhaps the most important factor in the reinvention of the Hottentot from slender to stout was the encounter with and subsequent exhibition by the English of a presumed archetype of Hottentot female beauty. Her presence as a symbol of black femininity helped transform the image of the Hottentot from thin to fat. It also helped make fatness an intrinsically black, and implicitly off-putting, form of feminine embodiment in the European scientific and popular imagination.

The woman went by the name of Saartjie "Sara" Baartman. The year of her birth is a point of contention, with most accounts citing 1789 but at least one suggesting she was born in the 1770s.[90] Sara was raised on

the farm of a colonist named David Fourie, a descendant of French Huguenots whose family had fled persecution under Louis XIV and settled
in Cape Town in the 1680s. Fourie himself was a ruthless murderer who
settled the area where Baartman's family had lived, and took possession
of land, cattle, and people by fiat. After his death, the Baartman clan was
broken up and sold to various slavers. Sara and her parents were sold
to a man named Cornelius Muller. Around 1803, a year after a bloody
Khoikhoi rebellion, many British left parts of the Cape, fleeing with the
remainder of their wealth and resources.

The economy at the Cape collapsed. Hendrik, a so-named Free Black
man who purchased Sara after her parents died, found himself deeply
in debt. He liquidated his once 400-strong holding of slaves, keeping for
himself only two, one of whom was Sara. To pay down his mountain of
debt, Hendrik decided to display Sara to British soldiers. These soldiers
came with the latest infantry in 1806. Their heads were aswirl with tales
of the insatiable and carnal nature of black women at the Cape, stories
that had been making their way to England for decades.[91]

So it was that Sara began her career as an exhibition for European titillation around 1806 while still in Cape Town. Her first shows took place
at the local Naval Hospital, where a large contingent of military men
found themselves immediately upon their arrival. An infirmary delight,
Sara would reveal her naked body to the soldiers for their last gasp of
sexual entertainment before welcoming sweet death. She was, according
to scholars Clifton Crais and Pamela Scully, "an early nineteenth century
exotic dancer," and for a fee, the dying men may have been able to touch
her or even have sex with her.[92]

The idea that Sara should be more than a sideshow for the sick and
dying at the Cape came from a Scottish surgeon by the name of Alexander Dunlop. Dunlop had lived in London as a youth, and after seeing
Sara's charms, he decided he could make considerable money off of her
if he could only get her to the Continent. Dunlop coerced the illiterate
Hendrik into signing a contract stipulating that he would accompany
Sara on a trip to London, serving as something of a handler, or show-
man. Sara, being the property of Hendrik, was not consulted on the matter. In 1810 the trio set sail for England.

London was the epicenter of Europe. The city was teeming with opportunities for the business-minded, salons for the philosophically

Figure 3.2. *Saartjee, The Hottentot Venus, Now Exhibiting in London, Drawn from Life*, 1810. Image courtesy of Bridgeman Images.

minded, and spectacles for those seeking lurid entertainment. With the display of Sara, Dunlop intended to exploit the intersection of all three. He promoted Sara as an erotic and scientific curiosity, a veritable "ethnographic freak show."[93] In his earliest posters for her show, she was billed as the "most correct and perfect Specimen of that race of people"—meaning the so-called Hottentot.[94] Moreover, as if to explain why the word "Venus" was part of her name, the bills touted the fact that she possessed the "kind of shape which is most admired among her countrymen."[95]

Contributing to the image of Sara as the "perfect specimen" of Hottentot woman, and by association all black women, was the voluptuousness of her physique. Together, Dunlop and Sara had worked to fashion

Figure 3.3. *Saartjee, The Hottentot Venus, Exhibiting in No. 225, Piccadilly.* Image courtesy of Mary Evans.

a suitably believable and yet exotic costume that was more fantasy than fact as it pertained to the garb of the Khoikhoi. Nevertheless, some iterations of her vestments were found to be disappointingly tame, and thus inauthentic, to London viewers anticipating something out of the African wild. Curious Londoners, however, were drawn to the exhibit by tales of her largesse, and especially the size and shape of her buttocks.

There had been a precedent in London for viewing persons deemed grotesquely oversized. In 1803 Daniel Lambert, said to have weighed over seven hundred pounds, had exhibited himself as the "fattest man alive," drawing enormous crowds.[96] But the fascination with Sara's size was different. She was simultaneously grotesque and exotic: a sexual specimen with a peculiar racial identity. For these reasons exhibitgoers came both to gawk at her proportions, especially her posterior, and to experience the sensory pleasure of touching her, which they could do for an additional fee. Although bustles exaggerating the derriere were fashionable in England at the time, there was something about the amplitude of flesh that, it was claimed, was amassed in her bottom and over her whole body, which made her a spectacle. Her figure was deemed "very different from the feminine standards of London" and its ladies' "long, slender lines."[97]

The exhibit was a smash hit in London for nearly a year, until controversy surrounding Sara's slave status derailed Dunlop's dream of riches that were quite literally built on Sara's backside. In 1811 the group took its act on the road, entering exhibits and fairs in other parts of England. They punctuated their travels with return engagements in Piccadilly. But the novelty of her act having worn off, Sara was often received with disdain or indifference when she was received at all.

Two years after her arrival in England, reviewers of her by then well-known show continued to marvel at the proportions of Sara, the conspicuously plump "Hottentot Venus." At the Bartholomew fair in London in 1812 a new rendition of an old ballad was issued in her honor: "Here, here the only booth in the fair . . . the greatest curiosity in all the known world—the Wonderful and Surprising Hottentot Wenus [sic] is here, *who measures three yards and three quarters round*."[98]

Sara was the first Khoikhoi to complete a successful run through England. The infamy of her physique would only increase in the coming years, when she made her way to Paris. It was there that she would encounter Georges Cuvier, the man responsible for turning Sara into an internationally recognized totem of racial and sexual savagery. Her "excess" fat was used as one sign of her primitivity.

Before Sara ever made it to Paris, she lost Hendrik. He had vanished a year into their stay in Europe. The following year, in 1812, Dunlop died, leaving Sara with not a single soul she knew from the Cape. Perhaps this was why she was willing to travel to France with Henry Taylor in the summer of 1814. It was only a few months after the defeat of Napoleon and the signing of the Treaty of Paris, and the British were excited about the possibility of resuming travels and touristry in the famed city.

Sara's status as slave or free was not questioned in France, largely because conditions had changed significantly since the Edict of 1716 and the Declaration of 1738. In 1777 Louis XVI supplied his last significant piece of legislation in an effort to resolve the matter. The declaration, known formally as the Police des Noirs, banned the entry of all "blacks, mulattoes, and other people of color."[99]

The prohibition on people with *any* black ancestry in the metropolis circumvented the question of slavery on French soil by granting only white persons rights as legal residents. This, of course, had disastrous implications for free black persons already living in France. And while the law was met with immediate resistance, it was nevertheless registered by the Parlement of Paris, something neither of the earlier edicts could claim. In any case, the law resolved very little. Slave owners continued to petition for the right to keep their slaves, which on occasion they were granted. Slaves themselves continued to petition the Admiralty Court of France for their freedom, which they were granted on occasion. This haphazard system remained in place until 1790, one year after the Revolution, when a November decree abolished this court.

Evidently, the French Revolution had not abolished slavery. France provisionally ended slavery in 1794, five years after its fabled revolution had declared liberty and equality for all.[100] The five-year waiting period for black freedom was in large part bought with the profits from overseas sugar and coffee plantations. By 1780, 40 percent of the Western world's sugar and coffee were being produced in French colonies. France's economic dependence on slavery meant that the question of liberty for blacks had been temporarily postponed, and it was further delayed by Napoleon in 1802 when he reinstated slavery.[101]

So when Sara arrived in France, after the passage of the Police des Noirs and during a revived moment of slavery, few questioned whether she was or should have been the human property of Henry Taylor. Not only were few questions asked about their relationship, their arrival was chronicled in the *Journal General de France*. The Hottentot Venus was by then a known quantity in Europe's bustling city centers. It was perhaps owing to Sara's fame as an ideal specimen of her race that Taylor was emboldened to send a letter to Georges Cuvier, the head of the Museum of Natural History, as well as something of a national treasure, inviting him to come to a show.

Cuvier was not a native Frenchman. Born in the German duchy of Württemberg to a strict Lutheran father, Cuvier had attended the illustrious Carolinian Academy in Stuttgart. Upon graduation in 1788, he secured a position as a tutor for a noble family in Normandy. In his free time, he performed independent zoological studies, the notes from which he sent to the professor and zoologist Étienne Geoffroy Saint-Hilaire at the Museum of Natural History in Paris. It was Saint-Hilaire who invited him into the fold at the museum in 1795. There he would begin a storied career in comparative anatomy that culminated in Cuvier being the first person to establish species extinction as a fact.[102]

Cuvier had a known passion for comparative anatomical studies. Sara was being promoted as both an erotic and a scientific curiosity. Nevertheless, he initially rebuffed Taylor's invitation. But some time later, he laid eyes on Sara for the first time. She was on display at a ball organized by Countess Du Barrier. For the occasion, she was wearing only feathers, giving her the appearance of an exotic bird. If Cuvier had previously been uninterested in Sara, the sight of her outfitted like an enticing fowl must have stimulated a deep and abiding interest in her that was to follow her long after she had been laid to rest.

Cuvier invited Sara to the Museum of Natural History, where he had planned to study her form and features in close quarters. She accepted the invitation, spending three days with Cuvier, who had had a few artists on hand to chronicle her behavior and sketch her most intimate parts. But Cuvier most wanted to see and measure her elongated labia. This she denied him.

Only after her death would Cuvier get his wish. Sara died in 1815. The exact date of her death is a matter of dispute, but according to Cuvier, it was December 29. He procured her body for an autopsy and claimed that the cause of death was excessive tippling.[103] Having her corpse at his disposal, he determined to dig into her body cavity to excavate the true nature of Sara, and by extension, her people.

Sara, in Cuvier's estimation, was not a Hottentot but a Bushman. He had decided this in the manner of his forebears, based on what he had read in diverse and contradictory accounts by European travelers about Bushman and Hottentot peoples. These accounts had set forth that only Bushmen had a *tablier* and "large and prominent buttocks."[104]

Unlike her handlers Dunlop and Taylor, Cuvier thought that Sara was an abnormal specimen of "her race," meaning in this case the Bushmen. Bushmen, he had read, were short, pockmarked, and "horribly

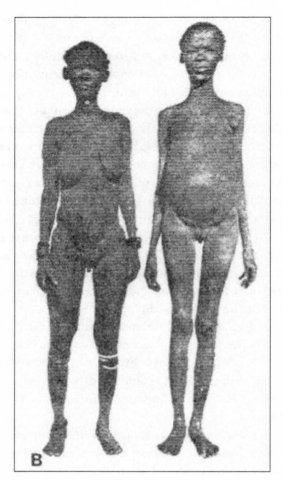

Figure 3.4. A photo of "Bushwomen" from 1912.
Cuvier and many others believed Sara to be a
member of this tribe.

thin."[105] What had impressed him about Sara, by contrast, was the vast-
ness of her figure. In his assessment, she was both taller and stouter
than the average Bushman. In a manner that recalled Buffon from
nearly a century earlier, Cuvier assumed that Sara's height and "bulk"
could be attributed to the easy accessibility of food in the region where
she lived, as he speculated that there must have been an "abundance of
food" at the Cape.[106]

But unlike Buffon, Cuvier found rotundity to be defective as opposed to alluring. "Her shape," he wrote of Sara, "is all the more shocking because of the enormity of her hips," each measuring larger than eighteen inches, "and by the projection of her buttocks, which was larger than a half a foot."[107] Her hips and bottom were, he adjudged, her principal "deformities," because while her knees were also fat and a little knocked in, her shoulders and back he found "graceful," her arms were "thin," and her stomach "didn't protrude excessively," a statement that reveals his unease at the very prospect that it might.

Cuvier was, indeed, generally disgusted by Sara's amplitude. This might have reflected some self-loathing on his part. As Elizabeth Kolbert explains in *The Sixth Extinction: An Unnatural History*, "During the [French] Revolution, Cuvier was thin. In the years he lived on the museum grounds, he grew stouter and stouter, until, toward the end of his life, he became enormously fat."[108] Arguably, Cuvier saw in Sara what he despised in himself. Or perhaps he was reflecting the heightened feeling in France and England that fatness was uncharacteristic of whites, and thus unbecoming in general. While these are things we can't know for certain, it does seem that he was in some small way comforted by the knowledge that the pockets of "excess fat" on Bushwomen's bodies were "already known" among other scholars, and therefore he had not been alone in bearing witness to them. The lesser-known explorers and writers Levaillant, Peron, and Jansens had been among those who had previously described the "fat mass resting underneath the skin" of Hauzannana people, into which Cuvier lumped the Bushmen and—more dubiously still—Sara.

The argument about fat lurking under the skin sounded stunningly similar to that of Virey's environmental-cum-biological armchair theorizing that made the Hottentots examples of black grotesquerie. This similarity could be due to the fact that Virey would have access to the same written sources as Cuvier. It could also have been that Virey had been present at the autopsy, which some scholars have suggested.[109] Alternatively, he may have received these ideas from Cuvier himself, since the two were contemporaries, and Virey cited the eminent zoologist in editions of his written works since 1824.

In any case, it was becoming part of the general zeitgeist that fatness was related to blackness. Thus, it was treated as evidence of barbarism, of a nonwhite affectation. Sara Baartman, as the Hottentot Venus, was considered a prime example of these relationships. If the Black Venus of the sixteenth century had been the low-status counterpart to the Venus de Medici, the Hottentot Venus was its antithesis. When Sara arrived in Paris, the *Journal de Paris* had warned potential showgoers that since "ideas of beauty vary according to the climate, amateurs should not expect to discover in the Hottentot Venus the Venus de Medicis."[110] Similarly, the *Journal de France* quipped that "if we were to be taxed . . . we would prefer the French Venus to the Hottentot one."[111]

When it comes to the Hottentot Venus, it is hard to separate fact from fiction. Showgoers flocked to see her because her supposed curious shape made her the apotheosis of Hottentot (and by proxy, black African) femininity. By this same measure, she was deemed the antipode of European femininity. But some exhibitgoers were disappointed to discover that she looked, well, just like any other woman. At least one Frenchman wrote that he had been hoping to see a monster, but complained that he had been bamboozled: "Instead of the imposing and majestic Venus of the Cape of Storms, I found only a svelte Venus."[112]

Whether fact or fiction, the purported size of her bottom, in tandem with her presumed general rotundity, placed Sara beyond the pale of fair-skinned, European norms of beauty. Racial theories had linked fatness to blackness in the European imagination. And they had also linked thinness to whiteness.

4

Birth of the Ascetic Aesthetic

Across the channel in England, a change was stirring. It was brewing in the teahouses and coffeehouses that served the fashionable and the well-to-do. It was foaming in the pubs among the boisterous and bleary-eyed patrons. It later spilled out onto the London streets. Troubled onlookers, disturbed by the entire affair, uttered its condemnation to like-minded intellectuals. In their opinion, England was becoming a society of caffeine-addled strumpets and drunkards who were growing more corpulent with each passing day.

This seeming spiral into debaucherous excess was openly lamented in early eighteenth-century England, but it had begun long before. It had been nearly a century since "white gold," the sugar cultivated by slaves in the colonies, had begun making its way back to England. And it had been fifty years since the first teahouses and coffeehouses gave a broader slice of the population their first taste of the adrenaline-tickling mix of caffeine and sugar.[1] The early eighteenth century was not the first moment at which this decadence was being witnessed. But it did mark the moment when a broad swath of social commentators began to push back against the social and moral decay that appeared to be the unintended returns of imperialism.

In Great Britain during what was known as the long eighteenth century (ca. 1680–1815), goaded by threats to the social and moral order, philosophers, physicians, and religious leaders began to redefine what they considered appropriate behavior and appearance in English society. This led to the development of what modern scholars have described as the "standards of taste."[2] The new standards detailed the rules of etiquette, which included, among other things, ideas about how well-mannered women and men should eat, drink, and otherwise comport themselves. In this milieu, gentlefolk were increasingly encouraged to show restraint in the oral appetite.

The new standards also detailed new ways of judging beauty. Beauty in the budding culture of taste was no longer merely a matter of individual impressions or mathematical proportionality.[3] For many British philosophers, judgments of beauty required the superior faculties of the rational (male) mind.

The codification of new principles of etiquette and new judgments of beauty had a special impact on women. For while men and women were encouraged to adhere to the new standards of behavior, when it came to judgments of beauty, English men were seen as the arbiters of taste, or those capable of creating the guidelines for judging beauty. English women were treated as its representatives.

In this way, what I am calling a new "ascetic aesthetic" was born. During the long eighteenth century, as eating and drinking less became evidence of refinement, so too did the thinner figures such behavior produced. Therefore, at the same time that gluttony and fatness were becoming associated with African women in scientific racial literature, the values of delicacy, discipline, and a slimmer physique were becoming associated with English women by the arbiters of taste and the purveyors of morality. Far from being a coincidence, the fear of being uncultivated, and thus like racial and national Others, lay at the heart of these developments.

* * *

By the early 1700s, London was home to an estimated three thousand coffeehouses and countless taverns. They buzzed with gossip and business deals in the making.[4] Incredibly, these places also played host to physicians, some of whom used their back rooms for medical consultations. George Cheyne, an eighteenth-century medical man, decided to one-up the average physician, using the coffeehouse as a platform for launching his own practice. As an unexpected consequence, he found himself both sick and growing fat. This spurred him to start the most visible medical campaign against overconsumption to date. The campaign was inspired by a spiritual awakening, and it attracted affluent English women by the droves.

Cheyne was not a native to the pub-and-café culture of smart Londoners. Born in Scotland in 1673, he had immigrated to London after finishing his studies at the University of Edinburgh. He arrived around

Figure 4.1. *Portrait of George Cheyne*, n.d.

the turn of the century, his goal at once noble and questionable: to make a fortune as a physician.[5] Since many business deals were transacted in taverns, and a fair amount of medicine was practiced in coffeehouses, he trolled these establishments for patrons of his own. Cheyne spent countless hours alternately among the heavily caffeinated and the heavily intoxicated, schmoozing and hobnobbing. Slowly he made a name for himself. In his own words, the only thing this mode of recruitment demanded of him was that he be able "to *Eat* lustily and swallow down much *Liquor*."[6] This seemed easy enough. To hear Cheyne tell it, he was "naturally of a large *Size*" and was readily "caressed" by the locals.[7]

This proved a mixed blessing. On the one hand, Cheyne was becoming a familiar figure about town. On the other, the size and shape of his own figure were changing in ways he bemoaned. To hear the good doctor tell it, he "grew daily in *Bulk* and in Friendship with these gay

Gentlemen" until he became "excessively fat, short-breath'd, lethargick and listless."[8] This description proved an understatement. In 1705, in what was undoubtedly a dramatic fashion, the doctor collapsed. He had complained of "vertiginous paroxysms," mixed with headaches, anxiety, and terror, and according to his own diagnosis, he was said to have caught "the vapours." The illness brought on a complex set of symptoms, which included "Heaviness in the Breast [and] a Grumbling in [the] Belly," accompanied by belching and occasional vomiting.[9] Their chief cause, according to Cheyne, was his voracious appetite for good food and strong drink.[10]

True, until that time, he had been observing the Bernard Mandeville philosophy of building a medical practice in London. The famed Anglo-Dutch moralist and essayist once wrote, "If you can Chat, and be a good Companion, you can drink yourself into Practice."[11] But only when he collapsed did it occur to him that while he had always been prone to corpulence, perhaps he should ease up on the supping and tippling. At the time of this event, Cheyne was thirty-two years old and weighed 34 stone, the equivalent of 476 pounds. Tragically, his many friends from his tavern and coffeehouse days, those merrymakers and roustabouts with whom he had tossed back quite a few, abandoned him immediately upon finding him infirm. This ordeal caused Cheyne considerable psychic distress. What really troubled him was not just concern that he had grown too fat or that he had recently lost all of his "Bottle Companions."[12] Rather, Cheyne feared that such indulgence in sensual pleasures contradicted the will of God.

Cheyne, as it turns out, came from a good Scottish family and had been reared in the church.[13] In the wake of his collapse, he reflected on his time with the "Free Livers" with whom he had enjoyed the finest of liquor and sweetmeats, and wondered whether he hadn't committed a grave moral misstep. He had been living for "sensual Pleasures" and "mere Jollity," which surely God would not have condoned.[14] He resolved to live so frivolously no more. No more spooning and dining and condemning his soul straight to hell. On the contrary. He would reverse course and cease his seemingly immoral overfeeding and obesity.[15]

Resolute, Cheyne turned to God for the inspiration to leave behind his indulgent ways. Happily for him, it wasn't long before God gave him a sign. It came in 1708, when the doctor happened to make the acquaintance of a clergyman, who explained to him that another doctor, a man by the name of Taylor, had cured himself of epilepsy by taking a diet exclusively of cow's milk. That was it. Cow's milk. Intrigued, Cheyne visited the doctor who was pursuing this experimental cure. Swayed instantly by the sight of Dr. Taylor's sobering dinner of a single quart of cow's milk, Cheyne left a changed man. He declared himself henceforth off meat, restricting himself to "a diet of milk with 'Seeds, Bread, mealy Roots, and Fruit.'"[16] And it worked. In a matter of months, his body was, as he put it, "melting away like a Snowball in summer."[17] Through this diet, Cheyne eventually shed between 16 and 18 stone, or between 224 and 252 pounds.

Thanks to this new regime, Cheyne was born again. He had been given a divine mandate to take it easy on the liquors and meats, and, like a good Christian, he followed. Accordingly, God rewarded him. Upon taking up his diet of milk, seeds, and fruits, Cheyne's health noticeably improved. "In five or six months, I was considerably recovered," he wrote, becoming, in his words, "Lank, Fleet, and Nimble."[18] He had had a near-death experience, but he now felt lithe, lean, alive. Nor was this a conversion story he saw fit to keep to himself. Cheyne quickly went about spreading the gospel of the milk and seed diet. Word spread like wildfire. Fashionable people throughout London, hearing of his miracle cure and seeing it in the (reduced) flesh, flocked to Dr. Cheyne's. His once fledgling practice was now vibrant and thriving, as would-be patients beat down his doors, insisting on one-on-one consultations to help them shed some of their own bulk.

Cheyne had finally found a winning formula. Previously, he had fought and scraped to make a name for himself, but now patients arrived in droves. He had managed to transform himself from an ordinary doctor into something more. He had effectively melded the roles of physician and priest, and was offering not just nutritional advice but a teetotaling vegetarian cure for the soul. His patients, for their part, had come looking for this combo cure. Women and men of means came to Cheyne seeking a remedy for their physical ailments (gout, listlessness, and frayed nerves) as well as their spiritual distress over the conspicuous consumption that they suspected was the root cause of their problems. That is to say, patients came to Cheyne in no small measure to confess their food sins. Cheyne, the almost former clergyman that he was, listened, gave advice, and in the end offered provisional absolution.[19]

* * *

To understand what led so many well-off English men and women to flock to a doctor who took up an extreme vegetarian diet and claimed that God told him to do so, it is necessary to look back to the sixteenth century. As noted previously, this was the period during which the English entered the slave trade and began reaping the bounty of sugar, spices, coffees, and teas that were being cultivated in the colonies. It is also important to remember that at nearly the same time, England was being touched by the Reformation.[20]

In England, the ideas of John Calvin did not make their way to the forefront of English consciousness until the 1550s, during the reign of Edward VI. This was some two decades after the watershed moment in 1534 when Henry VIII sought to annul his marriage to Catherine of Aragon, launching the Reformation. When Elizabeth I ascended to the throne in 1559, the chaos of the ensuing years led her to seek a "middle-way" between Catholicism and Protestantism, one she upheld for the duration of her reign. But like most compromises, this one did not satisfy the fervent. A budding group of English Reformed Protestants were among the visibly discontented. Some labeled them "Puritans" for their dedication to purifying the Church of England of any residual popery, and for their allegiance to a strict interpretation of the Bible.[21]

The number of abuses that quickened the blood of the Puritans were many. But high on the list was "intemperance," or the modern-day abuses of food and drink that attended the rising wealth in the metropolis. By the turn of the seventeenth century, vocal Puritans were disseminating voluminous tracts on the ills of pleasing the palate. One such tract was written in the early seventeenth century by a Puritan reformer named Thomas Muffet. Muffet had studied to be a doctor at Basel University.[22] Although trained as an entomologist, Muffet nevertheless wrote a four-hundred-page manual on how best to prepare food and then, apparently, deprive oneself of it.

His treatise, titled *Health's Improvement, or Rules Comprizing and Discovering the Nature, Method and Manner of Preparing All Sorts of Foods Used in This Nation*, amounted to a strangely repressive sort of food porn.[23] In it, Muffet reminds the reader of the grand and ill-fated excesses of older empires, including the Roman commander Clodius Albinus, who he claims ate "at one Sitting, 500 figs, 100 peaches, . . . 20lb weight of Raisins in the Sun . . . and 150 great Oysters." Yet, Muffet infers, he needn't have reached back to classical times to find such extraordinary and barbaric displays of gluttony. The English of his own time, he suggests, were also "making graves with their own teeth."[24] Citing the Greek theorist Heraclitus, he warns that "the wisest Soul dwelleth in the most empty Body."[25]

The use of the term "soul" is significant. As both a Puritan and a physician,[26] Muffet had provided a blueprint for the restrained, Calvinist-inflected orientation to diet and salvation that Cheyne was to tap into a century on.[27] Shot through Muffet's text are invocations to his countrymen that they remember it was God who had created the rules of regimented eating:

> The Invention of Diet [came] from a more worthy Teacher, yea, the worthiest of all, God himself. For can we imagine that he taught our Forefathers (having sinned), how to clothe their Bodies, and not how, and when, and wherewith to feed them? He that taught *Abel* how to diet Sheep, would leave him unskilful [*sic*] how to diet himself?[28]

The precise type of diet the English should adopt, Muffet added, depended largely on their health, youth, and vigor.[29] But the guiding principle for all was temperance, or avoiding overindulgence in food and drink. Indeed, he makes this point unequivocally in the last few pages of his dictum of damnation: "As for Temperance, which I can never enough reverence or commend, would to God [that it be] well practiced of every particular man."[30]

Muffet's declamation of what not to eat did not immediately gain popular interest and appeal. Published posthumously, his solemn assessment that overeating was leading to ruin in *Health's Improvement* entered the cultural conversation in the mid-seventeenth century. Its conclusions brought the nation a further source of dietary anxiety.

By the time George Cheyne began proselytizing on the ills of sumptuousness in the early eighteenth century, the English had been living with the ignominious notion that they had been "digging their graves with their teeth" (a widespread apparent bastardization of Muffet's phrasing) for well over a century. Muffet was the original proselytizing doctor on a mission to suppress eating among the English. Cheyne does not mention Muffet in his own work, yet he was indebted to the Puritan. Muffet had laid the groundwork for Cheyne's subsequent appeal, helping to generate a deep well of cultural foodborne shame that Cheyne would reanimate.

One notable aspect of George Cheyne's rise to prominence during the eighteenth century was that he had tremendous appeal among women. This was somewhat curious. While Muffet, fully a century earlier, had excoriated the orally fixated English, his condemnation centered largely on the habits of men. Reduced eating in England during the seventeenth century had been seen as the prerogative of men; it signaled a capacity for a Cartesian mind-over-matter approach that was largely viewed as the province of intelligent males. Cheyne, by contrast, made his greatest inroads among English women, particularly those of the aristocratic class.[31] Cheyne himself commented on this phenomenon with more than a little resignation. By the 1730s, he could count fashionable women among his most numerous and yet most recalcitrant patients. In a letter to his friend, the English writer Samuel Richardson, he bewailed the fact that, paradoxically, while he was massively popular among the women in his parish, their behavior could only be described as feckless:

> Those that know me and my late book will say I am . . . one of women's stoutest Panegyrists . . . and have found 50 Women for one man at Church and Sacrament, but . . . their being more used to Sickness they are rarely brought into the greatest Abstinence.[32]

Despite his dissatisfaction with their performance, Cheyne continued to take on high-class female patients and advise them on their food consumption. Selina Hastings, the Countess of Huntingdon and a leader in a Calvinistic wing of the burgeoning Methodist movement, became one of Cheyne's ardent followers. Over the course of many years, Cheyne sent the countess several letters, which almost always included diet advice. In one letter, written circa 1730, he counseled her to a regime similar to his own, telling her to "drink plentifully of sweet cow-hey all the day long."[33]

A few years on, it had become routine for Cheyne to recommend to the countess not only a limited diet but also fasting and even purging. In a letter dated August 3, 1734, he instructed, "When ever [sic] you find yourself colicked, griped, low-spirited, or want natural sleep, you must always have recourse to vomit." The doctor concluded that this method "of vomiting now and then, as you find necessity, will always prevent ail of consequence, and this with your diet, in one year will make you as well as you desire."[34]

For Cheyne, the goal was not for the Countess of Huntingdon or other women under his care to use purging and fasting to become as slender as possible. Cheyne's wish was that they might scrub their diets of any unholy excess. If they had to fast and purge to transform their bodies into a temple for the Lord, so be it. True, Cheyne had been thrilled about his own weight loss. But the self-described "Scotch man with an immense broad back" was not so delusional as to count himself in the thin, fine, intellectual class of Englishmen.[35] Even had he been so deluded, there were plenty of his contemporaries to disabuse him of this notion. Even though Cheyne had linked weight to spirituality, reminiscent of the way his seventeenth-century forebears had linked weight to reason, the man who some called the "Aberdeen Falstaff" considered trimming down a benefit but not the primary aim of a temperate diet.[36]

Cultivated women flocked to the dietetic pulpiteer partially due to their growing rates of involvement and greater responsibility in the church, which had increased since the Reformation.[37] Also a factor was their higher rates (real and imagined) of illness and susceptibility to disease in an age that increasingly demanded feminine delicacy.[38] And yet, while eating right for the restoration of mind, body, and spirit appeared to be the central objective, if Cheyne himself served as any indication, shedding pounds was not an unwelcome side effect.

Indeed, during the early Enlightenment in England, women would have had new reasons to be concerned about their weight. Several English philosophers and moralists were beginning to draft revisions to standards of taste, which included a reconfiguration of aesthetic ideals. The height of beauty, they suggested, should reflect the nation's moral compass as well as its racial caliber. Anything that could be construed as evidence of gluttony, they claimed, was beneath them. Therefore, it should no longer be revered. This touched off a backlash against "excess" fat, this time on women's bodies.

Joseph Addison and Richard Steele were among those interested in reforming the tastes of the modern man. As journalists, they wanted their message of social criticism and reform to be disseminated broadly, reaching those in the teeming pubs and coffeehouses where debauchery reigned. In 1711, the same year that the third Earl of Shaftesbury published his landmark treatise on proper aesthetic judgments, *Characteristics of Men, Manners, Opinions, Times,* they created *The Spectator.*[39]

The Spectator was a daily periodical that, among other things, served as something of a national etiquette manual. Its stated aim was to "enliven Morality with Wit, and to temper Wit with Morality."[40] As such, *The Spectator* offered moral witticisms intended as a correction to the dissolution of decency that appeared to be the result of colonial conquest and its attendant economic prosperity. The characteristically humorous advice on decency and proper conduct was offered by a fictitious character known as Mr. Spectator, who routinely guided the mostly male readership on the finer points of taste.

To that end, male readers routinely wrote to Mr. Spectator seeking counsel on managing their relationship to contemporary luxuries, especially food and drink.[41] Men who believed themselves to have grown grossly overweight and thereby ill, and who had, it seems, not discovered Dr. Cheyne, described their efforts to curtail their excesses and slim down. One man, who described himself as "very fat" and sick, detailed the length to which he had gone to change his gluttonous ways. Having devised a weighing chair that was inspired by the seventeenth-century Italian dietician Sanctorius, he explained,

> I used to Study, Eat, Drink, and Sleep in it; insomuch that I may be said, for these three last Years, to have lived in a Pair of Scales. I compute my self, when I am in full Health, to be precisely Two Hundred Weight, falling short of it about a Pound after a Day's Fast, and exceeding it as much after a very full Meal; so that it is my continual Employment, to trim the Ballance between these two Volatile Pounds in my Constitution. . . . I do not dine and sup by the Clock, but by my Chair, for when that informs me my Pound of Food is exhausted I conclude my self to be hungry, and lay in another with all Diligence. In my Days

of Abstinence I lose a Pound and an half, and on solemn Fasts am two Pound lighter than on other Days in the Year.[42]

Mr. Spectator, ever the lighthearted snark, replied that the man should let go of such neuroticism and choose instead exercise and Christian temperance to address his physical and (admitted) mental illness.[43]

But for all its humble and humorous Protestant-inflected counsel on men's struggles with diet and weight, *The Spectator* displayed a particular repugnance for gluttonous and fat women. Shaftesbury did not expend much energy trying to determine, for men, how they should judge a woman's appearance. *The Spectator*, however, took this up with relish. The general opinion seemed to be that big women should not be viewed as proper beauties in a nation that had deemed fatness immoral, irrational, and a precursor to illness.

The Spectator routinely featured letters by men railing against corpulent women as low and improper. In one instance, a man was incensed by the notion that women dared to appear in public wearing clothes that made them seem fatter. Per this man,

> The strutting Petticoat smooths all Distinctions, levels the Mother with the Daughter, and sets Maids and Matrons, Wives and Widows, upon the same Bottom. In the mean while I cannot but be troubled to see so many well-shaped innocent Virgins bloated up, and waddling up and down like big-bellied Women.[44]

This man's letter reveals the grotesquery associated with "bloated up, . . . big-bellied Women" in England. For although heavy men were being entrusted with the tools of reform, such as exercise and Christian temperance, fat women in *The Spectator* were commonly ridiculed for their intemperance and unattractiveness.

This much was revealed in a speech by the president of Oxford's so-called Ugly Club that was reprinted in *The Spectator*. The Ugly Club was made up mostly, if not exclusively, of men.[45] Among themselves they waxed poetic about their own ugliness, as if it were a badge of honor. But as the conversation turned to the appearance of women, they were quick to dismiss the (fat) women deemed undesirable by enlightened English standards of taste.

In the speech, one woman was ridiculed by the club's president for being too greedy and too big to be a beauty on his side of the English Channel:

> My Lady Ample is the most miserable Woman in the World, purely of her own making: She even grudges her self Meat and Drink, for fear she should thrive by them; and is constantly crying out, In a Quarter of a Year more I shall be quite out of all manner of Shape! Now the Lady's Misfortune seems to be only this, that she is planted in a wrong Soil; for, go but t'other Side of the Water, it's a Jest at Harlem [sic] to talk of a Shape under eighteen Stone. These wise Traders regulate their Beauties as they do their Butter, by the Pound; and Miss Cross, when she first arrived in the Low-Countries, was not computed to be so handsom as Madam Van Brisket by near half a Tun.[46]

The joke, it seems, about "Lady Ample" is that she is a fat woman in England. She is thus cruelly compelled by society's standards to adopt a strict diet and avoid the delicacies her palate craves. But if she were to go to Haarlem, in the Low Countries, she would find her fortune reversed. There, where they "regulate their Beauties as they do their Butter, by the Pound," a woman fearing herself to be too ample to be comely in England would fail to measure up to the women weighing nearly "half a Tun."[47] The open dig at the standards of taste in the Low Countries, including a probable reference to the full-bodied style rendered by Rubens, is further evidence of the elite English desire to create social distinctions on the basis of nation and appearance in the early eighteenth century. Fat, presumed to be the product of immoral and irrational intemperance, was considered lowbrow. In women, it was also comically unattractive.

The Spectator was one voice in a national effort to reinvigorate standards of taste with a renewed commitment to moral probity. It was a space where men's questions about their own (possible) moral turpitude could be explored, and their anxieties about the state of affairs in the country could be displaced onto the public appearance of women.

Although the periodical ran for only two years, it had a deep and lasting impact on the views of the newly affluent.[48] In its aftermath, men who admitted being influenced by the journalistic pair, by Shaftesbury, or in some cases by all three, would busy themselves with helping newly cultivated men determine just what a man of politeness and breeding should look for in a lovely lady. In the decades to come, whole new treatises on beauty would be written, and the beauties described therein would be very different from the fleshy models of the Spanish and Flemish masters.

* * *

No one, it seems, would have expected Joseph Spence to become a revered thinker in this regard. He was born into a family of minimal aristocratic status near the turn of the eighteenth century. He was educated, but according to contemporaries like the esteemed Samuel Johnson, only barely. But fortunately for Spence, his writing would eventually allow him to make the acquaintance of the very influential Alexander Pope, who, going against the grain of other intellectuals, decided to enjoy Spence's works.[49] Owing to his connection to Pope, Spence was elected to the Oxford Chair of Poetry in 1728. On the strength of Pope's recommendation, he was also given a chance to travel abroad with other members of the English jet set beginning in the 1730s. First making his way through Venice and Florence and later the Low Countries, Spence became a prolific and, some argued, comedic writer, even though his overall literary contributions as Oxford Chair of Poetry have been remembered as "unremarkable."[50]

The generally tepid reception he received may have been one reason Spence assumed the pen name Sir Harry Beaumont when he began publishing some of what would become his most widely read works. One of these works, *Crito, or A Dialogue on Beauty*, made its way to readers in 1752. In the book, Crito, the main character in this dialogue, is visiting his friend Timanthes and a mutual acquaintance by the name of Milesius. Taking up the dialogic style of writing so successful with its Renaissance predecessors, *The Book of the Courtier* and *On the Beauty of Women*, Spence set himself to the task of identifying true beauty for the eighteenth-century Englishman.

Crito begins with the expected genuflection to the classical models of beauty. He asserts that "the general Cause of Beauty in the Form or Shape in both Sexes is a Proportion, or an [sic] Union and Harmony in all Parts of the Body."[51] Crito then pronounces the Venus de Medici the example par excellence of feminine loveliness.[52] But in keeping with the concerns of the English during the eighteenth century, markers of racial and national origin were also cited as critical measures of attractiveness. The preferred skin tone, white enlivened with a hint of red, was an important feature of the pretty lady: "The Skin in general should be white, properly tinged with Red, with an apparent Softness, and a Look of thriving Health in it."[53] Although this appears to be a replication of the ideas found in Rubens's treatise on beauty, Spence is careful to distinguish between the heavyset models of beauty presented by the Flemish artist and those of his own nation and people:

> The greatest and most general Misleader of our Judgments, in relation to Beauty, is Custom, or the different national Tastes for Beauty; which turn chiefly on the Two lower Parts of it, Color and Form. It was from the most common Shape of his Countrywomen that Rubens, in his Pictures, delights so much in Plumpness; not to give it a worse name. Whenever he has to represent the most beautiful Women, he is sure to give them a good Share of Corpulence. It seems as if nobody could be a Beauty with him under Two Hundred Weight. His very *Graces* [sic] are all fat.[54]

In a clear departure from *The Book of the Courtier* and *On the Beauty of Women*, the Englishman in *Crito* demands that his model of beauty have both the proper color (white) and the proper form (a symmetrical figure that was not too fat). Yet *Crito* also reveals that the English model is not only distinct from those of other nations, it is also superior to them. There is a disdain in his prose as he describes the voluptuous women in Rubens paintings, as if to suggest that the Flemish mode of beauty is not only different but also lower.

It is not just the Flemish he derides for their aesthetic sensibilities, but also the colonial Others. Crito writes, "I would not have you imagine, that I would have any thing to do with the beautiful thick Lips of the good People of *Bantam* [sic], or the excessive small Feet of the Ladies of Quality in *China* [sic]."[55] In another reference, intended to be dismissive of African women, Crito indicates that one English woman, Miss C—, lacked the necessary charms to get on in England. But, owing to her dark complexion, she could nevertheless make a go of it in a presumably less civilized context. Miss C—, he quotes one man as saying, could be the "most charming woman in the world, if she were but a Negro."[56] It is evident, then, that in *Crito*, Spence is delineating a national and racial hierarchy of beauty. In it, English women were at the top. Women of other European nations were below them. And at the bottom were colonial racial Other women, specifically Asian and Black women.

Crito's articulation of a hierarchy of beauty was supported by another innovation: a scoring scheme. He claimed that even among English women, "a Scale might be settled, by which one might judge tolerably well of the proportional excellence in any of our most celebrated beauties."[57] Using this as a guiding principle, Crito scored, in beauty pageant fashion, the looks of reputable Englishwomen. A woman's skin color and her shape were the first points on which a woman was to be measured:

> I should assign to Lady B—, Eight for Color, Four for Shape, Twenty-five for Expression, and Ten for Grace; in all, Forty-seven; not quite half-way in the complete Sum of Excellence. To Mrs. A—, Eight for Color, Seventeen for Shape, Fifteen for Expression, and Twenty for Grace; in all, Sixty Degrees of Excellence. And to Mrs. B—, Eight for Color, Ten for Shape, Twenty-five for Expression, and Thirty for Grace; in all Seventy-three. And that is the highest Sum, that I could in Conscience allow to any Woman that I have ever yet seen.[58]

While *Crito* is commonly cited by scholars as an index of eighteenth-century English aesthetic tastes, few would claim that the work helped Spence make a splash intellectually. Horace Walpole, the art historian and son of Catherine Walpole, one of George Cheyne's most noted clients, wrote of Spence posthumously, "He was a good-natured man, . . . more like a silver penny than a genius. . . . [He] had read good books, and kept good company, but was too trifling for [much] use."[59]

Spence's disdain for fat women, whom he indicated fell outside national aesthetic norms, nevertheless did not lead him to trumpet slenderness. Every bit the classical romanticizer, he waxed poetic about the exquisite proportions of Venus de Medici. But cultural translator that he was, Spence did witness the new, and in his estimation alarming, trend of slimness. During his travels in Italy, Spence ran across a woman from his home country, whom he described only as an "English lady at Florence." This woman apparently had the gall to criticize the

Venus de Medici for "not being fine and taper enough."[60] Far from being a woman of questionable appearance, she was both a "beauty" herself and, according to Spence, representative of a new fashion of svelteness in England. Her ideas, he claimed, "proceeded from our beauties in England carrying this nicety generally too far."[61] The "nicety" he mentions is apparently the restrained eating of cultivated English women, and the excessively thin figures they created.

The English lady eventually came around and admitted her own, and by extension, English women's, aesthetic misstep. The lady, he writes, "had the grace to own herself in the wrong, and even to exclaim against the excess of this mode among us. The Venus de Medici, with all her fineness of shape, has what the Romans call *corpus solidium*, and the French embonpoint."[62] In a moment of revelation, the English lady at Florence realizes that the Venus de Medici's fleshiness should be something to strive for, not to scorn.

Spence may have meant this conversion narrative to represent something of a teachable moment for the women of England, but it didn't pan out that way. Spence does succeed, however, at chronicling the fashion of slenderness among women in England in the eighteenth century. It was the rise of the new ascetic aesthetic. Spence himself might not have advocated this "excess" of refinement. But again, he seemed to have been a better interpreter than innovator when it came to the topic of highbrow culture.

Already by the early decades of the eighteenth century, English women of good standing were slimming down. Many had incorporated diet- and weight-related ideals of decency into their own self-understandings. They had started taking the amount of fat on a woman's body as indicative of her cultivation, or lack thereof.

* * *

The letters of Lady Mary Wortley Montagu are a signpost of the early eighteenth-century wave of cultured women against fat. Lady Mary was born in London in 1689, and three days after her birth, she was baptized in St. Paul's Church, which before the 1662 Act of Uniformity had been the pulpit of the well-known Puritan minister Thomas Manton. In 1712 Lady Mary eloped with Sir Edward Wortley Montagu, a member of the Whig Parliament and ambassador to the Ottoman Empire. A few years

Figure 4.2. Jonathan Richardson, *Lady Mary Wortley Montagu*, 1718. Image courtesy of Bridgeman Images.

later she traveled with her husband to Constantinople, now Istanbul. It was among the Ottoman Turks that Lady Mary would gather the source material for her *Turkish Embassy Letters*, today regarded as the basis of her literary reputation.

In the letters, Lady Mary offers witty, if rude, observations on the difference between English and Turkish women in terms of their food consumption. In one instance, she reflects with alarm on the amount of food and drink she consumed on a given day, having a diet composed largely of milk: "I wake generally about seven, and drink half a pint of warm asses' milk. . . . I constantly take three cups of milk coffee, after that, a large cup of milk chocolate. . . . At five in the afternoon, I take another dose of asses' milk."[63]

Lady Mary's largely milk-based diet seems very similar to the diet championed by Dr. George Cheyne. As it turns out, Lady Mary and Countess Huntingdon, the latter an ardent disciple of Cheyne, traveled in the same social circles, although evidence suggests that they might have been frenemies rather than friends.[64] Lady Mary does not mention Cheyne by name, but the similarities between the items in her food diary and those recommended by the proselytizing doctor should not be dismissed.[65] Regardless of whether she received her dietary ideas directly from Cheyne himself, it is significant that the milk diet he is credited with popularizing had evidently become fashionable among a wide swath of haute English women.

Like many others who had adopted the milk diet, Lady Mary was of rather fine and fragile build. She had been a celebrated beauty in London prior to her departure for the Near East, but in 1715 her appearance was marred by smallpox. Nevertheless, given her reputation, it was with good reason that she presented herself as knowledgeable about the principles of beauty in England in her letters. And per Lady Mary, embonpoint was an appropriate form of embodiment only for non-English Others and not for an English lady. For instance, Lady Mary waxes lyrical about the beauty of Turkish women, seeming at first blush even to envy them. Turkish women, she rhapsodizes, "were exactly as proportioned as ever any Goddess was drawn by the pencil of Guido or Titian. . . . Their skins [are] shineingly white, . . . perfectly representing the figures of the graces."[66] Turks would have been considered part of the "first race" in early eighteenth-century racial categorizations. Therefore, her admiration of their "shineingly white" skins would not have been unusual.

While Lady Mary praises the complexions and figures of Turkish women, she nevertheless regards them as Other. She suggests that they possessed an ahistorical, or as described by Cynthia Lowenthal, author of *Lady Mary Wortley Montagu and the Eighteenth-Century Familiar Letter*, a "prelapsarian" and "sensuous" type of embodiment that she considers inappropriate for herself or other members of English high society.[67] Further proof that Turkish practices were incompatible with polite English society surfaces when Lady Mary attempts some of Turkish women's beauty practices. When she tries a face balm intended to restore the complexion, her face "swell'd to a very extraordinary size and all over [was] red."[68] Thereafter, she vowed to never again try this type of "unnatural" cosmetic aid, suggesting that her delicate English skin was not compatible with "Eastern magic."[69]

Arguably the best evidence of her sentiment that Turkish aesthetics and beauty practices were incompatible with English norms is that she declined an invitation to participate in the Turkish baths. Lady Mary refused to participate in this beautification rite since it required her to remove her stays. The naked freedom that made the Turkish women's (archaic) brand of beauty possible conflicted with her chaste, modern sensibilities. She was unwilling to forgo the latter to achieve the former.[70]

Her view that Turkish aesthetics were antiquated and improper for a proper English lady is also evident in her treatment of pudgy English women. Although she gushed over the fleshy and "sensuous" figures of Turkish women, and admitted that perhaps she and other like-minded English women were "refining too much," she is nevertheless repulsed by the sight of corpulent aristocratic women. Of one of these women, the Countess of Orkney, present at the coronation of George II in 1727, she writes,

> She that drew the greatest number of eyes was indisputably Lady Orkney. She exposed behind a mixture of fat and wrinkles; and before a very considerable protuberance which preceded her. Add to this the inimitable roll of her eyes and her grey hairs, which by good fortune stood directly upright, and 'tis impossible to imagine a more delightful spectacle. She had embellished all this with considerable magnificence, which made her look as big again as usual; and I should have thought her one of the largest things of God's making, if my Lady St. John had not displayed all her charms in honour of the day.[71]

There is no way to know if or how much the fat English women Lady Mary derides differed from the fleshy Turkish graces she commended. We do know that when praising the Turkish women, she used Titian as her reference point, and his models were known for being on the more voluptuous side. We also know that the racial and national identities of the women stood out as major distinctions. In a move that recalled Shaftesbury's hierarchy of beauty, what was considered beautiful among the colonial Others was a laughable affront to English propriety.

The slender physiques of refined English women may have been sneered at as excessive by men like Joseph Spence, but it was at the same time admired, recorded, and sanctified by other women and men of high station. After the 1740s the svelte ideal, this new ascetic aesthetic, was immortalized in the arts.

The eighteenth-century English artist Thomas Gainsborough was a bellwether of the new feminine aesthetic sensibility. A talented painter as a young child growing up in Sudbury, Gainsborough had amassed an impressive artistic portfolio even before he reached his teens.[72] In 1740, at age thirteen, he was off to London to study under the French painter and draughtsman Hubert-François Gravelot.[73] It was in London that Gainsborough made the acquaintance of William Hogarth, who would also become a mentor to the young artist.

Gainsborough had imagined himself to be a landscape artist. But when he landed in London, patrons of the arts weren't especially keen on investing in the landscape paintings of an unknown adolescent.[74] Consequently, he was forced to turn his attention to the more lucrative market of portraiture. Following an artistic path that mirrored that of the Renaissance master Peter Paul Rubens more than a century earlier, he was often commissioned to paint pretty young society ladies.[75]

Two of his earlier, iconic renderings of women appeared in couples portraiture. Between 1745 and 1750, Gainsborough painted *Conversation in a Park* and *Mr and Mrs Andrews*. The works appear to be playing on the theme of love and courtship among the refined. Giving the portraitist a chance to show off his skill in landscape portrayal, they are set in an idyllic countryside, the otherwise vacant setting occupied by a small bench on which the couples sit.

In *Conversation in a Park*, a lady of the upper crust sits demurely on the bench as her companion makes a play for her affection. The woman keeps her gaze fixed knowingly on the portraitist, gamely rebuffing the advances of the young man at her side. Her expression suggests she is not put off by her suitor, only playing the game of displaying a lack of interest appropriate to her station.[76] In *Mr and Mrs Andrews*, Gainsborough depicts a young married couple. Mrs. Andrews assumes a similar posture of coolness, her dress cascading out to cover almost the entire expanse of the bench. Her husband, standing, leans on one edge of her seat with a downward-pointing rifle held loosely in the crook of his arm, in a posture that conveys both ownership (of the fine Mrs. Andrews) and manly duty.[77]

In addition to the cavalier expressions and billowing dresses of the young ladies of leisure, the women in the two paintings are united by

Figure 4.3. Thomas Gainsborough, *Conversation in a Park*, 1748.
Image courtesy of Art Resource, New York.

their pale, lithe appearance. In a representation of beauty that had been uncommon among master portraitists of earlier generations, Gainsborough's ladies were thin and fine.[78] Their shoulders were rounded and sloping. Their slender and elongated necks were accentuated by the cut of their dresses. Their tiny waists almost disappeared into the folds of their gowns.

Gainsborough's representations of slim, sensible, high-society ladies were rousing and evocative. Between the 1760s and the 1780s, Gainsborough would paint dozens of them. His 1760 rendering of the English musician Ann Ford became an enduring and recognizable image of Ford's beauty and evidence of Gainsborough's talents. Befitting her life as an artist, Ford appears both refined and self-possessed. Her form is less delicate and her figure less slight than those of the

Figure 4.4. Thomas Gainsborough, *Ann Ford*, 1760.
Image courtesy of Bridgeman Images.

women in the two landscapes, but one would be hard-pressed not to call her slender.

Of Gainsborough's many and celebrated portraits of high-society ladies, not all of them were represented as svelte. His much-praised portrait of Lady Georgiana Cavendish, Duchess of Devonshire, depicts a buxom beauty, voluptuous and proportionate in the manner revered by the Renaissance masters. Since other portraits depict the duchess similarly, Gainsborough's illustration of her was likely his best attempt at representing her true shape. Yet a considerable number of the women who sat for Gainsborough were portrayed as being lithe and fine. His 1775 painting of Mrs. Lowndes-Stone and his 1777 portrait of the Honourable Frances Duncombe serve as two further examples. For some scholars, a sylphlike type of feminine beauty has become synonymous with the name Gainsborough.[79] Gainsborough may have tried to accurately reflect the slender forms of the wealthy women he painted. As Joseph Spence suggested, and Lady Mary attested, the women appeared to have had a preference for being svelte. Or he may have taken a bit of artistic license and imbued them with the lines of his preferred aesthetic. Either way, Gainsborough's body of work represents, among other things, a sustained meditation on the slender as beautiful.[80]

Gainsborough's influence on the history of art is unquestioned. And, whether or not he can lay claim to having commemorated the famed British author Lady Mary in his artistic portfolio, she too became an inspiration in the development of svelteness as a feminine beauty ideal.[81] This trend, already visible in eighteenth-century England, would reach new heights of popularity in the nineteenth century. By then, there would be much less ambivalence than had been seen among its earlier adherents. Nineteenth-century women would be proudly slender and profess a Protestant "Anglo-Saxon" heritage. And these women were to be found in the United States.

5

American Beauty

The Reign of the Slender Aesthetic

Sarah Josepha Buell never planned to become a writer. Born in 1788 in Newport, New Hampshire, and being a girl, she was barred from attending school. Instead, young Sarah received private tutoring from her older brother and her mother. That she had been denied a formal education ignited in Buell a passion for educating girls. She likely did not anticipate, however, that an enduring part of her legacy would be teaching women and girls not just to read and write but how best to comport themselves as modern Anglo-Saxon Protestant women. Integral to her teachings was that Christian temperance in food and drink was best in the eyes of God. And it bred the slender physiques that offered evidence of racial superiority.

Buell is a compelling starting point for a discussion of how in the United States, the ascetic aesthetic—born in eighteenth-century Britain—met with religious revivals, the expansion of racial theorizing, and the immigration of persons feared to be "part-Negroid" to make thinness a key goal for Anglo-Saxon Protestant women during the nineteenth century. As this history shows, some people in America—as in Britain—continued to push back against the fashion of excessive slimness. Nevertheless, many American women and men during the era began to regard svelte forms as a superior aesthetic ideal for white Christian women.

Convinced of the importance of a formal education for women at a time when such a thing was extremely rare, Sarah Buell became a schoolteacher during the first decade of the nineteenth century. A few years later, in 1813, she left this post to marry a lawyer named David Hale. She would later reminisce fondly of their time as a couple, reading together, writing poems, and discussing ideas. "The aim of Mr. Hale," she wrote, was to "enlighten my reason, strengthen my judgment, and give

Figure 5.1. James Reid Lambdin, *Sarah Josepha Buell Hale*, 1831.

me confidence in my own powers of mind."[1] Their wedded bliss ended in tragedy a mere nine years after it began when David died of a stroke, leaving Sarah to raise their five children alone. Because David Hale had not been a wealthy man, Sarah needed to figure out how best to feed and educate her young brood. She leaned on the writing skills she had been honing under her husband's tutelage. Gathering together a collection of poems she had written prior to her husband's death, she managed to have them published with the aid of her late husband's friends, the Free Masons.[2] In the 1830s, Sarah Hale was to make an indelible mark on English literature. The first year of the decade, she published her second book of poetry, *Poems for Our Children*. The book contained a nursery rhyme she had crafted, titled "Mary Had a Little Lamb," which would go on to become one of the most recognizable poems in the country.[3]

Poetry was only one vehicle through which Hale hoped to both earn a living and educate girls and young women. In 1828 she accepted a position as editor of *Ladies' Magazine*, a publication founded by the Boston-based clergyman John Lauris Blake. Its purpose, according to Hale, was to "prove the advantages of a general diffusion of literature among all classes and both sexes."[4] Accordingly, the magazine was largely literary, serving up poems, short stories, and a few minor biographies. Hale also included, against her will, a few pieces on women's fashion. She had apparently done so only to satisfy popular demand, writing, "There is no part of our duties as editor of a ladies' journal which we feel so reluctant to perform as to quote, or exhibit, the fashions of dress."[5] After a few years of including fashion plates in its pages, *Ladies' Magazine* clamped down on this form of entertainment, keeping its content oriented to the somber business of educating young ladies. Shortly thereafter, the bottom fell out of the magazine's revenues.[6]

There is no direct evidence that the financial problems that would ultimately signal the demise of *Ladies' Magazine* were caused by a lack of interest in (if not disdain of) women's fashion. Still, one can't help but notice that when *Ladies' Magazine* was bought out in 1836 by Louis Godey, it successfully merged with its former competitor, *Godey's Lady's Book*, which was renowned for its dedication to showcasing the latest in women's haute fashions. Due in no small part to its images of lovely rich women decked out in the best fineries, *Godey's Lady's Book* quickly became the most popular women's magazine in the country, a title it would retain for the rest of the nineteenth century.[7]

The popularity of *Godey's Lady's Book* was due to more than its display of sumptuous clothing and decadent jewels. Its appeal had a lot to do with its effort to create what the historian Benedict Anderson might describe as an "imagined community" of white middle-class Protestant women.[8] In the midst of the massive social upheaval of the mid-nineteenth century and the redefinition of just who was an "American," *Godey's Lady's Book* was a guidepost for such women. Conjuring the spirit of *The Spectator* across the Atlantic, the publication treated Christian ladies to burgeoning middle-class lighthearted entertainments. It suffused its merriment with lessons in the necessary moral principles for proper conduct.[9] The difference, of course, was that while *The Spectator* focused its moralizing rhetoric on the cultivation of men, *Godey's Lady's Book* focused on teaching girls and young women the rules of polite, white Christian society.[10]

Hale, as the publication's editor, wanted nothing to do with fashion plates for women of leisure. But questions involving said women's moral advancement were of great interest to her. She found it no less than her duty to instruct her female readers as to how to behave properly before the eyes of God. A central theme as it pertained to questions of correct conduct was "temperance" in eating and drinking. Articles on this topic often reminded women that they were the moral guardians of the home and the custodians of cuisine. Thus, it was their responsibility to check the indecencies, or indulgences, to which men were prone. In an article from 1839, written by a Mrs. Sigourney but featured in a section called the "Editor's Table," the author writes, "Excesses are too often indulged in . . . but can any man devise a more effectual check upon them than the presence of a woman?"[11]

While claims of women's moral conservatorship were common, still more common were reminders to women and young girls that they should check their own indulgences and excesses at the table. Although these arguments were prevalent under Hale's editorship, they had begun even before she took over. In an unsigned *Godey's* article from 1831, five years before Hale arrived, an anonymous author reminded readers of what she described as the "baneful effects of a protracted and abundant repast." She suggested that overeating, combined with the practice of tight-lacing one's corset—a bogus corrective to filling one's belly in the first place—were harmful to health. The solution, she offered, was "first, Temperance: a well-timed use of the table, and so moderate a pursuit," followed by gentle open-air exercise.[12]

It was, in fact, seen as more important for women to regulate themselves than to regulate their husbands. The reason being that for women, overeating was not just immoral and unhealthy, it could also destroy their beauty.[13] Another article from the same year makes a similar plea, noting that "Temperance includes moderation at table," before going on to excoriate some "well-bred" women for their crude excesses: "Their breakfasts not only set forth tea and coffee, but chocolate, and *hot* bread and butter." The author was not simply concerned about issues of immorality. She says that bread and butter, "when taken constantly, are hostile to health and female delicacy," and further reminds the reader that a "young beauty . . . as elegant as the Goddess of Love herself, would soon lose these charms by a course of inordinate eating [and] drinking."[14] This latter quote is a clear reference to Venus, the famed standard-bearer of Western beauty. The author was troubled by the prospect that well-born American women were eating in a way that was indecent, unhealthy, and, significantly, likely to breed the stout physiques that, counter to Renaissance notions, would be considered a detriment to the beauty of young damsels.

That the editors of *Godey's Lady's Book* would, in the 1830s, advocate temperance at the table can be better understood through an examination of the social context in which they offered their lessons. The 1830s fit squarely within the so-called Age of Reform, a period that extended roughly from 1815 to 1863 and was punctuated by several overlapping Protestant movements. The first of these was the Second Great Awakening, a Protestant religious revival that swept through the American South and Northeast between 1790 and 1850, and represented a rebellion against the secularism of the era. The Great Awakening inspired countless Americans to renew their religious commitments. But more important, its impassioned, often feverish appeals for its members to get to know the Lord and His word incited thousands to align themselves with sects of Protestantism, such as Methodism and Baptism, whose previous membership had been minimal.

At the same time, and arguably as an offshoot of the Second Great Awakening, the temperance movement was taking root. Visible as early as 1808 in New York and 1813 in Massachusetts, and budding in many of the same churches that the Great Awakening built, this movement initially aimed merely to limit the sale and consumption of liquor, but later advocated its prohibition. The movement's boosters asserted that the nation's moral fiber was weakening under growing unemployment, spousal abuse, indolence, and general apathy, all of which could be traced to rampant alcoholism.[15] By the 1830s, the temperance movement had birthed thousands of teetotaling organizations.[16]

Finally, the 1830s also saw the growth of another type of consumption-constricting movement, the Popular Health movement of which the Presbyterian minister and temperance advocate Sylvester Graham was the most notable figure. Graham would claim that a diet rich in animal foods was the cause of American dyspepsia, an allegedly widespread illness among the well-to-do. He also argued that stimulants such as tea, coffee, and spice, especially when combined with a meat-based diet, provoked a ravenous, un-Christian sexual appetite in men. But while many of Graham's lectures targeted men, women routinely made up the bulk of the audience at his sermons.[17]

Within the many and overlapping Protestant reform movements of the early nineteenth century, women came out in force. If the most prominent figures in these movements were men, women were the true foot soldiers for the cause. Middle-class women outnumbered men among converts in the Second Great Awakening, and they were also the main trumpeters of temperance and dedicated diet reform.[18] So it was that in the 1830s, when Louis Godey launched his lady's magazine, it was only natural that he should choose to explore, and exploit, a topic that the recently christened middle-class women held dear to their hearts. The genius of *Godey's Lady's Book* lay not simply in its ability to pick up on the era's spirit of reform. *Godey's* also enticed a newly hatched generation of women of means with the fripperies and frills of luxury, which would have been out of reach for the average American woman a generation prior.

The early nineteenth century had ushered in a new age of manufacturing in the United States. For the first time, items like clothing and shoes were being produced in factories. Those who labored in the factories constituted the bulk of America's emerging working class. At the same time, those who oversaw labor—for instance, those working in offices and as managers—came to form a separate class of people. These middle-class workers were separated from the working class (and the comparatively narrower strata of the upper class) in several ways that went beyond the jobs they held. Members of the middle class were distinguished by where they lived and the churches and schools they attended. And particularly for women, middle-class standing was identifiable via the finery they could afford to wear.[19]

It was the astute blending of moral lessons in proper Christian conduct with instructions on how to appear in public as a fashionable lady of the new middle class that made *Godey's* a sensation. Indeed, the magazine's success appeared to hinge on the combined talents of both Godey and Hale, since Hale's own fashion-free experiment had been a flop, and *Godey's Lady's Book* had floundered between 1830 and 1836, the years before Hale's editorship.

Sarah Hale may not have been a major figure in any of the reform movements of the nineteenth century. But as an Evangelical Christian, a temperance advocate, and a diet reformer, she was involved in all three of them. Rather than being a movement leader or foot soldier for these causes, Hale played her part by using *Godey's* as a platform for those who were actively engaged in these movements. Under her leadership, discussions of temperance expanded. In the magazine's "Editor's Table" feature, Hale promoted new and varied texts and treatises on temperance. *Godey's* could now boast entertaining fiction revealing the value of temperance, known as "Temperance Tales." It also featured recipes for the modern Christian woman. And fittingly, given Hale's interest in educating the youth, the gentle reader could find information on proper feeding and table manners for children. There was even a song titled "A Temperance Dinner to Which Ladies Were Invited." The song, composed by Oliver Wendell Holmes, M.D., echoed the doctor's solemn joy at the way the new woman chastely managed her household and her palate. "The days are no more," he noted, "when she watched for her lord till the revel was o'er. . . . The joys of his banquet to chasten and share . . . the rose of her cheek dissolved in his wine." The good women of today, he rejoiced, "breathe not the mist of the bacchanal's dream, But the lilies of innocence float on their stream."[20]

And yet what appeared in *Godey's* under Hale's guidance was not just an increase in the number of articles and essays on the proper amount to eat and drink to satisfy God, health, and the pursuit of beauty. These three topics had been addressed before Hale took over as editor. Under Hale came a fourth and previously little-considered aspect to being a right-minded, middle-class Protestant woman: the need to prove one's racial superiority as an Anglo-Saxon.

* * *

Theories of Anglo-Saxon supremacy can be traced to sixteenth-century England, coinciding with the Protestant Reformation. In their earliest manifestation, these theories were used to justify Henry VIII's bid to secede from the Norman papacy. Those favoring secession had argued that the original English people descended from a pre-Norman Germanic tribe known as Anglo-Saxons, a freedom-loving people who had originated civilizations, free institutions, and equitable laws.[21] The goal was to make a claim for ancestral difference, and thereby socio-legal independence, from the papacy. Although superiority was implied, this use of the term "Anglo-Saxon" preceded the use of the term "race," as it would be articulated more than a century later by François Bernier.

Yet the idea of Anglo-Saxon supremacy would resurface under a new racial and religious guise in the late eighteenth century. By 1776, a number of men in England were declaring themselves Anglo-Saxons. The firebrands were outraged this time not with the Norman papacy so much as the Norman Conquest itself, which they saw as evidence of foreign rule. The names of these rebels are mostly forgotten. But their ideas resonated forcefully with others of purported English extraction who felt similarly aggrieved by foreign rule—namely, the Americans. As a result, many of their central tenets were co-opted, refashioned, and promoted during the height of race making in America.[22]

No less a figure than Thomas Jefferson promulgated theories of Anglo-Saxon superiority. Jefferson was more than a self-identified Anglo-Saxon. He was a dedicated student of Anglo-Saxon history, language, and culture. In the midst of the American Revolution, Jefferson trumpeted the purported Anglo-Saxon value of freedom. In a now famous quote, he claimed some ancestral lineage linking Protestant Dissenters, the Whigs, and the Anglo-Saxons: "It has ever appeared to me that the difference between the Whig and the Tory of England is that the Whig deduces his rights from the Anglo-Saxon source, and the Tory from the Norman."[23]

Jefferson's claim underscores the common belief around the turn of the nineteenth century that Anglo-Saxonism was about more than anti-Catholic, anti-Royalist sentimentality. Anglo-Saxonism was seen as a matter of ancestral lineage, of inheritance. It was in this way that the term "Anglo-Saxon," while not described by its sixteenth-century forebears as a "race," easily lent itself to the project of racialization during the height of "racial formation" in the United States and Britain.[24]

That Anglo-Saxon would become a racial identity in the United States and England signaled an important break from the theories of race that had been crafted by the likes of Bernier, Diderot, and Buffon in France. For the first time, gradations *within* whiteness were being devised. As the nineteenth century approached, hierarchies and distinctions between elite whites (of Anglo-Saxon and implied Protestant heritage) and lowly whites (who were neither Anglo-Saxon nor Protestant) were articulated. In other words, there were now different categories of white people.

Perhaps predictably, given the racial politics of the time, the way to ascribe racial inferiority to another group of Europeans was to align them with one of the "colored races." And so, beginning in the nineteenth century, the authors of new racial theories claimed that Anglo-Saxons were the "pure" white race, whereas other Europeans, principally the Celtic Irish, were deemed an inferior or hybrid European race. These hybrid European racial inferiors were thought to be either "part African" or "part Asiatic," depending on the fancy of their creator.

British ethnologist James Cowles Prichard is of interest here for his treatment of the Irish as alternately "part African" and "part Asiatic." Prichard was well known as a theorist of human variability. One of his most widely read works, *Researches into the Physical History of Mankind*, was written in 1808, published in 1813, and polished over successive iterations between 1836 and 1841. It was in the 1836 and 1841 versions, as well as his 1831 text *The Eastern Origin of the Celtic Nations*—all of which followed his election to the Royal Society—that Prichard made notable contributions to theories of intra-white racial distinction. In *Eastern Origin*, for instance, the Englishman argued that language "must be allowed to furnish a proof, or at least a strong presumption, of a kindred race."[25] According to Prichard, the Irish "Celtic" peoples were linguistically, and thus racially, related to "Asiatics," people who today might largely be considered Arab or North African.[26]

Ten years later, in his 1841 reworking of *Researches into the Physical History of Mankind*, he offered further proof of the racial distance between the Celtic Irish and Anglo-Saxons, as well as the Celts' similarity to "Asiatic" or North African peoples. This time he chose to explore physical characteristics. In a section titled "Physical Character of the German Nations," Prichard states, "It is well known that the German nations are universally described by the ancients as a people of tall stature, robust form, with fair complexion, red hair, and blue eyes."[27] Characterizations of the Celts, he suggests, had been less consistent.[28] Nevertheless, according to Prichard, at the time he was writing, Celts "universally" had "dark hair, dark eyes, swarthy complexions, small stature."[29] This claim is reminiscent of the sixteenth-century English lore that Africans were little, low, and foul. And indeed, if Prichard had argued in *Eastern Origin* that Irish Celts were "Asiatic," he had also called them a "Semitic" people due to their purported ancestral relationship to

North Africans. In fact, in an unexpected move that revealed the vagaries of language for a respected philologist, he alternately considered the
Irish "Asiatic," "Semitic," and also "African": "Whatever else they may be,
the Semitic languages are, in the first instance, African."[30]

Prichard was one of the more notable British figures claiming sep-
arate and unequal origins between the racially unblemished Anglo-
Saxons and the not-entirely-white Celtic Irish. Prichard had claimed,
moreover, that physically, Anglo-Saxons were tall and robust, while the
Celtic Irish were small and swarthy. Still other theorists in England and
America would suggest that owing partly to their racial constitution, the
Irish were also a gluttonous and stout people.

* * *

The famed essayists Thomas Carlyle and Ralph Waldo Emerson were
important figures in the development of theories of Anglo-Saxon
supremacy and Irish inferiority in the middle decades of the nineteenth
century. Emerson was a native of Boston and the son of a clergyman.
Following in his father's footsteps, he became an ordained minister of
the Unitarian church in 1829. Two years later, after his wife died of tuberculosis, Emerson left the church. In 1833, seeking solace after his loss, he
traveled to England, where he met Thomas Carlyle.

Born in 1795, Carlyle was already a respected author by the time he
met Emerson. Carlyle lived with his wife on London's chic Cheyne Row
(no relation to George) in the city's elegant Chelsea section.[31] His father,
too, had been a devoted man of God, having been deeply and unwaver-
ingly Calvinist. Those who knew Thomas Carlyle claimed that his early
Calvinist upbringing had a profound influence on him.[32] It was in fact
Carlyle's reputation as, in Emerson's words, perhaps "the best Thinker of
the Saxon race" that led Emerson to seek him out.[33] The two, discussing
their shared spiritual and racial orientations, became fast friends. Each
crafted essays and delivered speeches that, according to the historian
Nell Irvin Painter, "outlined a transatlantic realm of Saxondom."[34]

Some of Carlyle's more noted essays on the topic of race were inspired by his travels to Ireland nearly a decade later. In 1846 he touched
down in the country in the midst of the Great Famine. He had long regarded the Celtic people as base and inferior. So, in his summary of the
causes of the famine, he pinpointed the gluttony and poor self-control

of the Celtic race. Specifically, it was the Irish appetite for the potato, which he called "potatophagi," that led to their ruin. This particular view of the Irish was not invented by Carlyle. Rather, his view of the Irish as little more than greedy potato eaters reflected centuries of anti-Irish stereotypes. Since the seventeenth century, English reformers had written disparagingly of the Irish as avaricious and gluttonous. The essayist William Camden, for example, described the Irish as "wilde and very uncivill," claiming that they were fond of profanity, violence, and gluttony.[35]

Carlyle, perhaps partly influenced by his Calvinist upbringing, was sickened by gluttony. On several occasions he expressed despair over what he described as "torpid, gluttonous, sooty, swollen and squalid England." He moreover lamented the "potbellied block-head this our heroic nation has become, sunk in its own dirty fat and offal."[36] For Carlyle, the difference between the overfed English and the greedy Irish was that in the Saxon people, Carlyle saw hope of reform. But the Irish predilection for overeating was constitutional, he believed. It was a deficiency that proved their inherent, intractable racial inferiority. Evinced in part by their greed, the degeneracy of the Irish was proof that they were closer to black than white. He concluded that the solution to the Irish question should be to "black-lead them and put them over with the niggers."[37] This would be, to Carlyle, a fitting solution, since in his infamous *Occasional Discourse on the Negro Question* he would also defame black people as indulgent and lazy.[38]

A handful of years later, Emerson would pick up where Carlyle and earlier Anglo-Saxon theorists had left off, making his contribution to racial theorizing. In his 1856 book *English Traits: A Portrait of 19th Century England*, he returns to the racial taxonomy popularized by Prichard, arguing that the Celts were of "Asiatic" origin.[39] And he advanced the ideas of his dear friend and colleague Carlyle when he described the Celts as short and dark. But Emerson did deviate from Carlyle in his conception of the Anglo-Saxon physique. For while Carlyle imagined that Anglo-Saxons in England and America were more similar than they were different, Emerson chose to highlight their presumed divergences. "At home," he began, "I am still struck with the superior animal vigor of the average Englishman; as if the English were pasture-oaks, and the Americans fine saplings."[40]

The view that the American breed of Anglo-Saxons was particularly svelte was by no means invented by Emerson. In 1810 Samuel Stanhope Smith, a Presbyterian minister and acquaintance of Thomas Jefferson,[41] wrote in the second edition of his *Essay on the Causes of the Variety of Complexion and Figure in the Human Species* that "in general, the habit of the Anglo-Americans is more slender than that of the natives of Great Britain or Ireland from whom the greater part of our population is descended."[42] Smith attributed the "Yankee" propensity for slenderness to the cold climate of North America, especially New England. Echoing the environmental theories of race popularized by Frenchmen like Buffon, Smith suggested that the cold climate had a slimming effect, as people in his environs could not sit lazily in the sun and enjoy the fruit of the land, as it was implied those of other races in hotter climates did.[43]

Emerson's position on the American Saxon physique, then, was not wholly unfamiliar. But there was one way Emerson did differ from many earlier theorists. Emerson took the position that the leanness of Americans was not just a fact, but was also preferable if the alternative was fatness. Indeed, Emerson may have looked slightly askance at the "slight, ill-woven" shapes of American men. But he, like Carlyle, despised gluttony. In his journals from the 1830s, Emerson had written, "One would think that the hog, that walking sermon upon Gluttony, was enough to turn the stomachs of all men from intemperate eating." He further questioned the religious commitment of the overeater, asking, "Was ever the full feeder ready for religion?"[44]

Later, in *English Traits*, he lamented the specific tendency of the English to overindulgence and stoutness. If "the English race," he wrote, is "the best of the breed," it could at times become "a little overloaded by flesh."[45] This tendency to corpulence was especially unfortunate as it applied to English women. As Emerson put it, "it is the fault of their forms that they grow stocky, and the women have that disadvantage."[46] Slimmer physiques, such as those found among American women, would be his preference. Emerson regretted that in England, by contrast, he noticed "few tall, slender figures of flowing shape, but [several] stunted and thickset persons."[47]

Therefore, while English and American Anglo-Saxons were supposedly blood brethren, sitting atop the racial hierarchy, the Americans were noted for their spare forms. It is worth noting that if Emerson was a tall and thin man, Carlyle too was described as a "reedy, stooped, six-footer."[48] Nevertheless, the racial lore of the time suggested that the English were a stouter breed of Anglo-Saxon than the Americans. By the mid-nineteenth century, this supposed general spareness of constitution, especially among women, would become a basis for extolling native-born Anglo-Saxon Protestant American women.

* * *

Sarah Hale had taken over the editorship of *Godey's Lady's Book* in the midst of these massive transformations in American religious and racial identity. After 1836, both Hale and the magazine reflected the times. As early as 1830, *Godey's Lady's Book* had spoken the language of temperance, urging women to curtail the amount they ate in the interest of God, health, and beauty. Upon the arrival of Hale some six years later, *Godey's* expressed a growing concern about the racial propriety of fatness.

The year Hale arrived at *Godey's*, the magazine published an article describing the relationship between overeating, femininity, and race. The article, titled "Chapter on Female Features," written by a woman named Leigh Hunt, reminded the reader that "the pleasure of even eating and drinking, to those who enjoy it with temperance, may be traced beyond the palate." Hunt's aim was to inform the reader that although eating to satiety and beyond could be enjoyable, greater rewards were to be reaped by keeping the appetite in check. Even better than gratifying the appetite, Hunt suggests, is to eat with moderation, so as to maintain one's appearance. Women of the "utmost refinement," Hunt intones, are far too frequently "wide of the mark."

Punning her way through the piece, Hunt makes it clear that "excessive" eating leads to a figure that would be undesirable for cultivated white women. With more than a hint of sarcasm, Hunt acknowledges that "there are fashions in beauty as well as dress." With this, she is suggesting that in other parts of the world, different standards of beauty apply. The place where fat women can be appreciated, it seems, is under the African sun, since in "some parts of Africa no lady can be charming under twenty-one stone," or approximately three hundred pounds.[49]

One of the authorities on beauty that Hunt relies on in this essay is none other than Lady Mary Wortley Montagu. As it turns out, Lady Mary's capacity for witticism, combined with her "desire to convey scandal" and underhanded slights, sometimes made her an uneasy model for American women. Yet her views on women's education and on beauty were printed again and again in *Godey's*, owing in no small measure to editor Hale's own reverence for her. Hale praised her in an issue of *Godey' Lady's Book*, suggesting that Lady Mary's work, along with other great works from Great Britain, "belongs to us, descendants of the Anglo-Saxons, as much as to the dwellers of that proud island." Hale would even translate a version of Lady Mary's *Letters* in 1856. Between 1836 and 1874, at least twenty-nine publications mentioned the inimitable Lady Mary, most revering her as an Anglo-Saxon foremother.

If Lady Mary received her fair share of recognition in *Godey's* as a model for Anglo-Saxon women, Ralph Waldo Emerson was also acknowledged. Many of Emerson's poems were published in *Godey's*. His famed disquisitions against overindulgence also made an appearance. In an essay on Thanksgiving temperance penned by an author identifying only as "S.G.B.," both Carlyle's and Emerson's treatises against overfeeding were met with appreciation. It is not without some irony that Hale, a proponent of temperance, would become the progenitor of the holiday most associated with overeating. S.G.B. considered this a perversion of the idea behind Thanksgiving. She inquired about the superfluous, fatty dishes that were its fare: "What are mince-pies made for? What enemy of mankind first prompted their composition? What inventor of patent dyspepsia medicine brought into use these promoters of the disease he would pretend to cure?" S.G.B. seems convinced that eating such food stood in opposition to the Thanksgiving, and the America, that reformers like Hale were aiming toward. She cites Carlyle and Emerson as beacons in the move against decadence. S.G.B. finds herself disgusted that mince-pies stuffed with three fat chickens were going to be served on Thanksgiving, and that such gluttony had not been eradicated by the teachings of "Carlyle, or Emerson, or any other destroyers of the old landmarks."[50]

While Anglo-Saxon women were often the focus of dietary reform, Irish women commonly were derided as irredeemably greedy and fat. An article from 1848 titled "Sketches from Real Life" describes a "Mrs. Bridget Notable," an Irish domestic. Mrs. Notable's heft was indicative of both her race and her low-class standing. According to the author, her "stature is somewhat low, and . . . she slightly inclines to embonpoint."

Embonpoint is a French term for "plump" or "fleshy." Mrs. Notable's weight was, per the author, "just enough so as to give her form and face that firm and massive texture which appears as if it could resist the 'wear and tear' of almost any amount of labor."[51]

Another article makes clear the anxiety surrounding the mere possibility that a boorish, fat Irish woman might somehow make her way into polite white society. The 1855 piece "The Fat Widow" describes the fear of an interracial relationship between a decent Scotchman and an older Irish woman:

> Some one mentioned that a young Scotchman, who had been lately in the neighborhood, was about to "marry an Irish widow, double his age and of considerable dimensions. "Going to marry her!" he exclaimed, bursting out laughing; "going to marry her! impossible! you mean, a part of her; he could not marry her all himself. It would be a case, not of bigamy, but trigamy; the neighborhood or the magistrates should interfere. There is enough of her to furnish wives for a whole parish. One man marry her!—it is monstrous. You might people a colony with her; or give an assembly with her; or perhaps take your morning's walk round her, always provided there were frequent resting-places, and you were in rude health. I once was rash enough to try walking round her before breakfast, but only got half way, and gave it up exhausted. Or you might read the Riot Act and disperse her; in short, you might do anything with her but marry her."[52]

In this and dozens of other articles in *Godey's*, the fear of an Irish woman managing to filter into hallowed Anglo-American communities is palpable. And yet it is brushed off through callous humor. Along with her race and age, the Irish widow's "considerable dimensions" make the pairing between her and the young Scotchman all the more preposterous. This helped to diffuse the sense of unease readers might have otherwise felt about the possibility of interracial mating during the height of Irish immigration to the United States.

Editor Hale, for her part, was less likely to critique the gross excesses and heavy weights of either Anglo-Saxon or Irish women. Choosing instead the high road, Hale would often herald good Anglo-Saxon women as guides toward the new way. She had written essays and encyclopedia entries on the virtues of the Anglo-Saxon Protestant woman, "God's appointed agent of morality," per Hale.[53] Thus it may not be surprising that after Hale was hired at the magazine, the issue of race, especially the racial superiority of Anglo-Saxons, was interwoven with narratives of morality, health, and beauty.

In an 1843 edition of the "Editor's Table," for instance, she presents Anglo-Saxon Protestant women as the source of the nation's moral and physical improvement.[54] "THIS is the age of action," she announces, adding that action must be taken to end the ignorance and indulgences that threatened our "great country." Appearing to reverse course on her previous position, the Fashion Plates were now going to be integral to, not a diversion from, reform. They were to batter the immoral excesses that fashion has elsewhere vaunted.

Crucial to this reformation is changing the short and stout models of beauty, including the Venus de Medici. Delivering a rare critique of the classical model of beauty as being "too full," the author saves her praise for the erect, lank bodies of Anglo-Saxons:

> We make it our particular aim to show, in our Fashion Plate, the better as well as more beautiful effect, of giving the natural forms of our female figures, in that perfect development which nature shows in her best models among us. That these forms are not precisely what is termed *classic—that* is, short and full as the Medicean Venus,—is the fault, if fault it-be, of nature. The Anglo-Saxon race of women are taller and slenderer than were the Grecian females; and, if we may credit history, far more lovely.[55]

This view, evidently, contradicts that of many of the so-called Anglo-Saxon forebears to whom Hale often paid homage. Even Lady Mary had praised the Venus, holding her up as the standard by which true beauty could be measured.[56] But in this "Editor's Table" article, the author suggests that "the Athenian women were proverbially ugly in person and repulsive in manners." It was incumbent upon Anglo-Saxon women, then, to serve as the flag bearers of a *new* standard of beauty, one rooted, "thanks to our benign religion and better civilization," in morality, health, and racial pride. "What we most need," the author concludes, is "to perfect our own system" in which we avow that "*delicacy must never be violated, health never sacrificed,* and propriety never disregarded."[57]

The new standard of beauty Hale seemed to hope for, that of the tall, slender, Anglo-Saxon Protestant woman, did arrive. It would come to be known in many New England circles as the "American Beauty." *Godey's* contributors would commonly describe this form of embodiment as such. This much was to be seen in an article titled "*Le Melange*: American Beauty," in which the author claims,

> There are two points in which it is seldom equaled, never excelled—the classic chasteness and delicacy of the features, and the smallness and exquisite symmetry of the extremities. In the latter respect, particularly, the American ladies are singularly fortunate.[58]

The "American Beauty" ideal was nevertheless fraught and contested. For although the author of this article, a British man, praises American women for their smallness, delicacy, and symmetry of features, he nevertheless found them "most deficient in roundness of figure."[59] His assessment of "American" women's delicacy and smallness as divine, and yet perhaps taken a bit too far, reveals just how conflicted he and many other men and women, especially those who were not American, were with the burgeoning slender aesthetic as an Anglo-Saxon Protestant American woman's ideal.

Figure 5.2. Fashion Plate, *Godey's Lady's Book*, March 1845.

Figure 5.3. Fashion Plate, *Godey's Lady's Book*, March 1878.

And yet the power of the slender aesthetic as an American beauty ideal lay in its repetition. *Godey's* was the earliest and most visible women's magazine to glorify an ideal rooted in the multiple and colliding factors of Protestant asceticism, scientific racism, and the proto-science of health and beauty. In subsequent decades, however, it was to be one of many sources to promote the thin ideal.

* * *

By the mid-nineteenth century, new women's magazines were starting to take off. Entering a competitive arena long dominated by *Godey's Lady's Book*, the new publications sought to carve out a slice of the magazine's considerable market share for themselves. Learning from Louis Godey, they decided that they needed a woman editor to speak to "women's issues." So when James, John, Fletcher, and Joseph Wesley Harper, collectively known as Harper & Brothers, decided after years of success in the publishing business to diversify their holdings by launching a women's magazine, it seemed only natural that they bring on a woman as the first editor. Their new publication would be called *Harper's Bazar* (spelled with one *a* in *Bazar* at first), and the editor would be an established female author named Mary Louise Booth.

Booth was born on Long Island in 1831, to descendants of French emigrants who had escaped persecution during the French Revolution.

Booth had learned to read by the age of five, and by her teens she had converted her affinity for the written word into a teaching position at a local school. A decade later, she resolved to put more time into writing and publishing her own works. In the 1850s she took off for Manhattan, where she would quickly befriend the suffragette leader Susan B. Anthony, join the women's rights movement, and accept a freelance writing assignment with the *New York Times*.[60] By the time Harper & Brothers tapped her to become editor of *Harper's Bazar* in 1867, Booth had already made a name for herself in the big city. In addition to being an occasional writer for the *New York Times*, she had also translated several works on French language, history, and aesthetics.[61]

Mary Louise Booth had none of the reservations that prevented Hale from promoting fashionable dress in her early years as an editor. Booth had herself worked part-time as a seamstress when she first arrived in New York. From the earliest issues of *Harper's Bazar* she tried to answer the pressing question of how a lady of a certain ethnic/racial and economic position might properly present herself in society. Within these queries, and *Harper's* responses, concerns about diet and weight were equal to those regarding whether or not crinoline was still making a go of it.

Under Booth, *Harper's Bazar* often addressed questions of how, and how much, a proper American lady should eat. A regular series titled "For the Ugly Girls" offered advice for those falling short of feminine demands in terms of appetite and apparel. In one article in this series, written in 1872, the author addresses "Yankee" women who include too many scrumptious pies "with crusts half lard and half butter" in their diet. Her advice was for these women to pick up a cookery book by a Professor Blot, who offered indispensible instruction on how to maintain one's weight, and by association one's attractive figure.[62]

While the author of this piece suggested that many American women ate too much fatty food, it is important to remember that the article was intended for the unsightly, those to whom *Harper's* wanted to give the chance, and the tools, to reform. This approach was not intended to undercut the position, dating back to the 1830s, that the average American woman was svelte, and that this was a preferable form of embodiment. Such was made clear in an 1877 article, "Our Women Growing Plump." The author writes, "Europeans generally concede that our American women are handsome," adding that Continental observers "particularly remark the tendency of our women to grow thin with years, while we remark the tendency of theirs to the accumulation of flesh as soon as they have passed their youth and often before that period."[63]

If there was any question as to which was preferred, the author makes it clear that the slenderness typical of women in the United States was preferable to the heaviness too often found in Europe:

> While we must allow that our women are, for the most part, lacking in roundness, there are few of us we imagine, who would not infinitely prefer the New-World slenderness to the Old-World stoutness.[64]

The author of this essay concedes that American women had taken the svelte ideal a bit too far in the 1840s, during the height of Irish Catholic immigration and the early years of the promotion of the new Anglo-Protestant thin ideal:

> Little more than a quarter of a century ago, young American women were ashamed to show a hearty appetite in public. They were infected with the Byronic philosophy; they wanted to be spiritual . . . and to look elegantly wretched. Many of them had half their wish; they looked wretched, but not elegant.[65]

However, according to the author, this ethereal over-refinement had recently been rehabilitated. By the time of his writing in 1877, a healthy, sleek figure was being cultivated in America. The "scrawny sallow peaked woman" of the past was disappearing. The new woman would be "comelier and rounder." Nevertheless, these new American women were "not likely to become gross and obese, as so many of their European sisters," but would instead aim for a vigorous leanness, and not a Byronic, peaked sickliness (referring to the gaunt British Romantic poet, Lord Byron).[66]

Under Booth's direction, *Harper's Bazar* reproduced similar ideas regarding weight, race, and aesthetics to those that would have been found in *Godey's Lady's Book*. *Harper's* reflected a kindred preoccupation with the "right" models of beauty, which were based on one's race and class status. For this reason, the magazine denounced the fatness of the "savage races" and exalted the more streamlined aesthetic of the Germans. This sentiment was to be found in an 1879 article titled "The Fixed Facts of Beauty." In it, the author informs readers that "it is idle to say that the laws of beauty are not fixed; that because the Turk sees beauty only in the obese and certain of the savages in the deformed, that therefore the laws of beauty are arbitrary." Betraying a none-too-subtle influence of English thinkers, the hierarchy of beauty implied here, placing Turks and "certain of the savages" near the bottom, is positively Shaftesburian. And the writer's reference to the Turk's fondness for voluptuous women may be another nod to Lady Mary Wortley Montagu, whose *Turkish Letters* were widely read by educated American women of the nineteenth century.

Instead of accepting the Turkish folly of what is termed "obeso-philia," the author asserts, "we must demand that taste be formed on the correct models . . . [and] approved by the most enlightened thought concerning which there can be but one opinion." More to the point, the author adds,

> One is not free in choice of form, or outline, not only because it will be universally admitted that what the most advanced, educated and refined race of any period has fixed as proper must be accepted as such by those who are still in a lower state of advancement, but because the principles governing form have been reduced to a science.[67]

In terms of which race was suited to offering the best models of mankind, the author points to the ancestral kin of Anglo-Saxons: "Germans have paid renewed attention to the matter, and, after patient research and trial, have announced a rule," which the author claims is the basis of true beauty. The verdict is that a woman must have some fat to avoid the scrawniness of the Reform years, and yet "beauty [is] to be found only in women where delicacy and littleness cause emotions of tenderness and protection taking them to be the admiration of beauty."[68]

These sentiments were found in other articles from the era. An essay in *Harper's* titled "Standard of Beauty" states, "It would be hard to establish any standard of beauty for the whole world and call it fixed." For neither "African savages" nor the "Turkish seraglio" who "stuffs herself till she is rolling in folds of fat" can understand the cultured beauty prized by the elevated races. According to the author, "what is held to be beauty by the most refined and intellectual of the world must be nearer the real article than any thing accepted only by a lower order of beings."

Mirroring ideas that had been promoted by German naturalist Johann Blumenbach, who popularized the term "Caucasian" near the turn of the century, the author proclaims Circassian women the most beautiful of all. Originating from the Caucasus mountains, these women offered the epitome of trim, refined beauty:

> The Circassian races, who take the Greek type as their model, with its slow and delicate curves, its perfect lines and slender elegance, have certainly something in their eye very different from the African races who want bulging and bountiful flesh.[69]

The author here goes so far as to reimagine the legacy of the classical Greek ideal, refashioning it, oddly, as the foundation of the slender aesthetic. In this way, this piece works to bolster the relationship between race and weight. Much like *Godey's Lady's Book* before it, *Harper's* promulgated the inferiority of African and Turkish races, said to delight in "bulging" folds of flesh. And it simultaneously claimed the superiority of trim white people.

Mary Louise Booth died in 1889 at the age of fifty-seven. The woman recruited to take over the leadership of the magazine was a poet named Margaret Elizabeth Sangster, who had much in common with Booth. The new editor was only seven years Booth's junior, and was a fellow author and native New Yorker. One notable difference between the two, however, was that Sangster's father, though born in England, had been raised in Ireland. In her autobiography, Sangster explains that her father left the country at the age of eighteen, landing first in Canada in 1804, then by 1810 in New York. Somewhere along the line he had left behind a wife and a son. He would later take Sangster's mother, the Scottish-descended Margaret Chisholm, as his second wife. Margaret Chisholm was described by her daughter as having hair a "real dark red, the Titian hue" and as "an extremely beautiful girl. . . . Her figure was always slight."[70]

As might be expected from Sangster's autobiography, under her editorship, *Harper's Bazar* continued the racially inflected emphasis on slenderness mixed with fat bashing that women's magazines had long

Figure 5.4. Cover art, *Harper's Bazar*, March 27, 1897.

been serving up. The work of a woman named Edith Bigelow, titled "The Sorrows of the Fat," was featured in an issue from 1897, and provides evidence of this ongoing trend. Describing the plight of large-bodied women who, in the face of tremendous odds, might hope to dress fashionably, Bigelow writes, "There are many stout women in the world. They must all be clothed. These two statements are incontrovertible: yet who ever invents appropriate clothing for them?"[71]

Rather than being an ally or empathizer, Bigelow suggests that this toxic state of affairs was the fault of the fat women themselves. Referring to fatness as a "crime" and a "deformity," she continues, "Fatness is a most undesirable state. It is dangerous to the vital organs, and it is destructive of vanity. . . . *I* say that to be fat—to be, oh, awful word *obese*—is to be miserable." Throughout her indictment, Bigelow italicizes the word *obese*, to remind the reader of the severity of the situation: "The stout lady of five-and-thirty has to remain stout. It is her nature—hereditary, possibly—and all she can hope for is not to become *obese*. That is the state all persons of refinement must shun."[72]

In this piece, the classical standard of beauty becomes, once again, the foil. Reversing course on the idea previously printed in *Harper's* that Venus was the foundation of the slender ideal, Bigelow's article is reminiscent of the assessment in *Godey's Lady's Book* that Venus would have been a little too chubby for the modern aesthetic sensibility. Of the new mode in fashion, Bigelow writes, "Venus herself couldn't fasten those bodices, and if she wore stays they would have to be made to order." If, Bigelow concludes, a lady wanted to be both fat and fashionable, she would have to repair not only to an earlier historical moment but to distant parts of the world. Only in the uncivilized "savage" world of Africa could a big girl be prized as a beauty, and therefore a fat society lady "will not be a social success unless she burnt-cork herself, don beads, and then go to that burning clime where women, like pigs, are valued at so much a pound."[73]

* * *

There was no mention in this article, nor in that of many others like it in *Harper's Bazar*, of Anglo-Saxons being the refined and thus "superior" race from which these fat ladies were barred membership. Unlike Hale, neither Sangster nor Booth could claim an Anglo-Saxon identity. But they didn't have to. By the final decades of the nineteenth century, new ideas about white racial superiority were emerging. The new racial theories, coming from the Americans, the British, and the French, would redefine the concept of whiteness for a new generation.

Since women's magazines served as a vehicle to foster an imagined community of elite white Christian women, the conspicuous near-absence of positive Celtic aesthetic representation in many women's magazines, in part owing to their presumed proximity to blackness, was about to be rectified. By the end of the century, the Celts had assimilated with Anglo-Saxons into the American mainstream. No longer deemed African kin, between the 1880s and the 1920s they were racially rehabilitated,

brought into the upper echelon of whiteness. The Celtic people had become simply northern Europeans, also known as Nordics, or sometimes
Aryans. They were joined with the Anglo-Saxon elite in being the exemplars of the tall and svelte "American Beauty" ideal. At the same time,
when it came to physical appearance, a new wave of poor immigrant
women from eastern and southern Europe were to become the new national enemy.

6

Thinness as American Exceptionalism

Elizabeth Bisland knew from a young age that writing was her calling. She was born into a genteel Louisiana family in 1861, the eve of the Civil War. Her mother, Margaret Brownson, had been known locally for her captivating beauty, and had herself been a small-time writer. Elizabeth, it was said, had inherited her mother's winning looks. And though it didn't bring her fame or riches, she had done her mother one better by managing to make a living from her prose.

Elizabeth Bisland wrote for some of the most respected publications of the late nineteenth century. Her written work has been largely forgotten, but it was a bellwether of the times. Picking up the thread left by the likes of Sarah Hale and Mary Louise Booth, Bisland had waxed lyrical about the beauty of white American women. Using language that reflected the most recent innovations in race science, Bisland, like other women and men of the era, suggested that it was not simply an Anglo-Saxon bloodline that created the superior beauty of American women. It was in fact their so-called Nordic or Aryan heritage that gave the characteristically svelte American woman her beauty.

Bisland's life and work provide a useful starting point for the exploration of turn-of-the-century notions of female beauty. As in prior decades, there was an ongoing debate regarding what constituted a beautiful face and figure. The aesthetic value of thinness continued to feature prominently in these discussions. Yet, interestingly, the assimilation of races like the Celtic Irish led to new justifications for old arguments. Along with peoples from other northern and western European nations, the Anglo-Saxon and Celtic peoples were believed to form part of the superior "Nordic" or "Aryan" race. The Nordics/Aryans were thought to be characteristically tall and lean.[1] And since the United States was viewed as the melting pot par excellence of the Nordic/Aryan races, thinness came to be viewed as a form of American exceptionalism.[2]

Under normal circumstances, Elizabeth Bisland would have wanted for nothing. The second child of nine, she spent the first few years of her life at her family's immense Palladian home, the home itself nestled comfortably in a vast grove of live oaks. Her family's considerable wealth and sparkling reputation meant that she and her siblings were poised to lead a comfortable existence.

But these were not normal circumstances. In 1863, when Elizabeth was just two years old, the Civil War rocked her small Confederate town. Her childhood was marred by the sound of gunfire. Her family scuttled constantly to and fro near the Louisiana-Mississippi border seeking refuge. Elizabeth thus spent her early childhood in hiding. Her mother, seeing the family's resources dwindling, decided to take up the pen to help make ends meet in the time of war.

It was in this context that Elizabeth began to find self-expression through writing. By the age of twelve, her secret written verses would be stashed throughout her house. By sixteen, she would get her first publication. To help out with the family finances, she eventually took a position at the *Times-Democrat* in New Orleans, effectively becoming the paper's department of women's issues.[3] Bisland left the paper around 1887. Feeling stifled in New Orleans, she set her sights northward. She moved to New York, and applied for a job at the *Sun*. The editor, who had his own ideas about the place of pretty young ladies in the order of things, tried to turn her away. But Bisland held firm, refusing to take no for an answer. The editor relented, and eventually gave her a few freelance writing opportunities.[4] By 1889, Bisland had also picked up a bit of piecework with the *World*, the most respected newspaper at the time. That same year, she landed a position as assistant editor at the newly formed magazine the *Cosmopolitan*.

The *Cosmopolitan* was launched in 1886. In the beginning, it sought to create a magazine devoted to cooking, home décor, and fashions for the entire family.[5] But this project failed to generate the interest its publishers had anticipated. It found itself teetering on the edge of demise before being bought out by a man named John Brisben Walker. In 1889 Walker released the rebranded magazine. Following on the heels of *Godey's* and other successful women's publications, the magazine turned its attention to social reform and, of course, women's fashion and etiquette.

There was another way in which the *Cosmopolitan* mirrored *Godey's* and *Harper's Bazar*: it posited a relationship between racial lineage and attractiveness. The *Cosmopolitan* was emerging during a new era in the development of racial ideologies. Beginning in the 1830s, *Godey's* had focused its attention on both praising the perfection of the Anglo-Saxon race and working to improve it. By 1889, when the *Cosmopolitan* was making a name for itself, the new science of race suggested that it wasn't just the Anglo-Saxons who deserved praise for their beauty. It was all the races originating from western and northern Europe.

* * *

The seeds for theories of northern and western European supremacy had been planted by French aristocrat Arthur de Gobineau, some four decades prior. In 1853 Gobineau devised a three-part system of race in which he segregated the world's peoples into black, white, and yellow groups. Echoing the work of earlier French race scientists, Gobineau placed black people at the bottom of the hierarchy, claiming their gluttonous nature to be one of their more base characteristics:

> The negroid variety is the lowest, and it stands at the foot of the ladder. The animal character appears in the shape of the pelvis. . . . Many of his senses, especially taste and smell, are developed to an extent unknown to the other two races. The very strength of his sensations is the most striking proof of his inferiority. All food is good in his eyes, nothing disgusts or repels him. What he desires is to eat, to eat furiously and to excess.[6]

The Frenchman's disgust for "gluttonous" racial Others, and black people especially, was par for the course during the period. What was new with Gobineau were his claims about the white race. For although whites were purportedly at the top of the tripartite system, there were divisions even within whiteness. The best of their members, he claimed, came from the pure-white Germanic subgroup he called "Aryans." Inventing what would later become known as a theory of Aryan supremacy, Gobineau saw himself as simply awakening the Germanic people to what he described as the awareness of their common origin.[7]

Gobineau's argument is strongly reminiscent of Anglo-Saxon theories of racial supremacy. But it differed in its assertion that in his native France, as in England, Celtic and Latin peoples had mixed with Germanic peoples.[8] This implied that contemporary Aryans, those most elite of white persons, were the descendants of Germanic *and* Celtic peoples. Even as Gobineau maintained Germanic superiority, he posited a form of racial closeness between Celts and Anglo-Saxons as northern Europeans and the superior whites. Relatedly, Gobineau suggested that southern and eastern Europeans were the inferior "hybrid" whites, indicating that although they are not as degraded as Africans, they were nevertheless "only civilized on the surface."[9]

When Gobineau put these ideas to paper in the 1850s, their impact was minimal. In the United States, the 1850s represented the height of Celtic Irish immigration and anti-Irish sentiment. But two events occurred near the turn of the twentieth century that profoundly affected shifting attitudes toward race in America. First, the number of Irish expatriates arriving in America began to decline. Irish immigrants had been coming to the United States in large numbers since the 1820s, with their numbers peaking around 1890. But their numbers began to dip around 1900. By the 1910s, the island could no longer claim its long-held status as one of the top two immigrant sending countries.[10] This eased their assimilation, since they no longer had the high levels of immigration that might have marked them as "perpetually foreign" by nativist Anglo-Saxons.[11] Second, and relatedly, a surge of migrants were arriving from regions that in earlier decades had sent few or no immigrants to America: southern and eastern Europe. Near the turn of the twentieth century, southern Italians and expatriates from the Russian empire had similar motivations for fleeing their homelands as had the Irish and Germans nearly a century prior.

In Italy, the nationalist movement known as the Risorgimento that began in 1815 culminated in 1861 with the fusion of the northern and southern regions of the Italian peninsula into a single unified nation. By many accounts, the marriage of the two regions played heavily to the favor of the north. Newly devised taxes, combined with the legacy of economic and political mismanagement in southern Italy, drove many residents of that region into abject poverty. The scramble for solutions to what many in Italy deemed "the Southern Question" led to a series of measures, among them an administrative centralization and a program of national improvements, to bring southern Italy into alignment with the new national economy and culture. But these measures proved, in general, to be ill-fated. The solution devised by southern Italian themselves by the end of the nineteenth century was simply to escape the ever worsening social conditions in their homeland.[12]

Imperial Russia, near the turn of the century, also witnessed a mass exodus of a subset of its population: the Jews. Jews of the Russian empire were leaving the country in record numbers. And while their flight was due to empire-building activities, the aim of these activities was very different from the nation-building activities in Italy. Rather than trying to unify two formerly disparate states (and, as it was described then, "distinct peoples"), the goal in imperial Russia was to purge what was described as the "alien" element. Through the pogroms of 1881–1884 that were repeated periodically from 1903 to 1919, Russia deployed an unofficial policy—which nevertheless involved the tacit cooperation of state officials—of exterminating or otherwise violently removing its Jewish population. The purported goal of the pogroms was to reinstate peace and a sense of community within the revolutionary environment that had arisen in the country after the assassination of the Russian tsar Alexander II. Many Russians blamed his assassination on "the Jews," and although there was never any definitive evidence to support this claim, one way peace could be achieved, according to the new tsar, Alexander III, was to reconstitute a "racially pure" Slavic nation.[13]

All of these events had a tremendous impact on immigration to the United States. Italy and the Russian empire, including people from present-day Russia, Poland, and Ukraine, a great many of whom were Jewish, sent the largest number of immigrants to the United States between the 1880s and the 1920s. The total Italian immigrant population jumped from 4,000 in 1850 to 44,000 in 1880. By 1900, nearly half a million people of Italian origin called the United States home. Statistics from the U.S. Immigration Commission showed that 2.2 million Italians came to the United States between 1899 and 1910, 1.8 million of them from southern Italy.[14] Immigration from imperial Russia followed a similar trajectory. In 1880 approximately 5,000 migrants from the Russian empire came to the United States in search of new lives. By 1891, that number had increased almost ten times, to 47,000. Between 1899 and 1910, nearly 1.8 million expatriates from the Russian empire disembarked on American shores. And significantly, while most immigrants at that time were male, nearly half of the Russian émigrés were female.[15]

This displacement and circulation of poor migrants, already considered unassimilable in their homelands, contributed to American fears that the national fabric was being sullied by foreign elements. Indeed, with the massive upheaval and dislocation of southern and eastern Europeans in the late nineteenth century came a considerable concern about limiting relations between "pure" whites and "hybrid" whites, who were believed in many instances to be part black.[16] Although this concern began with the Irish decades prior, it was expanded with the latest wave of immigration. The *New York Times* described immigrants from southern and eastern Europe as "undesirable" and a "drug in every market."[17] The development of racial theories had always been spurred by sociopolitical events. Thus it is hardly surprising that the massive upheaval of southern and eastern Europeans prompted a new generation of race scientists to rethink the world order.

In the new racial order, southern and eastern Europeans were vilified. Picking up on the work of Gobineau, observers deemed them inferior "hybrid" white races. According to the logic of existing theories about avarice and racialized depravity, southern and eastern Europeans were often considered corpulent.[18] Northern and western Europeans were praised, by contrast, for their intellect and beauty under the new racial regime. These Nordic or Aryan people were deemed tall and taut. There was a growing consensus that America was the place to find the best examples of the tall, svelte Nordic/Aryan type.

* * *

Just how much Elizabeth Bisland knew of these racial theories is hard to say. As a journalist, she was well-read. And by the time she was employed at the *Cosmopolitan* she was known for hosting literary salons reminiscent of the type François Bernier had attended when he was inspired to write the first ever racial classification schema. We do know, however, that Bisland herself had come from mixed, aristocratic, northern European heritage. On her mother's side, the Brownsons were descendants of the Asshetons, who had been made baronets by King James I. One of her ancestors, Ralph Assheton, was an English aristocrat and in-law to William Penn, founder of the Province of Pennsylvania. The credentials on her father's side were equally imposing. Through her paternal grandmother she could claim a relationship to the early Huguenot settlers of

South Carolina. She could also claim a kinship to the austere leader of the Scottish Reformation, John Knox, and his second wife, Lady Margaret Stewart, cousin of Mary, Queen of Scots.[19]

Given the intellectual climate and her own background, it might have been expected that when Bisland turned her attention to identifying the source of female beauty in the countryside, she emphasized their mixed Nordic heritage. In an article she penned for the *Cosmopolitan* in 1890, titled "Famous Beauties," she describes the beauty of American women as unrivaled: "It is equally and famously certain that the women [of America] surpass all others in the flower-like delicacy and perfection of their loveliness." The basis of American women's unmatched beauty, she contends, is their northern European racial makeup. For evidence, she offers the example of two purportedly famous American Beauties, explaining that "they both have Scotch blood in their veins. Mrs. Potter's being of both the Lowland Scotch and Celtic Highlander. Miss Anderson . . . being German and Scotch." While the women's racial makeup is the foundation of their attractiveness, the physical features that made them beautiful were their elongated, svelte physiques. According to Bisland, "both are tall and exquisitely slim."[20]

Here, Bisland describes thinness as a form of American exceptionalism. It is a type of beauty possible only in the United States, where the "best" of all races—those from northern and western Europe—had arrived as immigrants. These (desirable) immigrants had mixed and mingled to produce progeny who were tall, thin, and of unsurpassed beauty.

Bisland was not the only *Cosmopolitan* contributor to claim that American women of northern and western European descent were lithe, rangy, unparalleled beauties. In another piece from the same year, titled "Side Glances at American Beauty," Eleanor Waddle describes "native beauty as developed in America" as "the outgrowth of such heterogeneous elements, . . . a conglomeration of nationalities, the interfusion of so many races and types." In addition to the climate of America, this racial admixture gives the "ultra-Caucasian face an indescribably dazzling effect."[21]

Choosing, as had Bisland, to profile a few of these American beauties, Waddle shines the spotlight on an artist named Lilian Norton. Miss Norton is described as a "rare sort of beauty" and "highly cultivated." This is undoubtedly owing to her racial heritage, as Miss Norton, instead of going by her own name, is "known to the world as Nordica," indicating

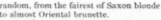

SIDE GLANCES AT AMERICAN BEAUTY.

BY ELEANOR WADDLE.

NATIVE beauty as developed in America is the outgrowth of such heterogeneous elements, such a conglomeration of nationalities, the interfusion of so many races and types, that any attempt to classify or even account for it, save as American, is futile. It is undeniable that climatic influences, freedom from old-world measures of restraint, and the diversity of our scenery random, from the fairest of Saxon blonde to almost Oriental brunette.

Some have assured us that "the skin of the native Indians is not only smoother, but more delicately furrowed, than that of Europeans"; thus proving a climatic advantage, witnessed in a softening of the national complexion, and producing in the ultra-Caucasian face an indescribably dazzling effect.

American beauty of to-day flourishes apparently alike in all localities. It crops out, like certain geological formations, in most unexpected places—on the sagebush plain, in the open prairie, in the atmosphere of smoky cities, or by the cruel sea—with equal but distinctive vigor. Its intrinsic merit alone recommends it, since there are no inequalities of rank to enhance its value, and the disparities of society frequently give place to its claim. Into this merit, however, enters largely the element of the picturesque, which obtains with a prevalence altogether sui generis. This is evidenced in the arts of dress and decorative effect, and in the selection of appropriate accessories.

The typical New-England girl, with demure eyes and charming Priscilla

Figure 6.1. Eleanor Waddle, "Side Glances at American Beauty," *Cosmopolitan*, June 1890, 193.

that she is a prime specimen of the Nordic peoples. Waddle also describes a Mrs. Adolf Dahlgren. Mrs. Dahlgren "is on the paternal side of French extraction." She is, moreover, "tall, slight and graceful in figure [with] gentle winning manners [that] elicit universal admiration."[22]

Evidently, Bisland was only one of the *Cosmopolitan*'s contributors to wax poetic about tall, slim Nordic American beauties. It is nevertheless a bit unexpected that Bisland would have inserted herself into this field at all. For though she was of aristocratic English and Scottish blood and had attracted many admirers, the English poet Rudyard Kipling among them, the writing she *is* remembered for lambastes the focus on feminine beauty.[23] A mere four years later, she published an article in the *North American Review* titled "The Cry of the Women," in which she suggests that women be allowed to lead the race to greatness. Her focus was not the look of the face or the size of the figure. Rather, it was the "beauty and importance" of women's intellectual and moral contributions.[24]

The *Cosmopolitan* was only one of the many publications to make claims about the beauty of Nordic/Aryan women. In many publications, as with claims of Anglo-Saxon superiority a generation earlier, women of northern and western European descent were said to manifest a peerless grace and a superior svelte figure, making them matchless American

Figure 6.2. Eleanor Waddle, "Side Glances at American Beauty," *Cosmopolitan*, June 1890, 194.

Comus so fittingly remarks, "To what end?"

Daily readers are familiar enough with Joseph Jefferson's reply to the Nashville reporter's insistent questions, "Where in America are to be found most intelligence, culture, and refinement?" and "Where are to be found the prettiest women in the world?" The famous comedian, when he designated Boston as his first answer, certainly did not intend to ignore beauty in favor of superabundant brains in that locality, as there are many glorious contradictions to such a statement; but Mrs. Emily Selinger and Mrs. Alice Kent Robertson merit comment as possessors of original beauty, accompanying remarkable mental vigor. These notable women occupy front rank in the artistic, literary, social, set of the Massachusetts capital; Mrs. Selinger as an artist and writer of genuine ability, and Mrs. Robertson as the president of the Saturday Morning Club, the gifted interpreter of Browning, and, latterly, Sophocles,—as King Creon in the Greek play Antigone,— in which part she achieved a decided success. Mrs. Selinger is a decided blonde with tawny hair,

violet eyes, and a warm color; while Mrs. Robertson is rich in coloring, with dark hair and eyes, and of tall stature.

Mr. Jefferson's response to the second

MRS. DA PONTE, OF NEW ORLEANS.

question varied the objective point somewhat in longitude as well as latitude. Turning to his son, who was standing near the reporter, he repeated the question to him. "My son, where are the prettiest women in the United States?" "In Nashville, Tennessee," came the prompt rejoinder. "That is my answer, also," asseverated the only Bob Acres, turning to his interlocutor; and undeniably he was very near the truth. The plateau of middle Tennessee is so favorable to the development of personal beauty that the bloom and elegance of their women is national in reputation.

No lovelier type of that region could possibly be selected than Mrs. Adolf Dahlgren, née de Morille. As her maiden name would indicate, she is, on the paternal side, of French extraction. Her beauty is of the typical patrician style, pale as an evening in autumn, with lovely golden hair, large gray eyes, and an uplifted expression of countenance that suggests spirituality of thought and feeling. Tall, slight, and graceful in figure, her gentle, winning manners elicit universal admiration.

Figure 6.3. Eleanor Waddle, "Side Glances at American Beauty," *Cosmopolitan*, June 1890, 195.

Beauties. And, if these connections between race, weight, and beauty had been popularized and disseminated in women's magazines for decades, by the turn of the twentieth century these ideas were becoming increasingly common in reputable academic and mainstream newspapers. The latest generation of boosters of the thin ideal relied on a new scientific language: eugenics. Prominent intellectuals asserted that the

slim Nordic/Aryan Americans were indeed the only group "fit" to reproduce. Their tendency to slimness was seen as an indication of such
fitness.

* * *

By the 1880s, as the number of southern Italians, Russian Jews, and
other southern and eastern Europeans landing at Ellis Island continued
to mount, so too did laws and policies intended to restrict the growth of
these populations. The restrictions took place on multiple fronts. Beginning in the 1880s, new laws were instituted that were intended to limit
the number of "undesirable" immigrants allowed to enter the United
States. This culminated in the Immigration Act of 1924, which severely
limited the number of visas that would be granted to immigrants from
southern and eastern Europe. Moreover, the act barred immigration
from several Asian countries.[25]

But, though a growing number of immigration restrictions were
cropping up, this left unanswered the question of what to do about the
population of low-caste, southern and eastern Europeans who were already in the country. The anxiety surrounding the possibility that the
dreaded "new immigrants" were not only living among but potentially
interbreeding with the Nordic population was in evidence at the highest levels of journalistic and academic authorship. In an article that
would be reprinted in a number of newspapers, including the *New York
Times*, Harvard professor and esteemed race scientist William Z. Ripley declaimed, "The Anglo-Saxon race is threatened with complete sub-
mergence" by those believed to be physically and mentally degenerate.
He feared that the Jews in particular were outliving and out-breeding
Anglo-Saxons, and thus threatening the future of the nation.[26] Restrictions on immigration, it seemed, were not enough. America also needed
a program aimed at curbing breeding with the constitutionally unsavory. These policies should also promote reproduction among persons
of good breeding stock.

Francis Galton had something for this. Galton was born in England
in 1822, thirteen years after his cousin Charles Darwin. Darwin's theory
of evolution would prove immensely influential to Galton's understanding of humankind. Like Darwin, Galton traveled far outside the con-
fines of the English countryside. But unlike Darwin, Galton used his

observations about human variability in various parts of the globe to theorize not only that humans had evolved to fit their environments, but that it might be possible, through selective breeding, to improve the mental and physical character of humanity. The way forward, it seems, was to discourage the reproduction of "inferior" peoples. But more importantly, civilized nations must encourage the better races to reproduce.

Galton's ideas about "better breeding" appeared in his 1883 book *Inquiries into Human Faculty and Its Development*. Coining the term "eugenics"—borrowed from the Greek *eugenes*, meaning "good in stock"—to describe propitious mating, Galton claimed that mental and physical characteristics, such as intellect and beauty, were inherited. Therefore, he claimed, it made sense for only the best of the human bloodlines to breed. The goal was to give "more suitable races or strains of blood" the best chance of "prevailing . . . over the less suitable."[27]

In the context of possible interbreeding between "old" immigrants from northern Europe and "new" immigrants from southern and eastern Europe, many American intellectuals viewed Galton's theory as sage advice. His ideas about promoting better breeding were largely transmitted to American audiences through Charles Davenport, a well-connected New England Puritan. In 1910 Davenport founded the Eugenic Records Office, a New York–based institute that collected information on the ancestry of American families.

Building on the work of Galton and other luminaries like William Z. Ripley, Davenport claimed that "Poles, Irish, and Italians" were of a decidedly different race from the native stock of white Americans, as shown through their color, stature, and propensity for crime and insanity.[28] The question of "stature" and its relationship to race was one he would return to frequently. For Davenport, obesity was a vile condition to be avoided. It was, moreover, racially inherited.[29] In his 1923 book *Body Build and Its Inheritance*, Davenport makes a clear distinction between the slenderness or medium build of the "Nordic" types and the fatness of the southern and eastern Europeans.[30] He writes that there is a "striking contrast" between the "slender Scotchman" and the "South Italian, Greek, or Russian Jew."[31] The latter groups, especially the women, suffer from an inherited tendency to fatness: "That fleshiness may be a true hereditary character is indicated by the existence of fleshy races of men. Examples are the South-Russian Jews, especially of the female sex;

and certain of the Chinese, who have strikingly short legs." He concludes that "the fact that the body reacts to food and climate must not blind us to the constitutional factors that are probably present in racial obesity."[32]

None of this would have been taken as particularly controversial within the scholarly community. Georges Vacher de Lapouge, a French sociologist and Davenport's friend and confidant, had expressed great anxiety regarding the racial future of America in the context of immigration from eastern and southern Europe.[33] But he had also expressed great hope. A follower of Gobineau's work, Lapouge claimed that the "Aryans" were the best of the races. And he believed that America was the nation par excellence to find these strapping, lissome peoples. In an article in the *American Journal of Sociology,* Lapouge writes, "In my view . . . the builders of the Aryan nation were of the type of 'Uncle Sam.'" This type is "lank-bodied, . . . usually blond, adventurous and aggressive."[34]

To these and other American intellectuals in the late nineteenth and early twentieth centuries, America was the land of the lofty race of lean Nordics or Aryans. They devised theories to confirm Nordic/Aryan supremacy—and southern and eastern European degeneracy. They simultaneously worked to promote the judicious mating of the superior peoples.

While politicians crafted anti-immigrant legislation and scientists generated studies on (eugenic) racial inheritance, artists and journalists also had their part to play. In the popular press, the question of the racial—and relatedly physical—character of Americans loomed large. In the spirit of American exceptionalism, they embraced the country as a melting pot of morally upright, democratic, and forward-thinking peoples. Yet they were clear to specify which nations, races, and peoples contributed to this arcadian melting pot: those from northern and western Europe. With women commonly being used to represent the nation, the emerging face and figure of American exceptionalism as seen in mainstream art and media was the trim Nordic woman.[35]

* * *

By the turn of the twentieth century, the name Charles Dana Gibson would be synonymous with feminine loveliness. He was born in 1867 in the Roxbury section of Boston. At an early age, he quit New England for

Figure 6.4. Charles Dana Gibson, *Picturesque America*, 1898. Image courtesy of Bridgeman Images.

New York, enrolling in the prestigious Art Students League in 1883. A mere three years later, the young artist had one of his sketches published in *Life* magazine.[36] In 1888, in the tradition of many great American artists and intellectuals, Gibson departed for Europe. In Paris, at the Académie Julian, he honed his craft and fine-tuned his artistic vision. In the 1890s, upon his return from Europe, his career as a draftsman took shape. It was during this decade that Gibson came up with a new icon of beauty, an image he called the "Gibson Girl." Like earlier American models, she was tall and graceful. But unlike earlier models, she was something of an athlete and an intellectual. The Gibson Girl was frequently depicted in pastoral scenes riding a bike or playing golf. She might equally be shown on a chaise lounge poring over a pile of books, or seated at a table composing letters to acquaintances. A representation of the late-century "New Woman," the Gibson Girl was commonly drawn with chin aloft, skillfully undertaking one of the many tasks demanded of the cultivated North American woman.[37] Before the century was out, the Gibson Girl would appear in multiple mainstream publications.

What made the Gibson Girl unique was that she gained widespread appeal in both the northern and southern parts of the United States. This was no mean feat. Although Louisiana-born Elizabeth Bisland had been a recognized beauty in the South who moved northward and continued to garner recognition for her looks, this was not necessarily a common trajectory. For decades, artists, journalists and other self-styled beauty experts claimed that different types of beauty were to be seen, and appreciated, in different regions of the country. Indeed, well into the 1890s, in the prominent southern newspaper the *Atlanta Constitution*, plump women, particularly those with the Venus's proportions, were celebrated.[38] In an 1888 article bearing the headline "Woman's Figure—Real and Ideal," the author describes the ideal woman's figure as that of the "Medicean Venus." This is not the Venus that was co-opted and retrofitted for *Harper's*. According to the author, the American version of the Greek ideal had the following measurements: "waist 23 inches or sometimes 24, bust 36 inches, occasionally 37, hip measure from 45 to 47."[39]

Another article from the same year in the *Atlanta Constitution* describes the appeal of the voluptuous actress Lillian Russell, born in the early 1860s. In her youth, Russell's beauty and talent were praised in many parts of the country. Over the years, however, she gained considerable weight. In the North, this apparently made her the subject of snide comments. In the South, however, her shapely, classical figure was defended: "Though New Yorkers speak of Lillian Russell's former beauty with a regretful sigh," the author states, "her charm is yet potent to those seeing her for the first time, for she still has with the aid of electric lights, etc, the face of a child and the figure of a Venus."[40]

In a later article, the author claimed that both class and race were what made the typically voluptuous southern belle. An 1895 article in the *Atlanta Constitution* revealed the clear difference between the North and South in terms of race and aesthetics. In "The Highest Types of Our Southern Beauty" the author intones, "Every one of [the] pretty southerners is a girl of high social position and has been a reigning belle in her own section." And it was not just class, but also racial lineage that generated the typically fleshy beauties in the region: "Mrs. Sterling's beauty is of the rich Circassian blond type. She is large and magnificently made."[41]

Yet the 1890s appeared to have been the turning point. By that time, even as many railed against the slender ideal, and voluptuous figures continued to be vaunted, there was a growing praise of slenderness in parts of the South.[42] Key factors were, again, the immigration of "stout" southern and eastern Europeans, and the growing relationship between Nordic/Aryan heritage, slimness, and beauty.[43] That is, even if immigration from southern and eastern Europe largely impacted the North, the South too, by the early 1900s, would receive a high number of immigrants from the Russian empire. This, combined with the greater circulation of newspaper articles by the end of the century, meant that the fear of immigrants from southern and eastern Europe was stoked in the South as well as the North.

It is partially for these reasons that the Gibson Girl captured the American imagination when it did. For although voluptuousness had long been praised in the South, areas like Atlanta were starting to see a new appreciation for slimmer models. Even the author of "The Highest Types of Our Southern Beauty," while praising the voluptuous Circassian figures, nevertheless describes an Alabama woman as a "slender and rather tall brunette, with a svelt [sic] figure," whose "beauty is of the most refined and aristocratic type." Of a woman from Virginia, deemed "rather small, of perfect figure," the author noted, "the type is decidedly the American girl, Gibson has made so familiar."[44]

The notion that the idealized "small" and "perfect figure" of American women was captured by Gibson was seen in several articles in the paper. An article from 1899 states, "Mr. Charles Dana Gibson first charmed the world with his original illustrations . . . [of a] type of American beauty Americans and foreigners admired as the highest type of the American woman."[45] Still another, written three years later, reminds the reader that the Gibson Girl was regarded as "the acme of American beauty and refinement."[46]

What is often underappreciated about Gibson is his own take on the relationship between race and beauty. Reproducing the notion of America as a melting pot of the "superior" races, Gibson believed that the refined and aristocratic air of the Gibson Girl had everything to do with her mixed-northern European heritage:

> What Zangwill calls "The Melting Pot of the Races" has resulted in a certain character. . . . They are beyond question the loveliest of all their sex.

Evolution has selected the best things for preservation. . . . Why should women not be beautiful increasingly? Why should it not be the fittest in form and features, as well as mind and muscle which survives? And where should that fittest be in evidence most strikingly? In the United States of course, where natural selection has been going on, as elsewhere, there has been a great variety to choose from. The eventual American woman will be even more beautiful than the woman of to-day. Her claims to that distinction will result from a fine combination of the best points of all those many races which have helped to make our population.[47]

The language of "natural selection" is certainly Galtonian, showing Gibson to be conversant with eugenic ideologies. Moreover, his description was indicative of the prevailing racial logic of northern European superiority. For although he suggests that America is exceptional as a melting pot of the races, he does not mention all the races in the brew, preferring to name instead only the one he finds most important: "The best part of her beauty will and has come from the nation of our origin— Great Britain."[48]

Describing the beautiful American woman as tall, trim, and first of Anglo-Saxon and later Nordic/Aryan racial lineage, had long been the norm in the North. By the turn of the twentieth century, this point of view was being widely disseminated in mainstream publications, gaining popularity in other parts of the country, and quickly becoming recognized as the American Beauty ideal. Odes to Charles Dana Gibson and his belles femmes appeared routinely in the *New York Times* and the *Atlanta Constitution*, but they were certainly not limited to these venues. Between 1895 and 1920, hundreds of references to the Gibson Girl appeared in publications such as the *Chicago Tribune* (135), the *Washington Post* (213), and even the *Los Angeles Times* (134).[49] The Gibson Girl, as drawn by the artist, represented the tall, trim American woman, foremost, in his own words, of British origin.[50] To the extent that thinness was becoming a form of American exceptionalism, the artistic portrayals of the Gibson Girl in the mainstream media were integral to making this association.

Gibson might have been rightfully heralded as an innovator in the field of feminine aesthetics. But by the time of his 1910 interview with the *New York Times,* his type of girl was being overshadowed by purport-edly newer models that nevertheless owed something to his inspiration. In a 1907 interview in the *Times,* for example, the artist M. Philip Boileau offers up his ideal beauty, one that seems very similar to Gibson's: "In his study of the American beauty, he leans toward the blonde, with the tall, slender, nervous nature that is so great a promise, and so alluringly different from any other type of woman in the world."[51]

In another article in the *Times* from 1911, yet another artist is credited with finding a "new type of beauty." But this beauty, as described, seems remarkably like the one popularized by Gibson. The author of the article says of the modern muse, "Miss Rasmussen is tall and slender. . . . That the ideal American beauty should be somewhat of a cosmopolitan is evidenced by the fact that Miss Rasmussen's Americanism comes from a blend of Irish and Danish blood."[52]

By the 1920s, the silhouette of the Gibson Girl was not enough. Writer Penrhyn Stanlaws reflected on the ideal of female beauty in 1923. He outright rejected what he saw as the frequently excessive size of the real-life women inspired by Gibson's drawings: "We or at least our fathers, were all in love with the Gibson girl, with her broad shoulders and her tiny waist who weighed from 110 to 175 pounds. No [sic] we show a most decided preference for the girl whose waist line is about 24 or 26 inches and who tips the scale at 110 to 120 pounds."[53]

The reference to the scale here is significant. Starting in 1891, public weighing scales started to appear in shops and in busy commercial districts. By 1913, scales made their entry into private homes.[54] For the first time in history, weight-conscious Americans could quantify their thinness and their corpulence. Many Americans were motivated by their physicians to find out their exact weight. This signaled a new front in the war on fat, one that was now to be waged in the field of medicine. For although doctors since the time of George Cheyne had been telling corpulent people to lose weight for God, and race scientists had been urging elite white Americans to stay slim for country medical science would in the twentieth century step in to tell Americans to get trim for health reasons.

Yet even in the medical field, descriptions of the relationship between weight and health were not motivated exclusively by medical findings.

The legacy of Protestant moralism and race science as it related to fat and thin persons loomed large. Indeed, many early to mid-twentieth-century physicians relied on moral and racial logics to rail against persons deemed too fat or too thin. But over time, a growing number did so specifically, and exclusively, to condemn fatness.

PART III

Doctors Weigh In

Good Health to Uplift the Race

Dr. John Harvey Kellogg did not set out to become the world's foremost purveyor of delicious breakfast cereals. He had, in fact, wanted nothing to do with the commercialization of his delectable foodstuffs. In his estimation, the array of vegetarian dishes that he and his wife, Ella, had lovingly crafted were to be shared with those in his ministry in Battle Creek, Michigan. Instead of turning a quick buck, the Kelloggs wanted to make more palatable the potentially joyless vegetarian fare his local Seventh-day Adventist church deemed essential for the maintenance of a robust body, ready for worship. Healthy eating, Kellogg was sure, would reform the sickly, frail young women populating the nation's cities. Reforming the nation's women was, he asserted, the only way to guarantee the preservation of the superior Anglo-Saxon race.

Kellogg was a major player in the increasing encroachment of medicine into questions of the proper diet and weight for the average American, a terrain previously dominated by race scientists and religious reformers. Rather than skirting or directly rejecting ethno-religious theories of the links between race, femininity, weight, and health, John Harvey Kellogg, a physician, eugenicist, and ardent Christian, combined all three. Like numerous other physicians, Kellogg believed that reforms to the American diet were long overdue. Yet for Kellogg and many other doctors, the problem was that far too many women of the fashionable classes were *underweight*. Invested in a form of what French philosopher Michel Foucault called "biopolitics,"[1] many physicians in the early years of medical reform aimed to help women of the fashionable classes gain weight for their health, and as a way to uplift the race.

* * *

Family misfortune led John Harvey Kellogg to devote his life to American health reform. His father, John Preston Kellogg, came from good

Figure 7.1. John Harvey Kellogg, n.d. Image courtesy of Ellen G. White Estate, Inc.

Puritan stock. He and his first wife, Mary, had headed west from New England in the 1830s in search of a greater expanse of land on which to raise their growing brood. They had settled on a 320-acre tract of land in an area of Michigan that, at that time, was home to only a few indigenous and white residents.[2] The rough-and-tumble nature of frontier life soon compromised Mary's health. The family called in a doctor from Flint, who recommended as a cure periodic bloodletting and inhaling the fumes of live coals.[3] John Preston Kellogg fared little better. After a few years of life on the plains, he developed an eye infection. The doctor who ministered to him dosed him with calomel, a substance that contained mercury. This did nothing for his puffy red eyes, but did cause his tongue to swell so that it lolled outside his mouth.[4] No thanks to the doctor in question, John eventually recovered. But the family was subsequently hit with one medical emergency after another, and the physicians at their disposal were of no help. In another two years, Mary would be dead of tuberculosis. Six years later, John and his second wife, Ann, would lose a daughter to a lung infection that a local doctor had misdiagnosed as worms.[5]

If the general ineptitude of local medical men left the family at their collective wit's end, the solution to their health problems seemed almost literally to be knocking at their door. It was, after all, the time of the Second Great Awakening, the Protestant religious revival that swept the United States in the early nineteenth century, captivating the likes of Sarah Josepha Hale. America throbbed with revivalist fervor. And a central goal for many people caught up in the movement was to transform what they deemed the intemperate American habits in food and drink. The reformers believed that if they could prevent Americans from stuffing themselves to the gills and tippling with abandon, and instead reorient American dietary habits in a way that honored God, it would be the best thing for the white race. It would at the same time offer further proof of the exceptionalism of the United States. These were, in effect, the principles that the Kelloggs' contemporary, Sarah Josepha Hale, had wanted to instill in her audience of like-minded upper- and middle-class Anglo-Saxon female readers of *Godey's Lady's Book*.

Hale had identified Lady Mary Wortley Montagu as her personal icon. And it seems that others in the health reform movement had also looked to eighteenth-century British figures for their inspiration. For it was during the mid-nineteenth century that American health reformers returned to the ideas of Dr. George Cheyne as they sought cures for what ailed them. The Reverend William Metcalfe, himself a British transplant, was one of the religious physiologists credited with popularizing Cheyne's dietary dicta on this side of the Atlantic. Cheyne had preached that eating right by God involved first and foremost not overeating. For one's portion-controlled meals, Cheyne had promoted a largely milk-based vegetarian diet, and to round out the regimen, he advised that one should drink plenty of water and take frequent baths.

Metcalfe, a teetotaling herbivore, had routinely preached sermons on the value of a Cheyne-ian lifestyle.[6] Its principles were central to the American Vegetarian Society, an organization he co-founded in 1850. Cheyne's work, benefitting from the proselytizing of Metcalfe and others, found a new audience in the United States. And while the vegetarianism that Cheyne advocated was met in America with a combination of zeal, resignation, and dismay, the water cure he popularized at his English baths proved immensely popular. The cure was rebranded "hydro-therapy," and hordes of health reformers churned out treatises touting the miracles of simply drinking and bathing in clean water. Whatever the intrinsic health benefits of clean water, this was clearly sound advice; the contaminated water supply and poor drainage were contributing mightily to the outbreak of cholera in the United States in the 1830s.[7] In addition to cholera, many Americans suffered from gout and dyspepsia fueled by the consumption of sugar and alcohol, making it arguable that many Americans had sipped and sopped their way to illness. A spare vegetarian diet and plenty of pure water were seen as the backbone of reform.

It should come as no surprise, then, that after suffering through years of medical negligence, the devout Kelloggs sought relief from their illnesses in the bosom of fellow parishioners. A proselytizing vegetarian preacher named Sylvester Graham blew through Michigan, lecturing on the ills of excess indulgence and the particular sin of meat eating. John Preston Kellogg was sold. He converted the family to vegetarianism. And around the same time, hearing tales of the miracles of the cold water cure, he began dabbling in the practice.

In 1852, the same year John Harvey Kellogg was born, John Preston found a new faith, one that miraculously merged his hydropathy and vegetarianism. The new sect did not yet have a name, but it did have a following, one that reached back to the feverish ecclesiasticism that had swept the Eastern Seaboard in the 1840s. Ellen White, one of the women who had borne witness to its development, and her husband, James White, touched down in 1855 in Battle Creek, Michigan. Shortly thereafter the new Church of Seventh-day Adventists began the business of expanding its ministry.[8]

White shared the same disdain for medical men as did the Kelloggs. She was also a Grahamite, and one of her key beliefs was that sickness was a punishment for sins. It was the Lord's righteous way of reminding His people that they had been abusing the body by eating, drinking, and (seemingly out of nowhere) masturbating with gross regularity. Ending forms of self-stimulation and taking up a vegetarian diet with a little hydropathy thrown in, she believed, was the way to purify the body of disease.[9] The message resonated with the pious residents of Battle Creek.

The sanctified body became central to the Seventh-day Adventist message in another way. For unlike most other Christian sects, the Adventists believed that the actual physical body would be spirited away to the heavens during the rapture. In this way, what they termed their "physiological rectitude" did not involve simply their health on Earth. It was designed to prepare them for the actual "bodily salvation" that was their due.[10]

John Harvey Kellogg had lived with the principles of Seventh-day Adventism his entire life. By the time he reached adulthood, Ellen White and the other senior members of the church were ready for him to make the leap from student to teacher. At the age of twenty, Kellogg was urged by his family and the Whites to attend Dr. Trall's Hygieo-therapeutic College in New Jersey. It was here that Kellogg and a few other young men from the church would learn the principles of treating the infirm through diet, exercise, and the healing properties of water.[11]

Still, the perception festered that the term "hygieo-therapeutic" in the school's title called into question the validity of another of its terms, "doctor." Even for a believer like young John Harvey, there was something decidedly unscientific, and arguably a little hokey, about the training he had received at Dr. Trall's. Despite the skepticism of traditional medicine on the part of his family and the Whites, John Harvey decided to continue his medical education. With the blessing of his family and some money from the Whites, he attended first the University Medical School in Ann Arbor, Michigan, and then the Bellevue Hospital Medical College in New York before getting his doctor of medicine degree in 1875.[12]

It was now that Kellogg felt truly prepared to do the Lord's work. First, he returned to the Western Health Reform Institute, founded by Ellen White in 1866, taking over as its superintendent in 1876. The following year, he rechristened the institute the Battle Creek Sanitarium, affectionately known as "the San." Then, working closely with a nurse named Ella Eaton, he set about creating a health-based dietary regime that would treat food and water as medicine. To Kellogg, this represented a major step toward righting the health of Anglo-Saxon Americans.

At the San, Kellogg and Eaton thereupon set out to create a menu of life-giving foods that no other place in the world could boast. They set up a satellite location, dubbed the Sanitas Food Company, where they toyed with food consistencies and generated rogue combinations of nuts and grains. Their experiments led to the creation of granola and early imitation meats. By changing the texture of the soybean, they were able to create soy milk. And, despite the lore surrounding George

Washington Carver, whom Kellogg would later come to know personally, the pair even developed and patented a form of peanut butter.[13] But it was, of course, for their process of toasting and drying a variety of cereals—wheat, rice, and corn—that they became best known.[14]

By 1905 the Kelloggs were making and selling an average of 150 cases daily of cornflakes alone.[15] Companies started by competitors sprang up overnight, the most viable of which was begun by a former patient at the San named C. W. Post, who would go on to achieve his own cereal-related fame. But fame and riches were not what they were after. Kellogg and Eaton had begun Kellogg's enterprise for the express purpose of furthering his own, and the church's, goals of what he termed "biologic living."[16] Eating the healthiest vegetarian fare and applying water liberally to the inside and outside of the body were the best ways to prevent illness in this life and to prepare oneself for the afterlife. It was a form of what Michel Foucault would later refer to as the "biopolitics" of medicine, with a spiritual payoff.[17]

Despite their commercial success, the Kelloggs were beset with difficulties from the start. Incredibly, only one year after coming on as superintendent at the San, Kellogg was already facing difficult questions regarding the viability of his medico-religious practices. The problem was simple. He appeared to be serving two masters: the church and the medical profession. Neither seemed overly impressed with his service. Members of the medical community had long regarded his practices with unease. Between 1877 and 1886, Kellogg defended himself against claims by the Calhoun County Medical Association in Michigan that his unorthodox practices at the San violated the American Medical Association's code of ethics.[18] The case was ultimately decided in his favor, concluding a tense, nine-year drama.

Slightly over a decade later, several of the more devout members of his own parish claimed that Kellogg, a facile surgeon, tried to infuse too much traditional medicine into his treatments at the San. They complained that his invasions into the diseased cavities of patients took up an increasing share of his, and thereby the San's, activities. By 1907, with church leadership fearing that his surgical practice was taking him away from the biblical ministering he ought to have been doing, he was asked to step down.[19] He split from the leadership the same year, although he was able to keep the San under his control.

The situation must have been distressing for Kellogg. His medico-religious take on physical and spiritual salvation was his entire raison d'être. For while he inherited his family's skepticism about conventional medicine when left unchecked, he was also certain that in the coming decades physicians would play a role in the preservation of the white race. To be sure, Kellogg's position on the preservation of white lives was a bit out of step with church leadership. Ellen White, after all, was a noted abolitionist who railed against what she described as the "high crime of slavery," writing that the church's goal should be to deliver "the gospel to the darkened regions of the world" as well as to the millions of people "in the very midst of us . . . who [also] have souls to save or lose."[20] And while the early settlers of Battle Creek had counted among them some pro-slavery advocates, members of the church were known for embracing abolitionism, as well as major anti-slavery figures. No less a personage than Sojourner Truth, herself a vegetarian and water-cure enthusiast, spent time with the Battle Creek Adventists. Inexplicably, given his politics, Kellogg doted on the ailing Sojourner affectionately during her final days.[21]

His devotion to the famed abolitionist aside, Kellogg showed minimal interest in the betterment of nonwhite races. He had studied the widely circulated works of race scientists and been a close reader of the writings of Cuvier. He believed in a hierarchy of races in which whites stood at the top. "Negros" and "Orientals," as he referred to these groups, were of inferior races, he believed, and therefore there was only so much that could be expected of them.

The medico-religious path Kellogg was charting was designed for the intended salvation of the human race through the uplift of its most valuable members: Anglo-Saxons.[22] So when he began laying out his plan for necessary improvements of humankind, Kellogg started at the top. The problem, he claimed, was that Anglo-Saxons were degenerating thanks to the vices of modern living. And who or what was largely to blame for this sorry state of affairs? Young, scrawny, Anglo-Saxon women. These wisps of femininity had taken the fashion of slimness too far. Their thinness was nothing short of an epidemic, and it was threatening the future of the nation.

Kellogg decided he would be an interventionist. He addressed Anglo-Saxon women directly with his plans for constitutional and racial reform in his 1891 book, *Ladies' Guide in Health and Disease: Girlhood, Maiden-hood, Wifehood, Motherhood.* The tract left few aspects of a woman's life unexamined. He wanted to make the case clearly that young, modish, and underweight women, far from being a model of femininity, were a threat to the entire master race. Even in the preface, he does not spare the rod. "The diseases of women," he states, have been on the rise, and consequently they now "constitute a large part of the practice of the majority of physicians, and probably contribute more to the support of the medical profession than any other class of maladies."[23] Identifying Anglo-Saxon women as critical vectors of disease, he then informs the reader that their frailty is their own doing, and undoing: "The suffering of civilized women from special diseases above those of other races, is due not to injurious climatic influences . . . but to a lack of physical culture, . . . improper dress, sedentary habits of life, errors in diet, too much excitement."[24]

The question of women's fashions, alluded to in his comment about "improper dress," could be seen as a direct dig at the hokum promoted by women's magazines. As far as he could tell, the corsets and other ridiculous garb in which these women swaddled themselves were in large part responsible for their "thin, flaccid, and powerless" figures.[25] Moreover, these practices in dress, he claimed, must have been a holdover from days of barbarity. Just as the "inferior races" continued to celebrate deformity as fashion, he complained, so too did far too many Anglo-Saxon women. By way of example, he offered a few illustrations of these barbarous practices among Africans, Asians, and Native persons.

Women's magazines were, of course, where many white women during the era might also have gleaned their dietary advice, if they had been following the dictates of *Godey's* and *Harper's.* Whether or not Kellogg was aware of this when he dismissed Anglo-Saxon women's nutritional choices as in "error" is uncertain. His objective as a licensed physician and health reform advocate was simply to right the ship. Regardless of where they had been getting their information, the "marked deterioration" in the physique of Anglo-American women was, from his vantage point, both pitiable and undeniable.[26]

But Kellogg had a cure for what ailed the sick, physically underdeveloped Anglo-American woman. In this he was aligned with the contributors to *Godey's* and many other women's magazines by claiming, curiously,

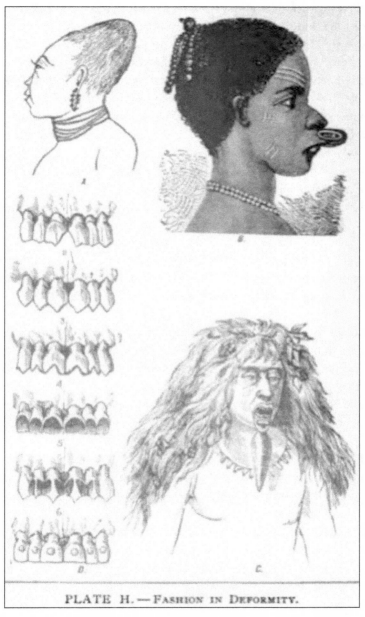

PLATE H. — FASHION IN DEFORMITY.

Figure 7.2. John Harvey Kellogg, "Fashion in Deformity," in *Ladies' Guide in Health and Disease*, 1891.

that these women had to first recognize that a critical source of the problem was overindulgence in the wrong foods. According to Kellogg, young ladies were "fond of pastry and knick-knacks," and "by the indulgence of this morbid taste, a large share of the young ladies of the day either actually become dyspeptics or lay the foundation for this disease."[27] But whereas the solution offered in *Godey's* commonly included an injunction to eat less in the name of temperance, Kellogg wanted young women to eat more, but of the right stuff. What they needed were "fruits and grains with plenty of milk" as well as "Graham bread, cracked-wheat . . . and other whole-meal preparations"—and of course plenty of good, clean water.[28] The latter point was important; Kellogg wanted to encourage the development of robust vigorous figures, not just added poundage. "Fine flour bread" was not advised because it was "fattening, not strengthening."[29] Obesity in general was considered a corollary of illness.

But for Kellogg, it was not excess fat but rather excess leanness, resulting from a poor diet, that was the existential threat facing Anglo-Saxon women, and by proxy the white race:

> In England and America, however, but particularly in this country, and especially in cities and towns, girls as a rule are found to be decidedly lacking in physical development. Observe the students of a female seminary as they pass along toward their homes at the conclusion of their hour of study. Notice how few possess shapely bodies, a strong, elastic, vigorous step, well developed waists, plump arms, broad backs, and a full chest.[30]

In his opinion, their underdevelopment was a marker of illness that would doom an otherwise exceptional nation full of superior peoples. And again, those afflicted were not few in number:

> The majority of young ladies whom we meet upon the streets have narrow backs, flat chests, round shoulders drooping forward, thin necks, scrawny arms, waspish waists, and an awkward gait. The ruddy bloom of health is rarely seen now-a-days except occasionally in some out-of-the-way country place.[31]

Clearly, when Kellogg offers advice to girls on how to eat right to build better physiques, the goal was not just that they develop "comely forms," although this too was desirable. The real concern for Kellogg was that Anglo-American women's "numerous deficiencies," shown by their want of fuller figures, were compromising the future of white America. He states this unequivocally when he proclaims, "The only hope for the race is in the future of its girls," whose diet and physiques needed massive overhaul.[32]

All of this was the stuff of mainstream eugenics. The concepts in *Ladies' Guide* were more or less in lockstep with the ideas of famed eugenicist Charles Davenport, who, as it turns out, was an associate of Kellogg's. Yet Kellogg had inherited a few ideas from Ellen White, such as her disdain for masturbation and the belief that it too played a mysterious role in illness, in that it caused infertility. Evidently, both Ellen White and Kellogg were deeply invested in controlling the vices of the "animal appetites," oral and sexual, specifically those of women.[33]

Related to the control of the animal appetites, Kellogg also maintained the position that if, for example, a white woman were to be so reckless as to have one child with a "negro," *all* of her subsequent children would be part black. Therefore, it was of utmost importance that white women breed only with white men to prevent what Kellogg called "bad blood" from seeping into the white race. He claimed that the "Hottentot," using the moniker as a synonym for blackness, were "blood clocks" in that they had a finite amount of potential, and, it was implied, their time on earth was running out.[34] If left to their own devices, he implies, African races would become extinct.

It is perhaps for this reason that Kellogg, like many eugenicists and other medical men of the era, spent far less time fretting over the state of black women, or black people in general, than had scientists and philosophers of earlier eras. Learned men of the eighteenth and early nineteenth centuries had claimed that black people were constitutionally inferior. Building upon these ideas, and given the socio-legal and political reality of black people in the mid- to late nineteenth century being a constantly disenfranchised underclass—cycling first through slavery and then through Jim Crow segregation (with only a brief respite during Reconstruction)—eugenicists like Kellogg had come to the conclusion that black people were doomed to die off. In this way, whereas racial scientific literature in the late eighteenth and early nineteenth centuries had made much of the physical and temperamental inferiority of black people, especially as it pertained to their presumed inability to control their base animal instincts, the eugenicists of the turn of the twentieth century devoted considerably less attention to them.[35]

Certain of black people's imminent racial demise, many, like Kellogg, chose to focus instead on improving the so-called superior white people, the Anglo-Saxons. Teaching them the proper principles of "biologic living," including whom to mate with, and what and how much to eat and exercise, would ensure their supremacy in this life and the next. Thus, a critical concern in the eugenic and general medical literature in the late nineteenth and early twentieth centuries was the health of well-to-do white persons, especially women.

* * *

Ladies' Guide represented Kellogg's sustained treatment of the question of the relationship between women's diet, their physical size, and the health of the race overall. Kellogg was a prolific writer, publishing multiple books and dozens of articles. Much of his early work, dating back to the mid-1870s, could be found in the publication of the Western Health Reform Institute, originally titled *Health Reformer*. In 1879 he changed the title to *Good Health*. Together, the publications ran from 1866 to 1953. In them, one could find more of Kellogg's thoughts on vegetarian diets as well as insights into how intemperance among black and indigenous peoples proved them to be lower on the scale of humanity: "The South is for prohibition because it has been forced to recognize that given whiskey, the negro is made a beast. The white man intoxicated sinks low enough in the bestial scale, but not so low as the negro or the Indian."[36]

Kellogg's status as a pioneer in the field of biologic living may have helped him to ultimately make his way into the mainstream of American medicine. Recall that between 1877 and 1886, he was viewed as an unorthodox and arguably unsavory personage in both the medical establishment and his church. As it was, he never fully mended relations with the Seventh-day Adventist leadership in Battle Creek.[37] But around the 1890s, he was finding redemption in conventional medical circles. Two years after the resolution of the row between Kellogg and the Calhoun County Medical Association, he was unanimously elected the group's president.[38] He also became a member of the American Public Health Association and the American Medical Association within a few years of getting his medical degree in 1875.[39]

Earning the support of the American Medical Association proved no small matter. The organization itself had been formed in 1847, coming on the heels of the Second Great Awakening. But according to sociologist Paul Starr, the group spent its first decades of existence embroiled in battles about who had the right to practice under its banner and what forms of practice would be sanctioned. Not until the end of the nineteenth century did the group move past its squabbles, giving homeopaths entrée into the organization. And in 1901 the association revised its constitution in a way that opened the organization up to thousands of new members. Its membership jumped from 8,000 in 1901 to 70,000 in 1910. By 1920 the association claimed that it represented 60 percent of all physicians in America, making it the profession's leading organization and marking the beginning of what is recognized today as organized medicine.[40]

Kellogg was an early member of the group and he had relationships with some of its leaders. In medical school, for example, he had studied under Dr. Austin Flint, who in 1884 became the association's president. Such connections likely helped him gain access to the association's recently created publication, the *Journal of the American Medical Association*, known as *JAMA*. Within a few years of its creation, the articles of a young Kellogg were being featured in its pages. One piece, from 1888, touted the benefits of an oxygen enema. Kellogg described the effects of oxygen administered to the rectum of a woman, aged fifty, who had been losing weight due to digestive distress:

> There was the steady decline in strength and flesh until the patient was reduced to a skeleton. . . . At this crisis, it was determined to make a trial of the oxygen enemata. . . . As a result, most marked improvement began at once. . . . The patient began to gain in flesh . . . and in a few weeks the patient was able to return to her home restored to health.[41]

Yet again, Kellogg identifies thinness as a corollary of illness. Proof of recovery was found in added flesh.

Only a few years prior, he had been sued by the Calhoun County Medical Association for his unorthodox practices at the San. Now, Kellogg's views on the value of a vegetable diet, exercise, clean water, and apparently oxygen enemas were endorsed by the medical community.

This much was clear when the *Journal of the American Medical Association* featured an image of the San on the cover of an 1889 issue. Praising the facility as the largest, "most thoroughly equipped" sanitarium in the country, the article reads more like an advertisement than an in-depth review of the San's facilities. Ironically, the backing of the facility by the mainstream medical community as a place where the sick could receive "modern, rational medical treatment" would precede a series of unfortunate events that were in store for Kellogg and the institution. But for the time being Kellogg must have been satisfied with the inroads he and the San were making.

In addition to the discussion of Kellogg's medical treatments and his none-too-subtle suggestions that slenderness in a woman was a sign of illness, his theories on race also appeared in mainstream medical venues. In 1914 his address to the American Public Health Association, titled "Relation of Public Health to Race Degeneracy," appeared in the *American Journal of Public Health*. The point of the address was to underscore what Kellogg described as the "remarkable depreciation of racial vitality and stamina" that had been occurring among the "civilized portion" of the human race.[42]

Yet another issue that concerned him was the fact that from generation to generation, Americans were growing shorter and thinner. Some estimates, he claimed, indicated that given a sample of five thousand to ten thousand "civilized" (read: white) people, "they would be found to weigh less in the aggregate at the present time than the same number of people weighed a generation ago."[43] The problem, he asserted, was that public health had been too concerned with treating acute illness, whereas chronic illness had been given short shrift. As a result, defective Americans—defective, that is, in terms of race, ethnicity, and class— were out-breeding people of superior stock. Consequently, he added, "It is no longer the fittest alone that survives . . . but the feeble individual who is afforded sufficient protection."[44] He asserted that "if race degeneracy is to be arrested," the only plan of action had to be one that incorporated "the new science of eugenics." Barring a consideration of the role of inheritance in disease, he concluded, "public health work must then inevitably tend to race depreciation."[45]

The tone of this article is decidedly less hopeful about the inevitable rise of the "superior" race than had been articulated in *Ladies' Guide*.

Figure 7.3. The San, featured in the *Journal of the American Medical Association*, 1889.

Some twenty years into his ministering, it is possible that his frustration about his bidding not being done was coloring his language. Still, this article and his earlier work shared a concern with the relationship between slenderness, illness, and race degeneracy. Anglo-Saxon women's growing "sterility," as he called it, served as further evidence of impending (white) racial doom.[46]

* * *

Kellogg was a highly visible and well-connected physician. He published eleven articles in *JAMA* between the 1880s and the 1920s, a number that suggests that his ideas were not dismissed by his contemporaries as quackery. In fact, his thoughts on the relationships between weight, health, gender, and racial prosperity were mainstream. For if the earlier generation of scientists had lamented the gluttonous and fat African, Kellogg and several of his contemporaries feared that Anglo-Saxon women had overcorrected. The over-refined woman ate too little good food, and was too slim.

Well into the 1920s, mostly male doctors saw themselves as fighting the uphill battle of the too-slight, empty-wombed woman that fashion had wrought. In 1927 Morris Fishbein, then one of the editors of *JAMA*, co-edited a book titled *Your Weight and How to Control It: A Scientific Guide by Medical Specialists and Dieticians.* The book was written in direct response to contemporary ideals regarding beauty, as is evident from the first sentence of the introduction, written by Wendell C. Phillips: "Any woman you ask can tell you the difference between weight and good looks."

He continues by posing the question, "How many understand why they may do themselves permanent harm by ridiculous unbalanced diets . . . or by reducing below the proper weight for their age and height?"[47] It was time for the fashionable norm regarding weight, that ubiquitous culprit when it came to women's well-being, to be laid to rest in favor of a more scientific approach to diet and health. As Phillips writes,

> The final warning . . . to American women, especially those in the breathless search for beauty, is: Do not blindly follow beauty ideals that endanger

your health and even your chances of motherhood. Before you roll off or starve off or steam off that pound of flesh, find out whether you shouldn't rather be putting it on.[48]

In a subsequent chapter, Fishbein too notes gravely, "The movement to prevent unwise and fanatical reduction in body weight must be considered as an activity of preventive medicine worthy [of] the consideration of every intelligent man or woman."[49] From his perspective, feminism was to blame for the svelte American girl; as he puts it, "Many observers are inclined to urge that the fad for slenderization is the result of the rise of feminism and the passing of some eleven millions [sic] of women out of the home."[50]

Like Kellogg, the authors of this book were concerned about the slimness, illness, and falling childbearing rates of Anglo-American girls, and what all of this signaled about the nation's health. Fishbein and company blame the nebulous but apparently allied forces of "fashion" and "feminism" for the trend. But while Kellogg saw slimness as evidence of the deterioration of the Anglo-American blend, Fishbein inadvertently reproduces the nineteenth-century race science found in the *Cosmopolitan* and other women's magazines, suggesting that slimness came naturally to young white American ladies. "The American girl is an end product of a mixture of races, predominantly Anglo-Saxon," he writes. "She is usually somewhat thin, often rather angular and not infrequently awkward."[51] While Fishbein was certainly in good company making this point, not all medical men claimed that the slender physique was "natural" for Anglo-Saxon women. But well into the twentieth century, a powerful contingency among them deemed it proof of poor health.

* * *

Back at the homestead in Battle Creek, things had taken a turn for the worse for John Harvey Kellogg. His foodstuffs having been long since commercialized, the lasting part of his legacy, he had hoped, would be his vegetarian, medico-religious interventions at the San. Unfortunately, by 1927, this model no longer proved profitable, and was thereby not viable, in the estimation of its now largely physician-run board. That same year, the San had announced its intention to devote its energies to the field of commercial medicine. But this shift failed to save them also. The Great Depression hit the San hard. With enrollments dwindling and debts running into the millions of dollars, Kellogg closed its doors for the final time in 1938. In one final irony, the water-cure specialist died of pneumonia in 1942.[52]

8

Fat, Revisited

There was something peculiar about Morris Fishbein's co-edited 1927 book, *Your Weight and How to Control It*. Alongside the attacks on ultra-svelte feminine figures that seemed to be the impetus for the book, it also included warnings against overweight. In the introduction, Wendell C. Phillips, former president of the American Medical Association, had been firm in his discussion of the ills of underweight and the role of beauty ideals as the source of said ills. Yet he seemed impelled to admit that overweight was also something to be concerned about.

The uneasy dance between the two messages was evident when Phillips stated, "Because weight control is so closely related to public health, the American Medical Association cooperated in the calling last February of the first Adult Weight Conference." According to Phillips, "All the doctors agreed in condemning the craze for the boyish form and the barber-pole figure at any cost. . . . Women have pounded and rolled, dieted and drugged themselves, and submitted to the tortures rivaling those of the Inquisition—all in the search for beauty."[1] To this, he added, "The conference expressed the opinion that underweight is more dangerous before thirty years of age and overweight after thirty."[2] Phillips does not bore the reader with details of the research that led to the conclusion that after thirty, being overweight is a serious health risk for women. Nevertheless, he sought to spread the message that young girls should stop dieting and prepare for motherhood. Meanwhile their middle-aged mothers might do well to lose a few pounds.

His approach had a great deal to do with the concept of "normal weight," which had been introduced to medicine just over a decade earlier. The word "introduced" is appropriate because the idea of a "normal weight" did not originate within the medical field. Rather, its rise can be traced to the actions and policies of insurance companies.

Starting around 1900, health insurance companies began cropping up in North America. As Paul Starr explains, health insurance had been a staple in western Europe since 1883. But it would be nearly two decades before Americans recognized the need for health insurance that would protect industry by reducing the number of sick workers while also stabilizing incomes.[3] In an effort to decrease risk, analysts working with insurance companies ran the numbers and discovered that policy holders who were considerably outside the average range of weight-to-height ratios represented the greatest mortality risk.[4] And in an age in which the vast majority of salaried employees were white and male, the result was that data on working-age, middle-class white men formed the basis of America's first "normal weight" tables.

In short order, what were known as "medico-actuarial standards of weight and health" filtered into the medical field. This occurred in part because physicians were employed by insurance companies to produce doctor-sanctioned reports on the link between obesity and mortality.[5] And since insurers could refuse to cover the "overweight," many doctors saw the standards generated from the reports as an expedient tool, and used them to determine who they wanted to take on as a patient.[6] While these developments were important in the growing effort to quantify a link between ill health and overweight, arguably the most important factor in the adoption of medico-actuarial tables came in the form of a Jewish American statistician named Louis Israel Dublin.

Dublin was born in Lithuania in 1882. His family emigrated to the United States in the mid-1880s, forming part of the wave of eastern Europeans arriving during that era. In 1909, just five years after receiving his Ph.D. in biology from Columbia University, he was snapped up by the Metropolitan Life Insurance Company, where he would remain for the next forty-three years.[7]

In 1912 Dublin was one of the principal architects of a new Standard Table of Heights and Weights, constructed from data gleaned from hundreds of thousands of policy holders at forty-three insurance companies. The researchers concluded that for people under thirty-five, being overweight could be good for health, whereas after thirty-five, it was a harbinger of illness.[8] The researchers at the insurance company, eventually to be renamed MetLife, overlooked what today is a recognizable issue in statistical analysis: small differences can become statistically significant when there is a massive number of people in the study. As a result, the statistical differences may not carry any practical significance for health outcomes.[9] Another major issue with the study was the relative dearth of women and racial and ethnic minorities included in the data. By the statisticians' own accounts, the 1912 sample included nearly twice as many men as women. And while separate weight tables were compiled for men and women, the same was not true for race. In fact, if the study included any nonwhite people, there is no indication of that fact, since the data included height and weight charts labeled "White Boys and White Girls."[10]

These issues aside, the Metropolitan Life tables were widely embraced. In fact, the very same life insurance tables were not only mentioned in *Your Weight and How to Control It,* they were reprinted in the book. This was done partly in an effort to prevent all women from seeking to be the same weight. According to Phillips, Mrs. William B. Meloney, at the time an editor at the *New York Herald Tribune,* revealed that she received more than two thousand queries a month on weight control, apparently most of them from women hoping to be a "size sixteen." As the sizing standards differed, there is some indication that this would have been a small size.[11] Phillips concluded that it was lunacy that "all American women were trying to pour themselves into the same mold." One had to consider family history as well as "height and age [and] . . . the general shape of her figure," he said, not to mention what he described as a woman's "racial type."[12] Notwithstanding the issue of race, the doctors assembled at the Adult Weight Conference—including Louis Dublin and the famed eugenicist Charles B. Davenport—did just that.

* * *

Fishbein's co-edited book indicates that many mainstream doctors were far more concerned about ultra-slimness than excess weight. Nevertheless, insurance tables indicating that extra fat was "deadly" could not be ignored.[13] By the 1920s, they had gained considerable traction in the medical field. This is evident in the proportion of *JAMA* articles mentioning underweight versus overweight individuals, which shifted dramatically after 1920. Between 1883 and 1920, only 56 articles mentioning obesity and 3 mentioning overweight were published, for a combined total of 59 articles containing those terms. However, between 1921 and 1940, that total ballooned to some 214 articles. The term "fatness" yielded totals of 359 articles before 1921, but shot to 530 between 1921 and 1940.

By contrast, between 1883 and 1920, 247 articles were published using the term "thinness," and only two with the word "underweight." This was a combined total of 249 articles. Between 1921 and 1940, that total had dropped to a meager 156.[14]

Nor was it simply the frequency with which slimness and fatness were mentioned in *JAMA* articles that shifted. So too did the thrust of the articles. In the earlier period, thinness was linked to ill health. Typical was an 1888 article titled "Medical Work among the Sioux Indians," by Dr. Frederick Treon. In this article he detailed the ravages of consumption among Native peoples, noting that the consumptive "grows weak, becomes emaciated, and often refuses food, while at other times it possesses a most ravenous appetite."[15] Clearly, thinness was related to the patient's illness. But lest we assume that the doctor's interest in the case was motivated solely by empathy, his comment was preceded by the following observation:

> In my experience it has been the exception to find among the Crow Creek Indians—who are of the great Sioux tribe, and known as the Yanktonai Sioux—a good healthy subject. I find, basing my belief on the death-rate for the past year, that in less than another century this particular band of Indians will be extinct, and so far as they are concerned the great Indian problem will have been solved.[16]

Like Kellogg, Treon made a clear connection between race and disease, reflecting the eugenic assertion that the nonwhite races would eventually die off due to their weak constitutions.

A *JAMA* article from 1900 focused on the question of frail, slight women. Considering them "physical[ly] degenerate," the author lambastes women of the cultivated classes who were evidently choosing delicacy at the expense of their health. By way of counterexample, he related the journey of a well-to-do American woman who had recently completed a two-hundred-mile bike trip. According to the author, this feat proved what "civilized women can do in athletics when she chooses."[17] It is significant that he used the term "civilized" to describe the status of the women in question, women who were white and well-off. It was well known, he noted, that "among savages . . . females have habitually the hard manual labor to perform."[18] And, he concluded, the luxuriating classes of women had to end the pretense of affected delicacy that undermined their muscular strength and physical endurance.

By the late 1910s, the tide was changing. A growing number of articles focused on excess fat. In a 1918 article titled "Food and Obesity," the author expressed annoyance with the proliferation of texts on the diets of fat people. "It is easy to assert in an offhand way as do the majority of writers on nutrition," he began, "that obesity or the deposition of fat in the body is due to 'superalimentation or the consumption of food in excess of the requirements,' and that is aided by 'insufficient exercise.'" If the article opened with a tone of seeming condemnation of the intense focus on obesity, the author switches gears rapidly, revealing that he too was bothered by the prospect of fat persons overeating. He wanted to suggest that it was not known whether their eating habits were the main factor in their weight, since many corpulent people claimed not to eat much, but if by some chance they could find evidence that obese people were "uneconomical" in their dietary habits, "there is an added force to the Food Administration's advice to our corpulent citizens to burn their own fat and thereby save fuel for the nation's fighters."[19]

The same year, a book titled *Diet and Health: With Key to the Calories* was published. The book itself was largely a treatise on calorie-restricted diets for those who wanted to avoid becoming unacceptably fat. The author, Lulu Hunt Peters, also described such a state of fatness as a "disease," writing, "It is true that being fat is a disease with some. . . . Those diseased individuals should be under the care of a physician."[20] Fortunately for her readers, Peters herself was one such physician. Thus, she gives a blueprint to reform the overly fat through caloric obsession: "Hereafter you are going to eat calories of food. Instead of saying one slice of bread, or a piece of pie, you will say 100 Calories of bread, 350 Calories of pie."[21] *Diet and Health: With Key to the Calories* would become the nation's first best-selling weight-loss book.

In a review of Peters's book that appeared in *JAMA*, the author wrote that the work "contains some good advice in simple language," adding, "It explains to the layman the meaning of the calory [sic] and the value of this knowledge in choosing diet for the treatment both of obesity and of undesirable thinness."[22] He followed this with the phrase "if in a person otherwise normal, [undesirable thinness] may be said to exist," as if the complaint of being too thin were difficult to imagine. This statement revealed that the author of the review, much like Peters herself, viewed excess fatness as a worse condition than unwanted slenderness. It moreover served as evidence of the growing anti-fat sentiment in the medical profession.

At least one article appearing in *JAMA* during the 1920s commented on the growing, and disproportionate, focus on fat. The article, written by Dr. William Emerson and Dr. Frank Manny, identified the arrival of the 1912 ideal-weight tables as the force behind the new interest in overweight: "The results of the medico-actuarial studies of 1912 were so significant in their bearing on the effects of overweight in adult life," the authors began, "that there has been a tendency to overlook the corresponding material which bears on the problem of underweight in the years at the close of the period of growth."[23] The article aimed to underscore the importance of the ideal-weight tables popularized by Metropolitan Life and their impact on the medical handling of the relationship between weight and health. While it achieved these objectives, the article was nonetheless not without flaws.

The authors concluded that for people in their twenties, "mortality increases about one percent for each pound below average weight for height."[24] But by the age of forty, a revolution occurred such that "weight below average, even as much as 30 pounds, may not be unfavorable." The finding that one's chances of dying switch over, that underweight is deadly at first and then turns into a life preserver in a matter of twenty years, may seem peculiar, or even preposterous. But the authors did offer the disclaimer that "more data are needed."[25] In the end, while Emerson and Manny set out, it seemed, to challenge the focus on overweight, the study largely confirmed rather than refuted the existing preoccupation with overweight as ordained by medico-actuarial tables.[26]

In a surprising turn of events, multiple articles cited fashion as the source of socially acceptable ideal weights. In an article from 1921, Dr. Elliott Joslin not only identified the fashion plate, first popularized in *Godey's*, as the original source of ideal weights, but claimed that the insurance companies were actually a step behind on this front:

The fashion plate makers are far ahead of insurance company presidents in their propaganda for a normal weight. All one needs to do is to glance at the morning paper to see ladies and gentlemen portrayed for our benefit, whose sylphlike figures are models of weight and height—nay more they are invariably a trifle below the standard weight.[27]

Unlike Kellogg or Fishbein, Joslin claimed that fashion served as something of a positive and health-inducing force in this regard. To Joslin, the sylphlike would be rewarded with good health for their troubles. Positioning obesity as a cause and not just a correlate of chronic illnesses such as diabetes, he claimed that the slender "might so bear the legend: Immune to diabetes."[28]

The medical antipathy toward fatness and especially toward fat women intensified after the insurance tables reached wide saturation. But these attitudes had actually emerged years earlier. Articles about obesity and overweight were present in *JAMA* since its earliest days, and in 1897, just six years after Kellogg published his *Ladies' Guide,* a Dr. John V. Gaff wrote an article for *JAMA* titled "Obesity as a Cause of Sterility." In it Gaff claimed that studies existed of "over two hundred cases of obesity associated with amenorrhea and sterility." In general, he avowed, obesity was the only probable cause of infertility. It was not just the poor reproductive rates of obese women that disgusted him, he also expressed an objection to fat women on aesthetic grounds. Citing the work of a British physician named James Paget, he wrote,

Women more often than men, as old and as ill nourished as these, make a far different appearance. With these the first sign of old age is that they grow fat, and this abides with them till, it may be, in a last illness sharper than old age, they are robbed of even their fat. These too, when old age sets in, become pursy, short winded, pot-bellied, pale and flabby; their skin hangs not in wrinkles, but in rolls and their voice instead of rising toward childish treble, becomes gruff and husky.[29]

This same quote from Paget appeared in another article in *JAMA* three years later.[30] But that author, A. W. Sherman, added with a touch of Greek philosophizing, "Hippocrates observed that 'enormous fulness [*sic*] of woman is responsible for their frequent sterility, and their slaves, who are lean, conceive as soon as they have connection with men.' The indolent habits and rich diet of the wealthy favor obesity and sterility, while the hardships and privations of the poorer classes favor leaness [*sic*] and large families."[31]

This was, of course, the exact opposite of the view expressed by Kellogg during the same era.

In the debates involving physicians whose work was being published in what was arguably the nation's most reputable medical journal, one thing remained: the belief that the bodies of elite women needed to be regulated by medicine. While physicians vacillated over the years in their estimation of whether middle- to upper-class white women were too thin or too fat, they could agree that the dietary habits and body size of these women had to be monitored. The reproductive capacity of these women was threatened due to their unwise choices, and the nation would suffer accordingly.

In 1930 Dr. Willard Stone, writing in *JAMA*, stated, "A nation's preeminence can be measured by the health of its people, and food habits have much to do with health."[32] Therefore, all Americans, and especially women "during pregnancy," had to eat in ways that ensured the "virility of the race." Using the language of eugenics, Stone adds that this is necessary if "a race of supermen is ever to be obtained."[33]

Social critics Barbara Ehrenreich and Deirdre English describe this type of messaging as "medical sexism."[34] Per the authors, as religious feelings and affiliations waned in twentieth-century America, medicine stepped in to fill the void, telling women, in effect, "how to live." Michel Foucault described these dictates on "how to live" as an integral part of the biopolitics of population management. In other words, women, and especially elite white women, had to discipline their bodies by learning the rules of diet and weight management—that is, how, what, when, and how much to eat—that first religion, then medicine mandated.

Never mind that prior to the late 1910s (elite white) women had been told overwhelmingly that they were too waifish, only to be told thereafter that they were too fat. This was despite the fact that a study by the U.S. Department of Agriculture on the weights of Americans showed relative stability between 1885 and 1955.[35] The point was that these women needed to learn the scientific management of their bodies. Their own health, along with that of their offspring, was the basis for the fitness of the race, and the nation.

*   *   *

The weight of middle- and upper-class white women had long been subject to intense scrutiny. But, in the medical field, the weight of racial

Others was an entirely separate issue in the sense that racial/ethnic minorities were rarely seen to matter at all. Indeed, racial/ethnic minorities were seldom included in medical analyses, much less the focus of them.[36] Kellogg and other eugenicists had thought that these groups might simply die off, eliminating the need to do any sustained research on them. Whatever the rationale, far fewer articles appeared in *JAMA* describing weight and health as they pertained to racial and ethnic populations prior to the arrival of the insurance tables.

However, since disease was increasingly linked to overweight in the medical literature after 1912, some physicians began to voice concerns regarding the excess fat of what were deemed the "inferior" races in ways that bore a striking resemblance to the racial scientific literature. The targets of these criticisms were typically immigrants from southern and eastern Europe and people of Jewish descent. Both groups had been deemed fundamentally and racially distinct from the average American. The scant articles that did spotlight racial and ethnic minorities offered few health solutions. These groups were commonly thought to be constitutionally diseased, and for this reason there was no rush to recommend changing their diet and body size. A 1912 article in *JAMA* was typical. The author, Dr. Henry Friedman, briefly bemoaned the impact on the nation resulting from the immigration of racial inferiors: "The great influx of Europeans into this country particularly interests us in the physical condition of these people . . . especially because that settlement here, in large number, might influence the physical character of the people already here."

The groups Friedman feared most were the southern and eastern Europeans. These groups, he claimed, were constitutionally inferior to Anglo-Saxons. Reproducing ideas that were found in the work of Arthur de Gobineau and like-minded proponents of Nordic/Aryan supremacy, Friedman asserted that "frequent intermixture or crossing with inferior blood from the African and Asiatic coasts is largely responsible for it."[37] These Mediterranean peoples were thus a menace to elite white society. Southern Italian immigrants were described as a septic mix of "Italian, Greek, and African" and as a result, "they are small, dark, and of a poor musculature." While in Friedman's opinion, these peopled lacked muscularity, they were not thin. On the contrary, he wrote, "very frequently there is an increase in fatty tissue. . . . This is the condition found in 'fat rickets' and obesity."[38] In this way, the "small" and "dark" immigrants from southern Europe were compromising national health by being obese.

Jews were also targets of fat phobia. Friedman had argued that Jews exhibited poor muscular development, which he claimed was a sign of excess fatty tissue.[39] And Dr. Elliott Joslin, the same physician who had praised the standards of the fashion plate, wrote in 1924, "The Jew, in my opinion, is not prone to diabetes because he is a Jew, but rather because he is fat. Jews are fat; though shameful to relate."[40] Even in his 1921 article in *JAMA*, Joslin claimed, "One has only to visit the Jewish quarter of a large Jewish city to be impressed with the frequency of obesity." He offered this explanation: "Overfeeding begins in childhood and lasts to old age. Very likely with the increasing affluence of the Jewish race in this country, permitting indulgence of their well-known fondness for style, obesity will tend to diminish along with diabetes."[41]

The relationship between Jewish identity and claims of undue fatness has been described in existing scholarship.[42] Yet interestingly, the relationship between fatness, disease, and inherent racial deficiency described in the medical literature did not appear to grow out of scientific findings but rather resulted from sentiment and impression. Curiously, Joslin admitted that he had almost no data to back up his assertions about Jewish people, allowing that "there are few statistics of the comparative weights of even a thousand Gentiles and a thousand Jews."[43]

* * *

Between 1883 and 1940 there was a remarkable dearth of articles in *JAMA* describing the relationship between weight and health for black Americans. A search of the magazine's archives reveals only one such article, from 1925, about a fat black woman who was deemed a case of "extreme obesity." Nevertheless, there were no connections made in this article between her weight and her race.[44] Again, during this era, the bulk of attention was paid to reforming the diets, and weights, of middle- and upper-class white people, especially women. The women in these groups, some authors claimed, had apparently been getting pseudo-scientific advice from women's magazines for far too long. It was high time the men of science intervened with their own advice.

Two decades after the 1912 medico-actuarial tables captured the attention of the medical community, Louis Dublin, working with A. J. Lotha, the vice president of Metropolitan Life, created a series of updates to the original tables. Using data culled from the company's policy holders between 1911 and 1935, new tables were published in 1937, and they were revised for the *Statistical Bulletin of the Metropolitan Life Insurance Company, 1942–43*. The key change after 1912 was that now "body frame" (small, medium, and large) was considered in addition to height and weight. How "body frame" was measured remains a mystery. One pair of medical historians has called the approach "pure fiction," as body frame was apparently not measured by the insurance companies themselves.[45] Nevertheless, the medical community continued to embrace the company's tables.

Since doctors were hoping to spread the good word on "how to live" to ordinary Americans, and especially to women, discussion of the tables and their implications was extensive. Louis Dublin himself wrote several articles promoting their use for mainstream publications, including the women's magazine *McClure's*.[46] In 1934 the *Washington Post* ran the headline "Weight Shortens Life of Women: Result of Studies Is Published." The article presented a review of one of Dublin's studies, which had been recently featured in *American Magazine*. While the article purported to detail the ill effects of being too fat or too thin, it leaned heavily on the risk of death associated with excess weight. Although the article concluded, "Women 25 years old who are 20 per cent below average weight have a death rate of 11 per cent greater than average," the rest of the piece was devoted to what was described as the greater concern, that of overweight: "In the older group, women who are 10 per cent overweight have a death rate of 22 per cent above the average. If they weigh 25 per cent above the average, the extra mortality jumps to 74 per cent, shortening life 6½ years." With the emphasis on the mounting risk of excess weight, the headline, "Weight Shortens Life of Women," was meant to suggest that it was overweight, not underweight, that shortened lives.

Metropolitan Life continued to participate in the creation of ideal-weight tables. In 1959 the company collaborated with other North American insurance companies for what was called the Build and Blood Pressure Study. From these data, they generated tables for what were now termed "desirable weights." It was also in the 1950s that another key figure in medicine was beginning his own work. Ancel Keys had doctorate degrees in both biology and physiology.

* * *

After teaching at Cambridge and later Harvard, Keys was ultimately hired by the U.S. Department of War to study, among other things, the effects of food deprivation on men. The result was the creation of the "survival K Ration" (the *K* stood for Keys), which would be given to soldiers during wartime.[47] Keys would later recruit civilians for an infamous experiment on the effects of underfeeding and how to slowly bring men back from near-starvation. The findings from this study were published in 1950 in *The Biology of Human Starvation*. The report catapulted Keys to national recognition.

Despite the fact that most of his work up to this point had been about the effects of limiting food, Keys was steadfast in his belief that a major concern for future generations would actually be the overabundance of food. Believing that the rates of heart disease among American businessmen owed more to their diet and weight than to the natural aging process, he undertook another landmark study, the Seven Countries Study, in 1958. In this study, Keys and his team of researchers examined the link between diet, weight, and coronary heart disease across seven nations. They found that overweight was associated with angina pectoris (a typical symptom of coronary artery disease) but not with either myocardial infarction (heart attack) or coronary death. The relationship between weight and mortality was U-shaped, indicating that the extremely slim and the extremely heavy had the greatest risk.[48]

Clearly, the situation was complicated. This much Keys allowed in his reflection on his research in a *Time* magazine cover story from 1961. In it, he claimed that obesity did not necessarily cause coronary heart disease. It was nevertheless, in his view, "ugly."[49] Here lay the heart of the matter. Like many respected medical professionals writing on the topic, Keys viewed obesity as unsightly. In other publications he described obesity as "disgusting" and "repugnant." Moreover, he described fat people as "clumsy" and their weighty bodies as "hard on furniture."[50] These statements make it hard to believe that his work in this area was fueled exclusively by medical findings on the complex relationship between weight and health, as opposed to his personal opinion that fat was unseemly and should be exorcised.

Keys's concern about obesity and its potential health effects persisted after his Seven Countries Study. He wanted to devise a more consistent way to measure overweight and obesity across different populations. He found the vagaries of the Metropolitan Life tables from 1912 to 1959 to belie the label "standard weight." Keys decided to look to history for inspiration, and he found it in the work of a nineteenth-century scientist named Adolphe Quetelet. In 1832 Quetelet had derived an index to assess weights across a given population, which became known as the Quetelet Index. The index was not designed to measure an individual's obesity.[51] Nevertheless, Keys determined that this index, which he renamed the "body mass index," would be a useful tool for measuring obesity in contemporary societies. In 1972 Keys published a landmark paper in the *Journal of Chronic Diseases*, making the case for the use of body mass index, or BMI. In his own assessment, BMI was a less than perfect measure. But it was good enough to replace what he described as the "industry-hyped" tables.[52] To Keys, the BMI, "if not fully satisfactory, [was] at least as good as any other relative weight index as an indicator of relative obesity."[53]

Going forward with this conclusion, Keys used his considerable influence in the American medical community to make the case for BMI over the ideal-weight tables. In 1980 he addressed a group of industry leaders in a speech in which he attacked medico-actuarial tables for their lack of representativeness, stating, "As has been pointed out repeatedly, the life insurance data are seriously flawed."[54] He then went after Louis Dublin, describing him and Metropolitan Life as a "major source of propaganda about the evils of overweight." He continued,

> The fact is that the tables of "ideal" or "desirable" weight are arm-chair concoctions starting with questionable assumptions and ending with three sets of standards for "frame" types never measured or even defined. Unfortunately, those tables have been reprinted by the thousands and are widely accepted as gospel.[55]

As it turned out, 1980, the same year Keys gave this speech, would mark the tail end of the reign of MetLife's standard-weight tables. That year, the U.S. Department of Agriculture continued to issue reports using the 1959 data. But in 1985, when the National Institutes of Health issued their weight-based health criteria, they used Keys's BMI, noting that it matched the criteria for "acceptable" weights from MetLife's 1983 tables. The year 1985 was one of the last years the tables were widely used.[56]

In 1995 the World Health Organization published a report on obesity, using BMI, that was based on a meta-analysis of seventeen international studies of hundreds of thousands of people. The report suggested that classifications of overweight by BMIs of 25, 30, and 40 should be established. The authors described such designations as an "arbitrary method of association between BMI and mortality."[57]

And arbitrary they did seem. In fact, BMI categories for overweight and obesity had been in flux between 1985 and 1995. Typically, age and gender were factors. In 1985, for example, "overweight-obesity" meant a BMI of ≥ 27.8 for men (e.g., height 5'5", weight 167 pounds), and ≥ 27.3 for women (e.g., height 5'5", weight 164 pounds). In 1990 the U.S. Department of Agriculture suggested that men and women should have one standard, and that the threshold for "unhealthy" weight should be lowered, to BMI ≥ 25 (e.g., height 5'5", weight 150 pounds) for people under age thirty-five, and BMI ≥ 27 (e.g., height 5'5", weight 162 pounds) for people thirty-five and older.[58]

In 1995 the World Health Organization published *Dietary Guidelines for Americans*. This delivered the system of assessing obesity that now dominates American medicine: "overweight (BMI ≥ 25), pre-obese (BMI: 25.0–29.9), class 1 (BMI: 30.0–34.9), class 2 (BMI: 35.0–39.9), and class 3 (BMI ≥ 40.0)."[59] In 1998 the NIH adopted these categories. The *New York Times* chronicled this shift in a 1998 article bearing the headline "U.S. to Widen Its Definition of Who Is Fat."[60]

Around the same time, after decades of relative neglect in medical research, the medical community shifted its attention to racial/ethnic minority populations. In 1983, the same year that the concept of BMI was starting to get attention on the world health stage, the U.S. Department of Health and Human Services drafted a reported titled "Health, United States, 1983." The report showed that while the health of the majority white population had been improving, there was a simultaneous, and disproportionate, "burden of death and illness experienced by blacks and other minority Americans."[61]

Two years later, Margaret Heckler, secretary of health and human services, released a report titled "Secretary's Task Force Report on Black and

Minority Health" that offered additional documentation of the "excess deaths" among African Americans, Native Americans, Asian Americans, and Latin populations due to illnesses, including cancer, diabetes, and cardiovascular disease.[62] The report included a series of recommendations, one of which was to "investigate factors affecting minority health, including risk-factor identification" as well as "education interventions."[63]

The response to the Heckler report was swift, and the question of risk factors would prove critical. In 1986 the Office of Minority Health was established to reduce the disparities in health outcomes between whites and racial/ethnic minorities. And in its report, "Healthy People 2000," published in 1990, the Department of Health and Human Services outlined its goals for reducing the disparity in the rates of chronic illness and mortality between people of color and whites. The stated goal was to "'close the gap' between whites and racial and/or ethnic minority populations."[64] Yet the mechanism for doing so proved myopic. For while a growing body of research indicated that the disparities in the health of white and nonwhite populations were due to social and environmental factors, "Healthy People 2000" had maintained its emphasis on individual behaviors and personal responsibility.

As Joseph Califano Jr., the former secretary of health, education, and welfare, and a representative describing the report, stated, "You, the individual, can do more for your own health and well-being than any doctor, any hospital, and drug."[65] "Healthy People 2000," published in 1990, made little mention of overweight and obesity. Yet it did list poor diet and lack of exercise among the leading causes of death. The next edition of the report, written in 2000 and titled "Healthy People 2010," did, by contrast, list obesity-related objectives for producing a healthy population. The report had identified obesity as a "leading health indicator." This conclusion, as chronicled by sociologist Natalie Boero in *Killer Fat: Media, Medicine, and Morals in the American "Obesity Epidemic,"* was due in no small part to the lobbying of private organizations, several of which were affiliated with weight-loss clinics, to place the issue of obesity on the national agenda, an action that would give them access to more federal funding for research and treatment programs.

Thus, two of the objectives in "Healthy People 2010" were to increase the number of Americans with BMIs of 18.5 to 25 to 60 percent of the total population and to reduce the number of Americans with BMIs of

30 or more to 15 percent.[66] And while giving a polite nod to the numerous factors that contributed to overall weight and weight gain, the authors homed in on presumed personal, behavioral failings, writing, "Obesity results when a person eats more calories from food (energy) than he or she expends."[67]

By 2000, the medical community had articulated several colliding ambitions. It had expressed the need for Americans to take personal responsibility for their health, the desire to get more Americans to a normal BMI, the need to perform more research on racial and ethnic minorities, and the hope of closing the health disparities gap. And so it might not be surprising that when obesity was identified as an "epidemic" following a 1999 article in *JAMA*, there was a spotlight on Latin American people, whose rates of obesity had increased.

Three years later, overall obesity rates, alongside increases over time, became focal points. Katherine Flegal and her colleagues at the Centers for Disease Control and Prevention released a report titled "Prevalence and Trends in Obesity among U.S. Adults, 1999–2000." Reflecting the growing interest in research on health disparities, the researchers devoted considerable space to spelling out differences in obesity rates by sex and race, concluding, "For extreme obesity, the increases were significant for men and women overall and for non-Hispanic black women."[68] This report, issued in 2002, was one of the earliest, highly visible studies of obesity by race and gender since the obesity epidemic had been declared. And, while rates of obesity were shown to have been mounting nationwide, black women were singled out as having significant increases in their rates of "extreme obesity."

Since at least 2000, scholars had shown that one reason black people tend to have higher BMIs than whites is that black people commonly have a greater bone mineral density, and/or muscle mass, than white people.[69] By 2004, authorities such as Paul Campos, author of *The Obesity Myth: Why America's Obsession with Weight Is Hazardous to Your Health*, had shown that while black women had higher BMIs than white women, they also had lower mortality rates at a given BMI.[70] These and other findings have led some scholars to conclude that there is a racial bias in the BMI classification system.[71]

Nevertheless, the findings about black women's obesity rates had touched a nerve. Since the height of the slave trade and the growth of

Protestantism, black women had been symbols of "savage" aesthetic inclinations and amoral appetites. Now that researchers found that black women had among the highest BMIs in the country; their size was also evidence of disease. The association between fatness and black femininity—which had been transmuted during the height of fat-baiting against "hybrid" immigrant populations in the nineteenth century— reemerged. Yet again, black women were to become the focus of fear, anxiety, and degradation over the size of their bodies.

Epilogue

The Obesity Epidemic

"Obesity Kills More Americans Than We Thought." This headline, from the health news section of CNN's website on August 15, 2013, commanded readers' attention. Accompanying the article is an image of a fat black woman. She is wearing a sleeveless top, revealing the dark, fleshy skin of her arms. A tape measure around her waist is being held together by a pair of delicate white hands reaching out from a white lab coat.

The image is a reenactment of what might be a typical doctor's visit. The black woman is the patient. Her visually identifiable status as "obese" brands her as a medical specimen. The white woman, her gender identifiable by her massive wedding ring, is her doctor. Her slim, dexterous hands and professional garb mark her as a medical specialist. No faces are visible—a photographic device used to denote the universality of the scene.

The CNN article detailed the findings of a widely circulated study of obesity published in the *American Journal of Public Health*. This study used a novel method to examine the relationship between obesity (defined as a body mass index of 30 or greater) and mortality. The investigators culled data from thousands of black and white Americans who had participated in the National Health Interview Survey between 1986 and 2006, performing a series of innovative tests to assess the link between a high BMI and the risk of death. Based on their findings, the study's authors concluded that obesity was the culprit behind 18 percent of deaths among adults between ages forty and eighty-five during the twenty-year time span.[1]

It was a landmark work, one that had the distinction of being the first to explore differences in the risk of dying from obesity by age, race, and sex. According to the authors, approximately 5 percent of black men died from obesity. This was followed by white men, with a death rate of 15.6 percent, and white women with a 21.7 percent death rate. Black

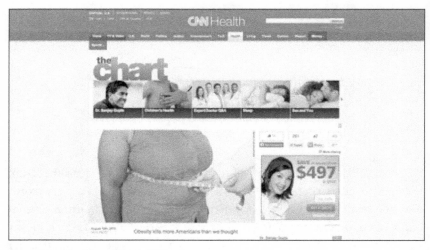

Figure E.1. *The Chart* (blog), CNN, Aug. 15, 2013.

women had the dubious distinction of leading the pack, with an estimated 26.8 percent of all deaths among them being caused by obesity.

Per the study authors, these figures should have represented a wake-up call for black women. African American women had long been recognized as having higher BMIs than any other subpopulation in the United States.[2] But many previous analyses had suggested that black women had a lower risk of illness and death from elevated BMIs.[3] This study provided evidence to the contrary, and signaled that black women should be working harder to trim their apparently outsized figures. In an interview about the findings, sociologist Ryan Masters, lead author of the report, underscored what he described as the substantial differences based on race or ethnicity. Still, he was careful not to let that finding overshadow the significance of the study for the broader population. Noting that excess weight was implicated in the deaths of nearly one in five American adults, Masters offered the following grim prognosis for the future: "We expect that obesity will be responsible for an increasing share of deaths in the United States and perhaps even lead to declines in U.S. life expectancy."[4]

Other television networks also carried the story, using doomsday-themed headlines intended to underscore the severity of the crisis. NBC News went with "Heavy Burden: Obesity May Be Even Deadlier Than

Thought." Fox News chose "Report: Obesity Kills More Americans Than Previously Thought."[5] Fox News emphasized the perils of obesity for African American women. In a conversation between Alisyn Camerota and Dr. David Samadi, the exceptionally high rates of obesity and supposed risk of death for black women was grist for the mill.

The coverage of a single study was extraordinary, especially given the fact that 2013 had been a watershed year for studies examining the link between obesity and mortality. In January of that year, a study appearing in the *Journal of the American Medical Association* and led by the epidemiologist Katherine Flegal of the Centers for Disease Control and Prevention (CDC) showed markedly different findings. The study, titled "Association of All-Cause Mortality with Overweight and Obesity Using Standard Body Mass Index Categories," set the medical community ablaze.[6]

The researchers performed a systematic review of ninety-seven studies completed between 1997 and 2012, the goal being to investigate the relationship between overweight/obesity and mortality. Based on this meta-analysis, the investigators concluded that overweight individuals had a 6 percent *lower* risk of death than those in the "normal" weight (BMI 18 to 25) category. People with mild to moderate obesity (a BMI of

Figure E.2. Fox News anchor Alisyn Camerota and Dr. David Samadi discuss the *American Journal of Public Health* article by Masters et al., Aug. 16, 2013.

30 to 34.9) had a mortality risk that mirrored that of people of "normal" weight. For Flegal, the findings may have seemed unremarkable. She was, in fact, the same researcher who had produced the 2002 report showing increases in obesity across populations and "extreme obesity" for black women. The 2013 study, by contrast, was race-neutral, and less ominous. In it, obesity seemed like less of an imminent death threat.

The response to the new study was swift. Letters to the editors of *JAMA* poured in. Dr. Wolfram Doehner, a cardiologist at the Charité Center for Stroke Research Berlin, declared the need for a new standard of obesity to assess what, if any, relationship existed between "excess" fat and health. As he put it, "It would be clinically useful to identify the true threshold for obesity becoming a significant mortality factor."[7] Nor was Doehner alone. A pair of physicians from the National Institutes of Health wondered whether the findings signaled a need for the medical community to shift its focus away from body weight altogether. Rather than searching for the exact amount of "excess" fat associated with illness and death, they suggested, perhaps it was time to end the long-standing assumption that fat was "bad":

> We also wonder if it is time to simply reject the notion that being over-weight or mildly obese is always bad for patients and to stop hounding such patients about their weight. If overweight patients keep their risk factors in control, they may outlive their lean friends.[8]

Letters questioning the utility of the current system of measuring obesity constituted a good portion of those published by *JAMA* in response to this study. Still, neither this study nor the praise it received attracted much attention in the press. What did receive attention were the views of one of the study's most vocal detractors, Dr. Walter Willett. Willett led a team of investigators who wrote to *JAMA* arguing that the Flegal study was flawed and may have underestimated the relative risk of death for people with elevated BMIs. The letter was just the beginning. Days later, Willett appeared on National Public Radio, stating, "This study is really a pile of rubbish, and no one should waste their time reading it."[9] His words were reprinted by other major news organizations, including the *Atlantic*. A few days after publishing an article discussing the controversial findings by Flegal and her team, *USA Today* played host to a debate between Walter Willett and Tom Frieden, director of the CDC, and presumably one of Flegal's superiors.

From the moment discussions of the study appeared in the popular press, Flegal was on the defensive. If Masters was presented as an important authority in much of the mainstream coverage of his study, reports featuring Flegal's study routinely questioned the conclusions. ABC News's "Is Being Overweight Really Bad for You?" for instance, positioned its report as a form of investigative journalism. Using insights offered by a panoply of experts with conflicting views, this and other news reports on the Flegal study ended on a note of uncertainty.

Within a few weeks of its publication, scholars affiliated with the Harvard School of Public Health convened a symposium on the Flegal paper that attracted an audience of more than two hundred. The symposium had one stated aim: to explain why the conclusions drawn from this study were "absolutely wrong."[10]

Months later, Katherine Flegal reflected on the academic brouhaha that surrounded her study and the negative media attention it sparked. In a May 2013 article in *Nature*, she admitted, "I was pretty surprised by the vociferous attacks on our work."[11] According to Flegal, the study was "not intended to have a message." She was not trying to change obesity standards or create obesity policy. Her job, as she saw it, was to provide accurate information based on existing data about obesity as the condition was currently defined.[12]

The stunningly divergent treatment of two obesity studies from top-tier medical journals may be shocking. Yet there is another piece to the puzzle that makes the reactions even more surprising. Ryan Masters was a newly minted Ph.D. who had, up to that point, published only a few large-scale studies of obesity. Katherine Flegal, by contrast, had been investigating the role of obesity in public health for two decades. During the course of her career, she has garnered more than 100,000 citations, making her one of the most-cited obesity researchers in the world.[13]

* * *

This tale of two studies underscores the nature of our contemporary relationship to fat. As we have seen, the current anti-fat bias in the United States and in much of the West was not born in the medical field. Racial scientific literature since at least the eighteenth century has claimed that fatness was "savage" and "black." To borrow a concept from Lisa Lowe, the phobia about fat "always already" had a racial element.[14] And, because women are typically reduced to their bodies, fat stigma has commonly targeted racial/ethnic Other women.[15] Protestant moralism and the disdain of indulgence contributed to the cacophony of pro-thin, anti-fat bias. The medical field has been the most recent institution to enter the fray.

In this way, fat phobia and the desire for slimness are about far more than empirical medical findings. They began as a way of instituting what Pierre Bourdieu called "social distinctions." That is, the elites of society have used the denial of food, along with "social censorships which forbid coarseness and fatness, in favor of slimness," to prove the superiority of those who sit atop the social hierarchy.[16] This analysis builds on Bourdieu's assessment by showing how, historically, diet and weight evolved as evidence of high-class or low-class standing.

This book also builds on the work of Michel Foucault, who explains how the state, through the institution of medicine, uses guidelines and principles regarding what to eat, and how much, as a form of social control.[17] As anthropologist Aihwa Ong has further articulated, as it pertains to "regulating individual and social bodies, modern medicine is the prime mover, defining and promoting concepts, categories and authoritative pronouncements on hygiene, health, sexuality, life and death."[18] This analysis builds on the work of Foucault and other scholars by revealing the centrality of race and gender to the creation of the "biopolitical" rules and regulations of weight management.

* * *

One question prompted by these findings may be whether racial and ethnic Others and especially black women knew about the weight-based aesthetic distinctions that were crafted using them as the target. A review of the literature reveals little to suggest that black women were aware of these distinctions before the twentieth century. For the majority of modern Western history, from the fifteenth to the nineteenth centuries, black people were kept enslaved and illiterate. Most of the black newspapers founded in the United States during the nineteenth century, such as *Freedom's Journal*, which began its first run in 1827, and the *North Star*, founded by Frederick Douglass in 1847, concerned themselves, fittingly, with abolition. After emancipation, questions of social, economic, and political rights continued to dominate black publications. In 1894 the *Woman's Era* became the first newspaper published by a black woman. As in many black women's newspapers and other publications well into the mid-twentieth century, economic and political power were the key issues.[19] Aesthetic concerns were less prevalent.

However, by the twentieth century, as described by sociologist Maxine Leeds Craig in her artfully rendered 2002 book *Ain't I a Beauty Queen? Black Women, Beauty, and the Politics of Race*, black people became more vocal about the vilification of black women's appearance in the predominately white mainstream media. In the mid-twentieth century, for instance, black people began to create beauty contests specifically for African American women as a way of instilling pride in the race. In these contests and elsewhere in black communities, considerable emphasis was placed on appreciating the beauty of brown skin and kinky hair. These were two of the key aesthetic elements reclaimed in the "Black Is Beautiful" movement, which was born in the 1960s.

Conversations about the relationship between race and weight, it seems, were far less prevalent. It is worth noting that some judges and contestants in the mid-twentieth-century pageants, as well as a few writers for magazines and newspapers during the period, did occasionally describe an appreciation for fuller-figured, more curvaceous women.[20] But there is little evidence of a sustained engagement with fat phobia as "black" or the slim ideal as "white" until the last few decades of the twentieth century.[21] This also coincides with more visible reclamations of "thickness" in the black community.

This suggests that, as has been shown throughout, discussions about racialized and gendered fat/slender bodies circulated largely in elite white spaces, and among white persons, prior to the mid-twentieth century. They served as a mechanism for white men and women to denigrate the racially Othered body. They also worked to police and applaud the "correct" behaviors of other white people, especially white women.[22]

This is the crux of the issue. The image of fat black women as "savage" and "barbarous" in art, philosophy, and science, and as "diseased" in medicine has been used to both degrade black women *and* discipline white women. For decades, white feminist scholars and historians focused largely on the impact of the "thin ideal" on middle- and upper-class white women.[23] They claimed that the thin ideal was oppressive, but also suggested that they did not know how it developed. This book endeavors to address that question, adding a much-needed intersectional component to the analysis of the development of fat phobia and the slender aesthetic, revealing race to be the missing element in many of these analyses. Indeed, the racial discourse of fatness as "coarse," "immoral," "black," and "Other" not only denigrated black women, it also served as the driver for the creation of slenderness as the proper form of embodiment for elite white Christian women. In other words, the fear of the black body was integral to the creation of the slender aesthetic among fashionable white Americans.

ACKNOWLEDGMENTS

I am deeply indebted to many people who helped this project come to life. First and foremost is my grandmother, Alma Jean Green. When I was younger, my grandmother would often ask me in an offhand fashion, "Why are all these white women dying to be thin?" She had no idea that her question would inspire several years of dedicated research and culminate in this book. Her love, support, and dry wit motivated me to undertake this project.

I also want to thank my extended family who have loved me and believed in me. Special thanks to my brothers and sister Chris, Derrick, and Desiree, all of whom are younger and in many ways wiser than myself. Another special thanks to Michael Strings, Jeffrey Strings, and Tammy Green, my uncles and aunt who are closest in age to myself, and the people I've felt I could always count on.

I want to thank the many scholars whose wisdom I have benefited from, including Lisa Park, Camille Forbes, Jeffrey Haydu, Christena Turner, Leonard Syme, Sandra Smith, and Bennetta Jules-Rosette. I would also like to thank scholars I have learned from, including Abigail Saguy and Robin D. G. Kelley. Thank you also to my graduate student assistants, Jessica Callahan and Estefani Marin.

The Africana Research Center at Penn State was the place where many of the ideas in the book were developed. I am grateful to the staff and faculty there, who were incredibly supportive, and for the platform the program provided for my research.

The University of California President's/Chancellor's Postdoctoral Fellowship Program also gave me the opportunity to meet and work with incredible scholars. From this program, I learned new methodologies and histories. I also learned new ways of thinking and writing about the topics presented in this book.

I want to thank the Hellman Foundation for providing a generous grant that allowed me to finish this project in a timely manner.

Lastly, because one of the most important, I'd like to thank Maria Charles. She was one of the first people to believe not just in the idea for the book, but in my ability to complete it. Because of you, Maria, I know what good mentorship looks like.

NOTES

INTRODUCTION

1 "Actually Starving," *New York Times*, Feb. 16, 1894.
2 Whorton, *Crusaders for Fitness*, 28.
3 Alcott, *The Young Woman's Book of Health*, 36.
4 Ibid., 37.
5 Ibid., 27.
6 Kellogg, *Ladies' Guide in Health and Disease*, 225.
7 Ibid.
8 "Are Girls Growing Smaller?," *Washington Post*, Jan. 22, 1888.
9 Brumberg, *Fasting Girls*; Seid, *Never Too Thin*.
10 Clarke, "Women's Health," 19.
11 "Are Our Women Scrawny?," *Harper's Bazaar*, Nov. 1896.
12 Ibid.
13 Ibid.
14 Chernin, "The Tyranny of Slenderness"; Orbach, *Hunger Strike*; Wolf, *The Beauty Myth*; Bordo, *Unbearable Weight*; Manton, *Fed Up*.
15 Campos et al., "The Epidemiology of Overweight and Obesity: Public Health Crisis or Moral Panic?" *International Journal of Epidemiology* 35, no. 1 (Feb. 1, 2006): 55–60, doi.org/10.1093/ije/dyi254.
16 Gilman, *Difference and Pathology*; Morgan, "'Some Could Suckle over Their Shoulder'"; Hobson, "The 'Batty' Politic."
17 Bourdieu, *Distinction*; Bourdieu, "The Forms of Capital."
18 Spelman, "Woman as Body"; Lerner, *The Creation of Patriarchy*; Wolf, *The Beauty Myth*.
19 Stoler, *Race and the Education of Desire*; Foucault, *The Birth of the Clinic*.
20 Chernin, "The Tyranny of Slenderness"; Gilman, "Black Bodies, White Bodies"; Orbach, *Hunger Strike*; Schwartz, *Never Satisfied*; Seid, *Never Too Thin*; Braziel and LeBesco, *Bodies Out of Bounds*; Griffith, *Born Again Bodies*; Campos, *The Obesity Myth*; Rothblum and Solovay, *The Fat Studies Reader*; Farrell, *Fat Shame*.
21 See Richard Klein, "Fat Beauty"; Saguy, "What's Wrong with Fat?"
22 Fortunately, many of the texts had been digitized, and were available through online digital archives. Thus, the articles from *Harper's Bazaar*, for example, were available through the University of California's Historical Newspapers Database. All of the *JAMA* and *New York Times* articles were located via archival searches on the respective websites for these organizations. Other digital archives included

the Accessible Archives of Pennsylvania, WorldCat, The Making of the Modern Word, and Nineteenth Century U.S. Newspapers (latter two managed by Gale Learning Group). Finally, Google Books and Google Scholar proved indispensible sources for primary and secondary source materials.

CHAPTER 1. BEING VENUS

1 As Joaneath Spicer explained, Katharina was most likely a slave, although she is commonly referred to in texts as a "servant." Spicer, *Revealing the African Presence.*

2 Ibid.; Bindman, Gates, and Dalton, *The Image of the Black in Western Art.*

3 Bourdieu, *Distinction*; Bourdieu, "The Forms of Capital."

4 Schreuder and Kolfin, *Black Is Beautiful.*

5 Ibid.

6 Official statistics are difficult to come by, but existing accounts suggest that by 1465 over a thousand slaves from Morocco, Mauritania, and Sene-Gambia were being shuttled to European city-states by the Portuguese; in the last few decades of the fifteenth century, nine hundred slaves per year were arriving from Guinea in Portugal alone. See Mark, *Africans in European Eyes*; and Nazeer Ahmed, "The Atlantic Slave Trade," *History of Islam* (blog), http://historyofislam.com, accessed Nov. 28, 2014.

7 Schreuder and Kolfin, *Black Is Beautiful.*

8 Bindman, Gates, and Dalton, *The Image of the Black in Western Art.*

9 Dürer, *The Writings of Albrecht Dürer*, 166.

10 Ibid.

11 There is some debate as to whether Katharina was the first African Dürer drew from a live model. The dating is uncertain, but some believe that he had drawn black men beginning around 1504–1508. Spicer, *Revealing the African Presence.*

12 Bindman, Gates, and Dalton, *The Image of the Black in Western Art.*

13 Ibid.

14 Ibid., 85.

15 Spicer, *Revealing the African Presence.*

16 Dürer, *The Writings of Albrecht Dürer*, 247.

17 Bourdieu, *Distinction.*

18 Bindman, Gates, and Dalton, *The Image of the Black in Western Art*, 86.

19 Dürer, *The Writings of Albrecht Dürer*, 166.

20 Ibid.

21 Bindman, Gates, and Dalton, *The Image of the Black in Western Art*, 86.

22 Ibid.

23 Tinagli, *Women in Italian Renaissance Art*, 2.

24 Wood, "Eine Nachricht von Raffael."

25 Tinagli, *Women in Italian Renaissance Art.*

26 Eco, *History of Beauty*; Sartwell, "Beauty."

27 Castiglione, *The Book of the Courtier*, 179.

28 Ibid., 179–80.

29 Ibid., 232.

30 Venus was the Roman goddess of love and beauty. By the late fifteenth century, with the Renaissance in full swing and neoclassical ideals coursing through the Florentine Academy and other schools retaining top artistic talent, "Venus" became shorthand for feminine beauty. See Eco, *History of Beauty*.

31 An earlier version of Venus was sculpted by Giovanni Pisano around 1300, apparently just on the cusp of the Renaissance in Siena. He named his figure Prudence, not Venus, although the representation bears stunning similarities.

32 Vasari also claimed that Raphael's death from "heatstroke" could be attributed to his obsessive amatory relationship with Luti. Modern scholars have suggested that his so-called heatstroke might have actually been syphilis, which would have made Luti the era's most infamous femme fatale. See Lathers, *Bodies of Art*.

33 John Brackett, "Race and Rulership: Alessandro de' Medici, the First Medici Duke of Florence, 1529–1537," in Earle and Lowe, *Black Africans in Renaissance Europe*.

34 Murray, "Agnolo Firenzuola on Female Sexuality," 200.

35 Ibid., 200–201.

36 Bembo, as noted above, makes similar claims about beauty in *The Book of the Courtier*. Artists in Urbino were well aware of Dürer. (Raphael, for example, once communicated his appreciation for Dürer's self-portrait, and Dürer attempted to send a collection of portraits to Raphael's studio in an effort to impress him. Raphael, sadly, had just died.) Firenzuola may have been acquainted with the mathematical theorizing of the German master, and like Dürer himself, arrived at the conclusion that beauty is elusive. See Wood, "Eine Nachricht von Raffael"; and "Portrait of the Artist as an Entrepreneur," *Economist*, Dec. 17, 2011, www.economist.com.

37 Firenzuola, *On the Beauty of Women*, 28.

38 Ibid., 49.

39 Ibid., 40.

40 Ibid., 60, 63, 67.

41 Ibid., 49.

42 Murray, "Agnolo Firenzuola on Female Sexuality."

43 Bindman, Gates, and Dalton, *The Image of the Black in Western Art*, 93.

44 Earle and Lowe, *Black Africans in Renaissance Europe*, 134.

45 Bindman, Gates, and Dalton, *The Image of the Black in Western Art*; Earle and Lowe, *Black Africans in Renaissance Europe*.

46 Earle and Lowe, *Black Africans in Renaissance Europe*, 134.

47 Ibid. Note that "buffoon" was a term used to describe exoticized persons collected at court and retained for courtly amusement. See also Beliles and Newcombe, *Doubting Thomas*.

48 Bindman, Gates, and Dalton, *The Image of the Black in Western Art*.

49 Crowe, *Titian: His Life and Times*.

50 "Biography of Tiziano Vecellio (Titian)," Tiziano Vecellio (Titian): The Complete Works, www.titian-tizianovecellio.org, accessed Feb. 27, 2018.

51 Bindman, Gates, and Dalton, *The Image of the Black in Western Art*; Earle and Lowe, *Black Africans in Renaissance Europe*.

52 Bindman, Gates, and Dalton, *The Image of the Black in Western Art*; Earle and Lowe, *Black Africans in Renaissance Europe*.

53 John Heath, "Diana's Understanding of Ovid's 'Metamorphoses,'" *Classical Journal* 86, no. 3 (Feb. 1, 1991): 233–43; Kline, "Ovid's Metamorphoses."

54 It is evident, however, that similar to Dürer, Titian saw a difference in the facial features of Africans and Europeans, as he attempted to provide the black woman with a stereotypically African physiognomy.

55 The African maidservant, while appearing in portraits of Judith by many painters, never became normative. Nevertheless, he suggests that in cinquecento paintings, "there are more images of black women in this role than in any other." Bindman, Gates, and Dalton, *The Image of the Black in Western Art*, 147.

56 Ibid., 2.

57 Ibid., 139.

58 The "Moors" were thought to be very fond of jewels and other forms of adornment. Therefore, Renaissance artists depicting blacks often showed them wearing jewels that were supposed to signify Moorishness, Africanity, or even Ottoman ties. Ibid., 131.

59 It is not for nothing that Titian's work was reminiscent of Dürer's. Titian was a known admirer of the esteemed German artist's work. Dürer was known to fear that his work was being hijacked by the Venetian, and though he never mentioned Titian by name, Titian's early success had been attributed by some contemporaries, like Giorgio Vasari, to his "study" of Dürer's work. Martin Gayford, "Rare Titian Confirms Durer's Fear of Venetian Thievery," *Bloomberg*, April 17, 2012, www.bloomberg.com.

60 Kim Hall, *Things of Darkness*.

61 David Dearinger and Stanley Ellis Cushing, *Acquired Tastes: 200 Years of Collecting for the Boston Athenæum* (Boston: *Boston Athenaeum*, 2006), www .bostonathenaeum.org.

62 Henry Louis Gates Jr., "When Black Venus Was the Ideal Standard of Beauty," *Root*, July 22, 2014, www.theroot.com.

63 The question of whether or not the mirror was intended to convey vanity is a point of contention. For more on the debate, see Schreuder and Kolfin, *Black Is Beautiful*, 198.

64 Firenzuola—through Celso—describes the two types of Venuses circulating since the classical era: the sacred and the profane: "Now note. Two Venuses were described by the ancients. One, daughter of the earth, operates in earthly sensual ways, and the acts of physical love are supposed to originate from her. The other, they said, is the daughter of heaven . . . celestial, chaste, pure and holy. And they claimed that from this second Venus comes . . . those things that are lovely, rather

than sensual." *On the Beauty of Women*, 37. This much was also represented by Titian in his painting *Sacred and Profane Love*. This might also be a precursor to the understandings of black women as "hypersensual" that were to be elaborated over the course of the next two centuries.

65 Fredrickson, *Racism: A Short History*.

CHAPTER 2. PLUMP WOMEN AND THIN, FINE MEN

1 On the term "proto-racist," Fredrickson, *Racism: A Short History*; Eliav-Feldon, Isaac, and Ziegler, *The Origins of Racism in the West*.

2 King Philip II named William of Orange stadholder (or governor) of Holland, Zeeland, and Utrecht in 1559. Putnam, *William the Silent*; Wedgwood, *William the Silent*.

3 Warnke, *Peter Paul Rubens*.

4 Ibid.

5 Israel, *The Dutch Republic*.

6 Earle and Lowe, *Black Africans in Renaissance Europe*.

7 Hard numbers are difficult to come by, but existing research suggests that the number of Africans arriving in western Europe expanded between the sixteenth and seventeenth centuries. Ibid.

8 The role he played as an envoy in this relatively minor mission would be the start of Rubens's secret career as a diplomat and negotiator of peace between the Spanish crown and Dutch forces some two decades later. Lamster, "The Art of Diplomacy."

   Vincenzo Gonzaga had no way of knowing that Rubens would become a masterful arbiter of peace. Nor could he know that Rubens's diplomatic entanglements would ultimately earn him the title of Lord, so fitting a man of his stature.

9 Lamster, *Master of Shadows*.

10 According to art historian Sally Hickson, the duke was quite a trendsetter. Upon hearing of his museum of high-end ladies, other royals followed suit, creating their own *collection privée* of court maidens. Teresa Pitman, "Facebook in the 1500s?," *At Guelph*, Nov. 26, 2010, http://atguelph.uoguelph.ca. See also Lamster, *Master of Shadows*.

11 Lamster, *Master of Shadows*, 15.

12 Ibid.

13 Ibid., 34.

14 Rosenthal, *Gender, Politics, and Allegory in the Art of Rubens*.

15 Schreuder and Kolfin, *Black Is Beautiful*.

16 Rosenthal, *Gender, Politics, and Allegory in the Art of Rubens*.

17 It is fascinating that while Ethiopia is black, its river god is white. Painting an African man as a "god" would have indeed been *hors de norme*. But more than a question of convention, it might also have been owing to an unwillingness to see an African male as equivalent to the white males present, even as the black nymph is equated to the white.

18 Schreuder and Kolfin, *Black Is Beautiful*.

19 Morrison, *Playing in the Dark*; Pinder, *Whiteness and Racialized Ethnic Groups*.

20 Vries and Woude, *The First Modern Economy*, suggest that its eminence was beginning to wane by 1550.

21 Ibid.

22 Schreuder and Kolfin, *Black Is Beautiful*.

23 Bindman, Gates, and Dalton, *The Image of the Black in Western Art*.

24 Rubens, *Théorie de la figure humaine*; Marwick, *It: A History of Human Beauty*.

25 This is a point of contention among scholars. Marwick argues that Rubens painted fat women because "he was intensely preoccupied with the texture of flesh," further claiming, "Rubens' representations of women were not primarily intended by him to be models of female beauty." Marwick, *It: A History of Human Beauty*, 18. I would argue that Rubens's depiction of sumptuous female body parts in *Théorie de la figure humaine* suggests otherwise. In fact, the section in which he describes such plump feminine body parts is titled "On the Perfection of Diverse Parts of the Female Body." The opening sentence of this section is "Here are the models of beauty that skilled artists, painters and sculptors, have determined for the feminine physique." Rubens, *Théorie de la figure humaine*, 50.

26 Rubens, *Théorie de la figure humaine*, 177.

27 Ibid., 50–51. The aesthetic praised here was not invented by Rubens. Long blond hair and milky-white skin had been an ideal, particularly among the English, since the Middle Ages. Brewer, "The Ideal of Feminine Beauty." What I am trying to show here is that Rubens's ideology about whiteness represented a break from earlier Renaissance masters, like Dürer, from the Low Countries.

28 Rubens, *Théorie de la figure humaine*.

29 Ibid., 45.

30 For additional research on physical distinctions, see Shilling, "Educating the Body"; Lamont and Lareau, "Cultural Capital"; Wacquant, *Body and Soul*.

31 Ben Phelan, "Dutch East India Company: The World's First Multinational," *Antiques Roadshow*, PBS, Jan. 7, 2013, www.pbs.org.

32 Ibid.

33 The ample proportions of one woman from the so-called Hottentot tribe would come to electrify the entire Western world in the nineteenth century, as detailed in chapter 3.

34 Schreuder and Kolfin, *Black Is Beautiful*, 92.

35 Herbert Klein, *The Atlantic Slave Trade*.

36 Gikandi, *Slavery and the Culture of Taste*.

37 Ibid.

38 Derrida, *Margins of Philosophy*.

39 Lerner, *The Creation of Patriarchy*.

40 The first black Africans designated as "slaves" arrived in 1555. The group of five black men, however, were more like intelligence agents and emissaries. They were brought to England on an official mission to learn English. Having attained a

sufficient mastery of the language, they were to return to their West African land, an area that would later be known as Ghana, to serve as interpreters and liaisons to English traders trying to enter a field long dominated by the Portuguese and the Spanish. Fryer, *Staying Power*.

41 Boemus, *The Fardle of Facions*; Fryer, *Staying Power*.

42 Arguably, the most authoritative historical work on the subject came from a Spanish-born Moor named Leo Africanus. In his widely disseminated text, *A Geographical History of Africa*, translated into English in 1600, he claimed that Africans were more prone to sensual excess than any other people in the world. Earle and Lowe, *Black Africans in Renaissance Europe*. The notion that blacks were sexually and orally overindulgent became integral to the English view of Africans. It formed the heart of their "proto-racist" conception of blackness. Fredrickson, *Racism: A Short History*. The term "race" was not yet in wide circulation. It had been used by the Spaniards in the fifteenth century to describe people of Jewish or "Moorish" ancestry. In sixteenth-century Spanish colonies it morphed into a way of delineating a descent-based social hierarchy, a "caste trio" of whites, indigenous laborers, and black slaves. Silverblatt, *Modern Inquisitions*. The term was to be defined and redefined again and again by various western European powers. Beginning in the eighteenth century, the English would become major figures in generating the so-called racial differences that would become a linchpin of English colonial management. Smedley, *Race in North America*; Fields and Fields, *Racecraft*. The long-standing association between blackness and carnality would prove critical.

43 The English had yet to build up their own stable of esteemed painters—largely relying instead on the mastery of painters from the Low Countries for their portraits. Dalton, "The Black Emperor."

44 Fryer, *Staying Power*, 140.

45 Erickson, "Representations of Blacks and Blackness"; Reilly, Kaufman, and Bodino, *Racism: A Global Reader*.

46 Paul Edwards and James Walvin, *Black Personalities in the Era of the Slave Trade* (New York: Springer, 1983), 9.

47 Chaudhri and Jain, "History of Cosmetics," 164; Mia De Graaf, "Why the Virgin Queen Wasn't Really Pale and Interesting: Paint Tests of Portrait Show Elizabeth I Had Rosy Red Cheeks," *Daily Mail*, June 11, 2014, www.dailymail.co.uk.

48 Erickson, "Representations of Blacks and Blackness."

49 Ibid.; Bindman, Gates, and Dalton, *The Image of the Black in Western Art*.

50 Ibid.

51 A "masque" is like a musical performed at court; see Bindman, Gates, and Dalton, *The Image of the Black in Western Art*.

52 Ibid., 235.

53 Ian Smith, *Race and Rhetoric in the Renaissance*, 138.

54 Although Hermia is not identified as black, Lysander derides her for her proximity to blackness qua her darkness and small stature. He uses the *idea* of black femininity here as a slur.

55 Shakespeare, *A Midsummer Night's Dream*, Act 3, Scene 2.

56 Bindman, Gates, and Dalton, *The Image of the Black in Western Art*.

57 Ibid., 243.

58 Black, *The Atlantic Slave Trade in World History*.

59 Ibid.

60 Rivard et al., "Sack and Sugar, and the Aetiology of Gout."

61 Ibid.

62 Gilman, *Fat Boys*.

63 D. Haslam, "Obesity: A Medical History," *Obesity Reviews* 8 (2007): 33.

64 Rivard et al., "Sack and Sugar, and the Aetiology of Gout," 421.

65 Sydenham and Wallis, *A Treatise of the Gout and Dropsy*.

66 Ibid.

67 Ibid.

68 By the 1788 edition of this text, George Wallis had corrected this assumption, claiming that sugar was one of the "poisons" contributing to rates of gout. Sydenham and Wallis, *A Treatise of the Gout and Dropsy*.

69 Rivard et al., "Sack and Sugar, and the Aetiology of Gout."

70 The relationship between overeating, obesity, and gout was also being taken up in Italy. In 1558 Luigi Cornaro, a self-proclaimed former glutton once "at death's door," attributed his improved health to his drastically reduced food intake. Gilman, *Obesity: The Biography*. In the early seventeenth century, an Italian physician by the name of Sanctorius Sanctorius developed a weighing machine known as the Sanctorian Balance. He ate, slept, and wrote in this cage-like device, in an effort to keep the body in "proper Poise" by never eating too much. The experiment ultimately failed. Porter, *Flesh in the Age of Reason*.

71 Estill, "Proverbial Shakespeare."

72 Shakespeare, *Love's Labour's Lost*, 1.1.24–27.

73 Estill, "Proverbial Shakespeare."

74 Shakespeare, *Julius Caesar*, 1.2.189–92.

75 Potter, *The Life of William Shakespeare*, 5.4.161–63.

76 Letters to Princess Elisabeth of Bohemia, 1647–49, *Early Modern Texts*, www.earlymoderntexts.com, accessed Feb. 27, 2018.

77 Ibid., 22.

78 Descartes's ideas were taught at Cambridge universities. Indeed, Cartesianism was perhaps strongest in England, where members of the Cambridge Platonic school waxed intellectual about its implications. Porter, *Flesh in the Age of Reason*.

79 Edward Craig, *Routledge Encyclopedia of Philosophy: Index*.

80 Shapin, *The Scientific Revolution*, 37.

81 Ibid., 38.

82 Ibid., 39.

83 Ibid., 38.

84 Lamster, *Master of Shadows*.

85 Joan Altabe, "Rubens' Fleshy Females," *Ft. Myers Magazine*, Sept. 2006, www
    .ftmyersmagazine.com.

86 Porter, *Flesh in the Age of Reason*.

CHAPTER 3. THE RISE OF THE BIG BLACK WOMAN

 1 See Paul Baines, *The Long 18th Century* (London: Arnold, 2004).

 2 Foucault, *Discipline and Punish*; Bartky, "Foucault, Femininity, and the Modern-
    ization of Patriarchal Power."

 3 Bernier, *Travels in the Mogul Empire*.

 4 Around the time Bernier and Gassendi met, the priest was embroiled in an
    intense exchange with Descartes, against whose *Meditations* he had written an
    aggravated treatise. These culminated in a set of objections to the text that were
    published with Gassendi's name, but without his consent. To hear Gassendi tell
    it, Descartes's premise of "I think, therefore I am" lacked *bons sens*. To Gassendi,
    all understanding about the world was born first of sensory experience, and was
    tortured and elaborated upon after the fact. Kearns, *Ideas in Seventeenth-Century
    France*. Their bitter back-and-forth continued for the next several years.

 5 Bernier, *Travels in the Mogul Empire*.

 6 Ibid., 51.

 7 Ibid.

 8 Since the Middle Ages, the term "race" was used as a way to describe a breed
    or stock of domestic animals. Smedley, *Race in North America*. In the fifteenth
    century, during the rise and expansion of Spain's colonial enterprise, the Spanish
    began to apply the term "race" (*raza*) to human groups believed to have a shared
    ancestry. In Spanish colonies, people of "Moorish" or "Jewish" ancestry were
    routinely designated as separate from European colonists.

    The term entered the French lexicon in the late fifteenth century and was
    first used to describe the distinctive character of the king and his descendants.
    Peabody and Stovall, *The Color of Liberty*. It was later extended to others of no-
    ble birth. These men and women were labeled with the advantageous moniker
    noblesse de race (noble race), distinguishing them as gentlefolk of "good breed-
    ing" from the vulgar common folk, for whom there was no need to ascribe any
    special characteristics befitting their distinction as a race.

 9 Peabody, "*There Are No Slaves in France*."

10 Ibid.

11 Iyengar, *Shades of Difference*.

12 There is some contention on this point. While Iyengar, in *Shades of Difference*,
    identifies him as a polygenist, Joan-Pau Rubies, in "Race, Climate and Civiliza-
    tion," asserts that his training with Gassendi (a monogenist) and his writings in
    Gassendi's defense prove him a monogenist. Rather than attempting an adjudica-
    tion of this debate, I am suggesting here only that he was evidently familiar with
    the claims of polygenists, whether or not he subscribed to them.

13 Bernier, "A New Division of the Earth."

14 Ibid.

15 Ibid.

16 Ibid.

17 Ibid.

18 Ibid.

19 Bernier's racial schematic was curious in many respects. Despite his contention that physical and regional differences were interconnected, by the end of the tract the first race contained people from four separate continents (after adding American Indians), extending to most of the world's landmass. The Lapps, meanwhile, stood alone as a unique race of mankind. The doctor-cum-explorer never attempted to explain the disparities in numerical or geographical representation that his schematic introduced. See Bernier, "A New Division of the Earth"; Stuurman, "François Bernier."

20 Bernier, "A New Division of the Earth."

21 Ibid.; Peabody and Stovall, *The Color of Liberty*.

22 As he also stated in *Travels*, the "nature of the semen . . . must vary with specific races and types." Bernier, *Travels in the Mogul Empire*, 249.

23 Hannaford, *Race: The History of an Idea in the West*; Boulle, "François Bernier and the Origins of the Modern Concept of Race."

24 As Stuurman notes, not only was Bernier building on a legacy of men philosophizing about women's appearance, he had been implored on one previous occasion by Jean Chapelain, founding member of the esteemed Académie Francaise, to write as much as he could about "Oriental women." Stuurman, "François Bernier," 5–18.

25 Because of the uncertainty surrounding which African group a given author was referring to, in this chapter I will maintain the original "Hottentot." I also see the use of this false moniker as a way of describing an invention, a fantasy of the European imagination, rather than a real people.

26 Baker, *Race*.

27 Bernier, "A New Division of the Earth," 248.

28 Ibid., 249.

29 Ibid.

30 Ibid.

31 Ibid.

32 Smedley, *Race in North America*; Stuurman, "François Bernier"; Curran, *The Anatomy of Blackness*.

33 Clark, *State and Status*; French, *Frog Town*.

34 According to Sue Peabody, the law's legitimacy remained ambiguous in cities like Paris, where the Parlement refused to register the law. There were fewer ambiguities in the Parlements of Dijon and Rennes, where the law was registered. Peabody, *"There Are No Slaves in France,"* 19–22.

35 Jean Piveteau, "Georges-Louis Leclerc, Count de Buffon," in *Encyclopedia Britannica*, 2015, www.britannica.com.

36 Ibid.

37 Pagliaro, *Racism in the Eighteenth Century*; Fowler, *New Essays on Diderot.*

38 Buffon, *Buffon's Natural History.*

39 Ibid.

40 Ibid., 278.

41 The Peabody text (*"There Are No Slaves in France"*) uses a translation of the original French to "plump." The Barr (1797) translation uses the word "bulky."

42 Fields and Fields, *Racecraft.*

43 He further divided "black Africans" into two races: the Negroes and the Caffres. The Caffres included the Hottentot as well as black people of East Africa, Mozambique, and Madagascar. The Negroes included people from West and Central Africa, including countries such as Senegal, Angola, and Congo.

44 Buffon, *Buffon's Natural History.*

45 The land of the (white) Moors, by contrast, was less abundant. According to Buffon, survival for Moors required both effort and industry. This cultivated "meager" physiques but inquisitive and "ingenious" minds. Ibid., 279.

46 Baddam, *Memoirs of the Royal Society.*

47 Ibid.

48 Buffon was Carolus Linnaeus's main rival and detractor. If Linnaeus's system of classification ultimately gained traction over that of Buffon, Buffon enjoyed several years of esteem due in part to his post at the Jardin du Roi. Sloan, "The Buffon-Linnaeus Controversy."

49 Buffon, *Buffon's Natural History*, 279.

50 Ibid., 280–81.

51 Foucault suggests that at any given historical moment, a specific meaning will attach to certain bodies. Frequently, this meaning is produced within the halls of power—for example, within the disciplines of science, medicine, or philosophy. However, its origins are often obscured. And, because they are attached to bodies, the meanings are easily naturalized. This is how bodies become "legible," or understood in a particular way, within a given society. Foucault, *Discipline and Punish.*

52 Curran, *The Anatomy of Blackness*, 20.

53 See also "Denis Diderot: Philosopher and Writer of the French Enlightenment," 2015, British Humanist Association, https://humanism.org.uk.

54 Roger, *Buffon*; Fowler, *New Essays on Diderot.*

55 Jean-Baptiste-Pierre Le Romain, "Negroes" (1765), in *Encyclopedia of Diderot and d'Alembert: Collaborative Translation Project*, https://quod.lib.umich.edu.

56 Curran, *The Anatomy of Blackness.*

57 Quoted in Christopher Forth, "Fat, Desire and Disgust in the Colonial Imagination," *History Workshop Journal* 73, no. 1 (2012): 214.

58 Ibid.

59 That many of the more recognized accounts of lazy, corpulent black Africans were being produced by French and British authors should come as no surprise. As

had been the case during the Spanish-Italian reign of the sixteenth century and the Dutch-English reign of the seventeenth, there was a relationship between the British-French dominance in philosophical and scientific production and their dominant position in the transatlantic slave trade. Gikandi, *Slavery and the Culture of Taste*. Indeed, it is not for nothing that the height of the slave trade for the British and the French (ca. 1726–1825) overlapped with the High Enlightenment. Similarly, the onset of the African slave trade had coincided with the High Renaissance. Sharp, "Fascinating Database about the Trans-Atlantic Slave Trade." In each case, the immense profits from overseas plantations and chattel slavery were part of the rising tide lifting the colonial powers' boats. The profits from the slave trade contributed to the availability of luxury goods and leisure time and literacy as well as intellectual production. Gikandi, *Slavery and the Culture of Taste*. And, if it gave the British and French the resources for knowledge production, it also gave them the capacity to produce forms of knowledge that would reify their dominant political and social position.

60 Long, *The History of Jamaica*.

61 On page 352, he claimed that the blacks from "Negro-land," or "Guiney," were different from the dark-skinned native-born Creoles. He backtracks on this statement a mere two pages on.

62 Long, *The History of Jamaica*, 352.

63 Ibid., 373, 271.

64 Ibid., 361. In another example of Long's vagaries, in some passages of the text, he describes blacks as being somewhat abstemious. Citing the work of a man named Jobson, he writes, "The common people in Guiney eat only *once* a day, which is after the sun-set. They hold, that eating seldom, and in the cooler part of the day, is a good preservative of health" (562). Moreover, in other parts of the text, Long suggests that it is the Europeans in the colonies who are commonly the most voracious. Of the Spaniards, he remarks that they have a "too plentiful flesh diet" (557) and regale themselves with spirits beginning at 11:00 a.m., and sometimes devote the entire day to tippling (562). Englishmen too, he contends, arrive in the colonies and find "their appetite unusually keen," purportedly due to the climate. A number of these men have been "stimulated by the sight of several dainties they have been before unacquainted with; thus strongly solicited to gratify their palates" (529). They in turn "may fall into hurtful excesses, if they are not on their guard" (529).

65 Ibid., 372.

66 Royal Society Library, *Catalogue of the Scientific Books*.

67 Partially inspired also by the travelogues of his former coauthor Sonnini de Manoncourt, who offered his own analysis of the looks and behavior of Egyptians and Guyanese in his travelogues.

68 Virey, *Natural History of the Negro Race*, 4–5.

69 Ibid.

70 Rousseau, Sebastian, and Porter, *Exoticism in the Enlightenment*.

71 In 1614 the Italian physician Santorio wrote in his text *De statica medicina* that black skin was caused by the presence of black bile. In 1687 this belief was revived by the Italian Malpighi, who claimed that this black bile was akin to a "mucuous liquor" found beneath the skin of black people. Pagliaro, *Racism in the Eighteenth Century*. The humoral theory posited a balance between the four humors, or bodily fluids, that impact temperament. It is believed to have originated with Hippocrates.

72 Radden, *The Nature of Melancholy*.

73 Virey, *Natural History of the Negro Race*, 25.

74 Ibid.

75 Ibid., 47.

76 Virey, *Histoire naturelle du genre humain*, 243.

77 Merians, *Envisioning the Worst*.

78 Other authors have described the looseness of the term "Hottentot," which was applied, sometimes indiscriminately, to people of various tribes in southern Africa. Baker, *Race*.

79 Virey, *Histoire naturelle du genre humain*, 242–43.

80 Ibid., 244.

81 Baker, *Race*.

82 Sparrman, "Account of the Hottentots"; Matthew Carey, ed., *The American Museum, or Universal Magazine: Containing Essays on Agriculture, Commerce, Manufactures, Politics, Morals and Manners; Sketches of National Characters, Natural and Civil History, and Biography; Law Information, Public Papers, Intelligence: Moral Tales, Ancient and Modern Poetry* (Mathew Carey, 1791).

83 Sparrman, "Account of the Hottentots."

84 Ibid.

85 Crais and Scully, *Sara Baartman and the Hottentot Venus*.

86 It is also worth mentioning that the British had been arriving in South Africa since at least the sixteenth century, issuing negative polemics on the look, character, and mores of South Africans, but not, routinely, with "excess" appetites. Merians, *Envisioning the Worst*.

87 Quoted in ibid., 177.

88 Ibid., 180.

89 Ibid., 210.

90 Crais and Scully, *Sara Baartman and the Hottentot Venus*; Willis, *Black Venus*.

91 Stoler, *Carnal Knowledge and Imperial Power*; Crais and Scully, *Sara Baartman and the Hottentot Venus*.

92 Crais and Scully, *Sara Baartman and the Hottentot Venus*, 48–51.

93 Ibid., 72.

94 Ibid., 80.

95 Qureshi, "Displaying Sara Baartman."

96 Bondeson, *The Two-Headed Boy*; Crais and Scully, *Sara Baartman and the Hottentot Venus*.

97 Crais and Scully, *Sara Baartman and the Hottentot Venus*, 80.

98 Emphasis mine, quoted in Crais and Scully, *Sara Baartman and the Hottentot Venus*, 110.

99 Peabody, *"There Are No Slaves in France,"* 7.

100 Sue Peabody reminds that we ofttime "anachronistically conflate freedom and social equality." Ibid., 8. Lawyers and magistrates might have fought to end the ancien régime in favor of freedom from despotic tyranny, but that didn't mean for them *social equality* or equal access to all rights for all applicants. The abstract principle of liberty did not imply to them that everyone had a right to be treated equally. See also Dubois, "Inscribing Race in the Revolutionary French Antilles."

101 Peabody, *"There Are No Slaves in France."*

102 Kolbert, *The Sixth Extinction.*

103 Cuvier, "Femme de race Boschismanne"; Bancel, David, and Thomas, *The Invention of Race.*

104 Cuvier, "Femme de race Boschismanne," 2.

105 Ibid., 3.

106 Ibid.

107 Ibid., 4.

108 Kolbert, *The Sixth Extinction*, 33.

109 Merians, *Envisioning the Worst.*

110 Crais and Scully, *Sara Baartman and the Hottentot Venus*, 124.

111 Ibid.

112 Ibid., 127.

CHAPTER 4. BIRTH OF THE ASCETIC AESTHETIC

1 While the existence of taverns in London predates England's entry into the slave trade, the expansion of sweet offerings like sack, made possible by the transatlantic slave trade, generously expanded the pub-and-strumpet scene. Rivard et al., "Sack and Sugar, and the Aetiology of Gout."

2 Elizabeth A. Bohls, "Standards of Taste, Discourses of Race, and the Aesthetic Education of a Monster: Critique of Empire in *Frankenstein*," *Eighteenth-Century Life* 18, no. 3 (1994): 23–36; Jones, *Gender and the Formation of Taste*; Gikandi, *Slavery and the Culture of Taste.*

3 Gikandi, *Slavery and the Culture of Taste.*

4 "London's Coffee Houses," History TV, www.history.co.uk, accessed Feb. 27, 2018.

5 Porter, *Flesh in the Age of Reason.*

6 Ibid.

7 Ibid.

8 Ibid.

9 Guerrini, *Obesity and Depression in the Enlightenment*, 6.

10 Cheyne, *The English Malady.*

11 Guerrini, *Obesity and Depression in the Enlightenment.*

12 Stuart, *The Bloodless Revolution.*

13   If one were to ask which church, the answer to this would be somewhat less clear. Cheyne had lived through the Glorious Revolution of 1689 in Scotland, which reinstated Presbyterianism as the dominant religion. Prior to that, between 1660 and 1689, Scottish Episcopalianism had reigned. This had unseated—you guessed it—Presbyterianism, which enjoyed a full twenty-two years atop the religious pyramid, after the overcoming of Episcopalian authority by James VI. Therefore, as to the question of Cheyne's religious upbringing, it seems reasonable to assume that his parents might have been either Episcopalian or Presbyterian. Guerrini, *Obesity and Depression in the Enlightenment*. In any event, he was likely to have been exposed to a heavy dose of Calvinist teachings.

14   Guerrini, *Obesity and Depression in the Enlightenment*, 6.

15   Ibid.; Cheyne, *The English Malady*.

16   Stuart, *The Bloodless Revolution*.

17   Guerrini, *Obesity and Depression in the Enlightenment*, 6.

18   Cheyne, *The English Malady*, 337–38.

19   Stuart, *The Bloodless Revolution*.

20   The Reformation was touched off by German monk Martin Luther in 1517. Luther, fed up with the indulgent practices of the Roman Catholic Church, pinned ninety-five theses slamming said practices on the door of St. Peter's Basilica university chapel. He was excommunicated for his efforts in 1521. In 1524 he formed his own church, Lutheranism. Martin Luther's ideas were not to be confined within German borders. Inspired by his ideas, the French Protestant John Calvin produced his own writings on the topic. Central to his theology, subsequently known as Calvinism, was a reverence for the awesome power of God, human pre-destination, and the necessary role of ascetic discipline in the lives of the morally upright. Calvinism promptly spread throughout much of Europe, descending on Scotland (as previously noted), as well as France and the Low Countries.

21   Dewey D. Wallace, ed., *The Spirituality of the Later English Puritans: An Anthology* (Macon, GA: Mercer University Press, 1987); "Puritanism," in *Encyclopedia Britannica*, last modified Jan. 3, 2018, www.britannica.com.

22   A specialist of entomology, he took a particular liking to spiders, which many believe is evinced in the nursery rhyme "Little Miss Muffet," which he allegedly wrote for his daughter Patience.

23   This book was edited by Christopher Bennet, and saw its first posthumous publication in 1655.

24   Moffet, James, and Oldys, *Health's Improvement*.

25   Ibid.

26   Muffet (sometimes spelled Moffett or Moffet) was, in fact, the personal physician to the Earl of Essex. The earl famously took part in the English Armada in 1589, following the Spanish Armada the year prior. Edward Larocque Tinker, "New Editions, Fine and Otherwise," *New York Times Book Review*, Oct. 5, 1941, 28.

27   And, if his ideas feel similar to those of Robert Boyle and the Cambridge Platonists, it is worth noting that not only was Muffet's book first published when

Boyle had just moved to Oxford, but there is some speculation that Boyle himself might have been a Puritan. Marshall, *Puritanism and Natural Theology*.

28 Moffet, James, and Oldys, *Health's Improvement*.

29 Muffet posited three types of diets: a Full Diet, for the young, strong, and grow-ing; a Moderate Diet, for those in decent health but who are no longer engaged in rigorous exercise; and a Thin Diet, for the infirm. Moffet, James, and Oldys, *Health's Improvement*.

30 Ibid.

31 Guerrini, "The Hungry Soul."

32 Wild, *Medicine-by-Post*.

33 Cheyne, *The Letters of Dr. George Cheyne*.

34 Ibid., 43.

35 Ibid., vii.

36 Ibid., xxiii.

37 During the Reformation, John Calvin, like his predecessor Martin Luther, had rele-gated women to the rigorously reimagined space of the home. In addition, women were now seen as the spiritual equals of men, and accordingly given a greater role and voice in the church. Furthermore, since the priest had been removed from his perch as salvation broker, women were now afforded direct access to the word of God. Since women were now necessary in-home interpreters of God's word, their literacy had soared by the early eighteenth century. Wiesner, "Beyond Women and the Family." This gave them both the motivation and the skills to invest themselves in the movement for right-minded eating in the name of the Lord.

38 Jones, *Gender and the Formation of Taste*.

39 In *Characteristics of Men, Manners, Opinions, Times*, Shaftesbury claimed that beauty had tiers. The first two tiers of Shaftesbury's hierarchy are of particu-lar interest. They might be considered "natural beauty" and "moral beauty," respectively. McAteer, "Third Earl of Shaftesbury." Natural beauty was "sensual," unthinking, and pleasure-based. Shaftesbury, *Characteristics of Men, Manners, Opinions, Times*; McAteer, "Third Earl of Shaftesbury." Men of low breeding, who were "poor-spirited, lazy and gluttonous," would follow its sensualistic command. Shaftesbury, *Shaftesbury* (Cambridge University Press edition). It would not, and could not, advance the common good. By contrast, moral beauty bespoke a certain type of goodness, a virtue. English gentlemen, who were "Men of Breeding and Politeness," should seek a type of moral beauty in women. Bindman, *Ape to Apollo*; Gikandi, *Slavery and the Culture of Taste*. This kind of beauty had the capacity to advance the common good. Moreover, the earl had made it clear that the people capable of discernment were certainly not the "lazy and gluttonous" men of far-off continents. Nor could residents of other European nations neces-sarily be trusted. Men of breeding came from the elite of British society.

Addison himself was a former mentor of Shaftesbury. There is some debate as to whether Addison and Steele were writing against the earl, or hoping to build upon his political and ideological project.

40 Pratt, "'To Enliven Morality with Wit.'"

41 The man, describing himself as a "Valetudinarian"—one who is anxious about their health—admitted that of late, he had grown "very fat" and contracted gout. In an attempt at self-cure he had read Dr. Thomas Sydenham's work on gout. But finding no relief (since, as previously explored, Sydenham's advice was dubious at best), he turned to the more drastic means of Sanctorius, the seventeenth-century Italian who devised a pair of chairs that hung on springs and scales. This letter writer appeared to have gone over the edge by devising his own weighing chair. Still, as evidenced in Mr. Spectator's response, a measured temperance that was neither sacerdotal fasting nor self-flagellation was routinely advocated in the *Spectator*. In fact, Mr. Spectator would commonly reference the advice of another sixteenth-century Italian dietician, Luigi Cornaro, who was the intellectual forebear of Sanctorius. Cornaro too would promote temperance in eating to achieve health and longevity. As articulated in *The Spectator*, Cornaro offered "the most remarkable instance of temperance toward the procuring of long life." Steele and Addison, *The Spectator*.

42 Steele and Addison, *The Spectator*, no. 25, March 29, 1711.

43 Ibid.

44 Ibid., no. 127, July 26, 1711.

45 In *The Spectator* there was one instance of a woman writing in to declare herself ugly enough to warrant access to this Ugly Club. But there is no evidence that she, or any other woman, ever gained access to this club, if it did, indeed, exist. Steele and Addison, *The Spectator*.

46 *The Spectator*, no. 32, April 6, 1711.

47 Ibid.

48 Pratt, "'To Enliven Morality with Wit.'"

49 James Sambrook, "Spence, Joseph," in *Oxford Dictionary of National Biography*, 2010.

50 Ibid.

51 Beaumont, *Crito, or A Dialogue on Beauty*.

52 Ibid.

53 Ibid.

54 Ibid.

55 Ibid, 8.

56 Ibid, 51.

57 Ibid.; Prince, "The Eighteenth-Century Beauty Contest," 254.

58 Ibid.

59 Walpole, *The Letters of Horace Walpole, 366*.

60 Jones, *Gender and the Formation of Taste*, 25.

61 Ibid.

62 Ibid.

63 Montagu, *Lady Mary Wortley Montagu*.

64 Tytler, *The Countess of Huntingdon and Her Circle*.

65 Cheyne was not the only doctor promoting a restricted diet for women in England at the time, but he was arguably the most recognizable. Guerrini, "The Hungry Soul."

66 Lowenthal, *Lady Mary Wortley Montagu*.

67 Ibid., 103.

68 Ibid.

69 Ibid.

70 Ibid.

71 George Paston, *Lady Mary Wortley Montagu and Her Times* (1907), 335.

72 "Thomas Gainsborough Biography," Biography.com, www.biography.com, accessed Feb. 27, 2018.

73 Emil Krén and Daniel Marx, "Gainsborough, Thomas," Web Gallery of Art, www.wga.hu, accessed Feb. 27, 2018.

74 "Thomas Gainsborough Biography."

75 He would later pick up more than a few tricks from the scenic renderings in the works of Peter Paul Rubens, whose work Gainsborough studied closely during the 1760s. Postle, *Thomas Gainsborough*.

76 The Louvre offers a rich treatment of the scene depicted in this painting. *Conversations in a Park*, Louvre online, www.louvre.fr, accessed Feb. 27, 2018.

77 *Mr and Mrs Andrews*, National Gallery online, www.nationalgallery.org.uk, accessed Feb. 27, 2018.

78 It is worth noting that Gainsborough was inspired by the master French painter Jean-Antoine Watteau, who himself had been known for his paintings of slight and refined women and who had been the teacher of Gainsborough's own mentor, Gravelot. Perl, *Antoine's Alphabet*.

79 Bob Spitz, *The Beatles: The Biography* (Boston: Little, Brown, 2012); Madsen, *Chanel*.

80 This break from classical standards in eighteenth-century art was purposeful, if we are to believe one of Gainsborough's mentors, William Hogarth. Hogarth himself had written, in 1753, *The Analysis of Beauty: Written with a View of Fixing the Fluctuating Ideas of Taste*. Hogarth's treatise hadn't exactly been groundbreaking, but it was a pushback, albeit ambivalent, against the so-called false classicism of the age. Voogd, *Henry Fielding and William Hogarth*; Eco, *History of Beauty*.

81 There are those who have speculated that he painted an image of Lady Mary Wortley Montagu at one time, but if this is the case, surviving evidence has proven elusive. See N. D'Anvers, *Thomas Gainsborough: A Record of His Life and Works* (G. Bell and Sons, 1897).

CHAPTER 5. AMERICAN BEAUTY

1 Hale, *The Ladies' Wreath*.

2 Ibid.

3 According to Peggy Baker, director and librarian of the Pilgrim Hall Museum, there is some controversy over who wrote the poem. While Hale maintained that

it was her invention based on events in her own life, others at the time stepped forward to claim ownership of a few of the rhyme's verses. Peggy Baker, "The Godmother of Thanksgiving: The Story of Sarah Josepha Hale," Pilgrim Society and Pilgrim Museum, 2007.

4   Hale, *Ladies' Magazine.*

5   Endres and Lueck, *Women's Periodicals in the United States,* 115.

6   Ibid.

7   Okker, *Our Sister Editors*; Stella Blum, *Fashions and Costumes from "Godey's Lady's Book"* (North Chelmsford, MA: Courier, 2013).

8   Anderson, *Imagined Communities.*

9   Okker, *Our Sister Editors.*

10   Ibid.

11   Lydia Sigourney, "Editor's Table," *Godey's Lady's Book,* Nov. 1839.

12   "On the Female Form," *Godey's Lady's Book,* Dec. 1831.

13   This was in keeping with the view of women as the "body" and beauty as important to valuations of a woman's worth that have been witnessed since the dawn of patriarchy. Spelman, "Woman as Body"; Lerner, *The Creation of Patriarchy.*

14   "Mirror of the Graces," *Godey's Lady's Book,* Feb. 1831.

15   Fletcher, *Gender and the American Temperance Movement*; McCue, *Domestic Violence.*

16   The temperance movement was budding near the turn of the nineteenth century, and by the 1830s could count thousands of churches and local organizations in its number. "Temperance Movement," in *Encyclopedia Britannica,* last modified Sept. 26, 2017, www.britannica.com.

17   Schwartz, *Never Satisfied.*

18   Lindley, *You Have Stept Out of Your Place*; McCue, *Domestic Violence.*

19   Blumin, *The Emergence of the Middle Class*; Mark Roth, "The Historic Roots of the Middle Class," *Pittsburgh Post-Gazette,* Nov. 20, 2011, www.post-gazette.com.

20   "Editor's Table," *Godey's Lady's Book,* Jan. 1850, 40.

21   Later theorists would elaborate upon his initial claim. English author Richard Verstegan, for example, wrote in his 1605 book *Restitution of the Decayed Intelligence* that the Germanic peoples had settled England in AD 449, nearly six centuries before the arrival of the Norman rulers in 1066. Therefore, the English were German descendants, and should be recognized as Saxons. Banton, *Racial Theories*; Smedley, *Race in North America.*

22   Smedley, *Race in North America.*

23   Gossett, *Race: The History of an Idea.*

24   Omi and Winant, *Racial Formation in the United States.*

25   Prichard, *The Eastern Origin of the Celtic Nations.*

26   Prichard was not the first to make this claim. In fact, according to his text, "writer upon writer" had claimed that Celtic languages shared a kinship with "Asiatics," who, in this instance, were Palestinians, Phoenicians, Persians, and Egyptians, groups that today would be recognized as Arab or African. In this way, the aim of

these works had been to suggest that the "Eastern origins" of the Irish made them linguistically and thereby racially similar to these groups, and thus distinct from the English.

27 Prichard, *Researches into the Physical History of Mankind*, 391.

28 Whereas the ancients described the Celts as tall, fair, and blue-eyed (much like the "Germanic nations"), he argues that this characterization would not match the way Celts would be described in the nineteenth century.

29 Prichard, *Researches into the Physical History of Mankind*, 189.

30 Prichard, *The Eastern Origin of the Celtic Nations*, 353.

31 A. O. J. Cockshut, "Thomas Carlyle: British Essayist and Historian," in *Encyclopedia Britannica*, last modified Aug. 18, 2017, www.britannica.com.

32 Stanford Gwilliam, "Thomas Carlyle, Reluctant Calvinist" (PhD diss., Columbia University, 1965); Martin, *Modernism and the Rhythms of Sympathy*.

33 This in itself is interesting, since Carlyle was born in Scotland. But, in order to better his racial positioning, he reminded people that he was a southern Scot, and thus Anglo-Saxon. It was the northern Scots who, he claimed, were of the Celtic race. Painter, *The History of White People*, 156, 154.

34 Ibid., 161.

35 Ashcroft, Griffiths, and Tiffin, *Post-Colonial Studies*.

36 Carlyle, *The Sayings of Thomas Carlyle*.

37 Catherine Hall, *Cultures of Empire*, 208.

38 Carlyle, *Occasional Discourse on the Negro Question*.

39 Painter, *The History of White People*, 165.

40 Emerson, *English Traits*.

41 Beliles and Newcombe, *Doubting Thomas*.

42 Samuel Stanhope Smith, *An Essay on the Causes of the Variety of Complexion and Figure*, 45.

43 Ibid.

44 Emerson, *Journals and Miscellaneous Notebooks*, 5.

45 Emerson, *English Traits*, 76.

46 Ibid., 71.

47 Ibid.

48 Painter, *The History of White People*, 154.

49 Leigh Hunt, "Chapter on Female Features," *Godey's Lady's Book*, April 1836.

50 S.G.B., "Thanksgiving," *Godey's Lady's Book*, Nov. 1863.

51 "Sketches from Real Life," *Godey's Lady's Book*, March 1848.

52 "The Fat Widow," *Godey's Lady's Book*, Dec. 1855.

53 Lerner, *The Creation of Feminist Consciousness*; Booth, *How to Make It as a Woman*.

54 This essay was unsigned. But, being part of the Editor's Table series, presumably if it were not written by Hale, it would have been approved by her.

55 "Editor's Table," *Godey's Lady's Book*, May 1843.

56 Montagu, *The Letters of Lady Mary Wortley Montagu*.

57 "Editor's Table," May 1843.

58 "Le Melange: American Beauty," *Godey's Lady's Book*, Dec. 1852.

59 Ibid.

60 Scanlon and Cosner, *American Women Historians*.

61 Ibid.

62 "For the Ugly Girls," *Harper's Bazar*, Nov. 30, 1872.

63 "Our Women Growing Plump," *Harper's Bazar*, Aug. 4, 1877.

64 Ibid.

65 Ibid.

66 Ibid.

67 "The Fixed Facts of Beauty," *Harper's Bazar*, April 5, 1879.

68 Ibid.

69 "Standard of Beauty," *Harper's Bazar*, Feb. 8, 1879.

70 Sangster, *From My Youth Up*.

71 Edith Bigelow, "The Sorrows of the Fat," *Harper's Bazaar*, Apr. 3, 1897.

72 Ibid.

73 Ibid.

CHAPTER 6. THINNESS AS AMERICAN EXCEPTIONALISM

1 In practice, most race scientists would use one or the other of these terms. However, each term was intended to refer to Germanic-descendant northern Europeans. Indeed, by the early twentieth century in the United States, the terms were often used interchangeably. See Grant, *The Passing of the Great Race*.

2 American exceptionalism is the view that, as a nation of immigrants who tout Christian values and maintain ostensibly democratic principles, the United States is "exceptional" among nations. Byron Williams, "The Myth of American Excep-tionalism and the Uniqueness of America," *Huffington Post*, Dec. 27, 2015, www .huffingtonpost.com.

3 Edwin Anderson Alderman, Joel Chandler Harris, and Charles William Kent, *Library of Southern Literature: Biography* (Atlanta: Martin and Hoyt, 1910).

4 Ibid.

5 The *Cosmopolitan* was launched in 1886, but took on new life in 1889 under John Brisben Walker's headship. "Cosmopolitan Magazine," in *Encyclopedia Britannica*, last modified Aug. 17, 2017, www.britannica.com.

6 Gobineau, *The Inequality of Human Races*, 205.

7 Arendt, *The Origins of Totalitarianism*.

8 Ibid.

9 Gobineau, *The Inequality of Human Races*, 74.

10 U.S. Census Bureau, "Region and Country or Area of Birth of the Foreign-Born Population, with Geographic Detail Shown in Decennial Census Publications of 1930 or Earlier: 1850 to 1930 and 1960 to 1990," March 9, 1999, www.census.gov, accessed Jan. 22, 2018.

11 Sociologist Tomás Jiménez explains how high levels of immigration among Latinx populations contribute to the perception that persons from these groups are foreign-born. Jiménez, *Replenished Ethnicity*.

 Another way the Irish were able to assimilate was by supporting chattel slavery. As existing scholarship shows, this represented an effort to separate themselves from the Africans thought to be their racial peers. By maintaining an investment in black enslavement, Irish Catholics could establish a racial barrier between themselves and black Africans, and thus affirm that they were bona fide white Americans. By the late nineteenth century, the Irish in America had managed to distance themselves from black Americans. They had also amassed enough social, political, and economic resources to be better able to coexist with Anglo-Saxons in mainstream society. Ignatiev, *How the Irish Became White*; Roediger, *The Wages of Whiteness*.

12 Guglielmo, *White on Arrival*.

13 "An Indictment of Russia: The Great Empire Marching Back to Barbarism," *New York Times*, Sept. 14, 1891.

14 U.S. Immigration Commission, "Statistical Review of Immigration, 1820–1910," in *Reports of the Immigration Commission* (Washington, DC, 1913), 66–71.

15 Ibid.

16 The reasons for the outcry about "hybrid" immigrants appear to have been practical. Throughout the nineteenth century, between slavery and Jim Crow segregation (despite the brief respite brought by Reconstruction), black people were kept in an inferior social, political, and economic position. In this way, the fear of black sexuality remained, but the threat of (romantic or social) intercourse between white people and black people was at least mitigated by legal means. The real threat, for many eugenicists, was the hyper-breeding patterns of undesirable southern and eastern European immigrants, and potential unregulated inter-breeding between these peoples and northern European peoples.

17 "Undesirable Immigration," *New York Times*, June 21, 1884; "The Rush to America," *New York Times*, May 4, 1902.

18 Donaldson, *Varronianus*; Haddon, *The Natural History of Man*.

19 Alderman, Harris, and Kent, *Library of Southern Literature*.

20 Elizabeth Bisland, "Famous Beauties," *Cosmopolitan*, Jan. 1890.

21 Eleanor Waddle, "Side Glances at American Beauty," *Cosmopolitan*, June 1890.

22 Ibid.

23 Painter, *The History of White People*, 270.

24 Elizabeth Bisland, "The Cry of the Women," *North American Review* 158, no. 451 (1894): 757–59.

25 Brawley, *The White Peril*.

26 "Future Americans Will Be Swarthy," *New York Times*, Nov. 29, 1908.

27 Galton, *Inquiries into Human Faculty and Its Development*, 25.

28 Painter, *The History of White People*, 270.

29 LeBesco, "Quest for a Cause," 65–74.

30 He also reproduced notions of the relationship between race and weight that had been articulated by Frenchmen like Buffon over a century prior. Davenport claimed that "Nilotic negroes," or persons from northern Africa, were the "slenderest on earth." But of less interest to him than north or sub-Saharan Africans was the critical question of the vigor of build of the European races. Davenport, *Body Build and Its Inheritance*, 7.

31 Ibid., 7.

32 Ibid., 69.

33 Hecht, *The End of the Soul*.

34 Lapouge, "Old and New Aspects of the Aryan Question," 345–46.

35 Women represent the nation not only because of their reproductive capacity, but also owing to their visibility, historically, as "bodies." See Spelman, "Woman as Body"; Floya Anthias and Nira Yuval-Davis, eds., *Woman-Nation-State* (Basingstoke: Macmillan, 1989); McClintock, *Imperial Leather*; and Ranchod-Nilsson and Tétreault, *Women, States, and Nationalism*.

36 "Charles Dana Gibson, 1867–1944," National Museum of American Illustration, https://americanillustration.org, accessed Feb. 27, 2018.

37 In the 1890s, the "New Woman" was an educated and independent woman. In the context of debates about the "Woman Question," or what role women would have in society over the coming years, the New Woman—and the Gibson Girl as her artistic embodiment—was depicted as a Renaissance woman, ready to take on more of a visible role in the public sphere. *The Gibson Girl's America: Drawings by Charles Dana Gibson*, exhibition, Library of Congress, March 30, 2013, www.loc.gov.

38 The *Atlanta Constitution* is one of the longest-running, most-esteemed southern newspapers. I do not intend to use it here to represent the entire South. But it does represent an example of the evolution of representations of race and weight in at least one major southern market.

39 "Woman's Figure—Real and Ideal," *Atlanta Constitution*, Aug. 27, 1888, 5.

40 M.A.A., "Life in New York," *Atlanta Constitution*, May 20, 1888.

41 "The Highest Types of Our Southern Beauty," *Atlanta Constitution*, Oct. 13, 1895, 7.

42 Well into the 1930s in the South especially, women and men praised fleshy forms of the Venus type. Curvaceous beauty Lillian Russell maintained a regular syndicated column, "Lillian Russell's Beauty Secrets," which was originally published in the *Chicago Tribune*. Kershner, "Jim Kershner's This Day in History." In it, she often discussed the value of a fleshy form. Moreover, women seeking advice on how to gain flesh frequently wrote in to newspapers and magazines into the early twentieth century. Tara, *The Secret Life of Fat*.

43 To be sure, the South had long kept a racially Othered population, that of the black slaves. But black women in the South were rarely depicted in mainstream newspapers as a bona fide aesthetic threat to white women. The situation was wholly different for southern and eastern Europeans. Since they had no long-standing kinship ties to existing white families and also had a "hybrid"

or degraded white racial identity, their settlements in the region meant the possibility of unintentional race mixing and the degradation of proud Anglo-Saxon stock in the South.

44 "The Highest Types of Our Southern Beauty."
45 "Fads and Fashions," *Atlanta Constitution*, April 30, 1899.
46 "The Gibson Girl," *Atlanta Constitution*, Nov. 8, 1902.
47 "Gibson Girl Analyzed by Her Originator," *New York Times*, Nov. 20, 1910. It must have been with some confusion that he credited Israel Zangwill's play *The Melting Pot* with his claims of British ascendancy. Zangwill, who was born in London, was from a Russian Jewish family. His esteemed play rejects the kind of hierarchical thinking Gibson displays in this quote. He embraced the view that Celts, Slavs, Jews, Gentiles, blacks, and Asians could all live together in harmony.
48 "Gibson Girl Analyzed by Her Originator."
49 Data found from a ProQuest historical search, 1895–1920, July 4, 2016.
50 It is important to distinguish the artistic portrayals of the Gibson Girl from either the models he used or the real-life women who modeled themselves after his artwork. The models he used, one of whom was his own wife, Irene Langhorne, could be rather voluptuous. Women on the street who adopted the Gibson Girl aesthetic in terms of dress, hair piled high, and aristocratic bearing, came in a range of body sizes. Nevertheless, his images of the Gibson Girl cut a trim figure.
51 "American Beauty Analyzed by Artists," *New York Times*, Sept. 29, 1907.
52 "Harrison Fisher Discovered a New Type of Beauty; It's a Healthy, Full Blooded Out-of-Door Girl and He Found a New Model for It Out in California," *New York Times*, Jan. 22, 1911.
53 Quoted in "Our Girls Are Psycho-Eugenic," *New York Times*, Sept. 18, 1923.
54 Stearns, *Fat History*.

CHAPTER 7. GOOD HEALTH TO UPLIFT THE RACE

1 Per Michel Foucault, biopolitics is the politics of the state, often through the institution of medicine, informing its citizenry on "how to live." This includes how much they should eat, what they should eat, and how much they should exercise in order to optimize their healthful (read: productive) years. Ong, "Making the Biopolitical Subject"; Foucault, *The Essential Foucault*.
2 Wilson, *Dr. John Harvey Kellogg*; Markel, *The Kelloggs*.
3 Schwarz, *John Harvey Kellogg*; Wilson, *Dr. John Harvey Kellogg*.
4 Schwarz, *John Harvey Kellogg*, 10.
5 Wilson, *Dr. John Harvey Kellogg*, 20.
6 Iacobbo, "History of Vegetarianism."
7 John Noble Wilford, "Cholera Epidemic in New York City in 1832," *New York Times*, April 15, 2008, sec. Science, www.nytimes.com.
8 Wilson, *Dr. John Harvey Kellogg*.
9 Larson, "Revisiting Ellen White on Masturbation."
10 Wilson, *Dr. John Harvey Kellogg*.

11 John Harvey Kellogg Papers, Michigan State University Archives and Historical Collections, accessed Feb. 27, 2018, http://archives.msu.edu/.

12 Ibid.; Wilson, *Dr. John Harvey Kellogg*.

13 "Dr. John Harvey Kellogg—Inventor of Kellogg's Corn Flakes," University of Texas Health Science Center at San Antonio, last modified June 8, 2017, http://library .uthscsa.edu/.

14 Ibid.

15 Ibid.

16 Schwarz, *John Harvey Kellogg*; Wilson, *Dr. John Harvey Kellogg*.

17 Foucault recognized that frequently, Christian asceticism requires similar forms of "techniques of the self," or discipline required to meet the biopolitical exigencies of modern government, as does medicine. So it is not surprising that Kellogg, as both a Christian and a doctor, connected these two forms of "care for the self." Foucault, *Technologies of the Self*; Ong, "Making the Biopolitical Subject"; Foucault, *The Essential Foucault*.

18 Schwarz, *John Harvey Kellogg*, 35.

19 Wilson, *Dr. John Harvey Kellogg*.

20 Delbert W. Baker, "Black Seventh-day Adventists and the Influence of Ellen G. White," in *Perspectives: Black Seventh-day Adventists Face the Twenty-First Century*, ed. Calvin Rock (Hagerstown, MD: Review and Herald Publishing, 1996), 22; Ellen Gould Harmon White, *The Southern Work*, 20.

21 Wilson, *Dr. John Harvey Kellogg*, 214.

22 Ibid.

23 Kellogg, *Ladies' Guide in Health and Disease*.

24 Ibid.

25 Ibid., 231.

26 Ibid.

27 Ibid., 215.

28 Ibid.

29 Ibid., 142.

30 Ibid., 224.

31 Ibid.

32 Ibid., 169.

33 Tompkins, *Racial Indigestion*; Strings, "Obese Black Women as 'Social Dead Weight.'"

34 Kellogg, *Ladies' Guide in Health and Disease*, 392.

35 This is not to suggest there was no interest in black people, for, as shown above, even Kellogg spared a few words for them. Moreover, by the mid-twentieth century, sterilization campaigns came to target women of color, and black women in particular. Roberts, *Killing the Black Body*; Stern, *Eugenic Nation*. Here, as in the previous chapter, I am showing that a great deal of the eugenic language near the turn of the twentieth century in the United States revolved around building up the "superior" white race.

36 John Harvey Kellogg, "A Ban on Rum in the South: To Save the Negro from Bestiality the White Men of the Southern States Are Becoming Sober Themselves," *Good Health* 42 (1907): 522. For Kellogg's writings on vegetarianism, see, e.g., "The Absolute Vegetarian Diet of Japanese Monks," *Good Health* 56, no. 1 (1921): 364.

37 Wilson, *Dr. John Harvey Kellogg.*

38 Schwarz, *John Harvey Kellogg.*

39 Fee and Brown, "John Harvey Kellogg"; Schwarz, *John Harvey Kellogg.*

40 Starr, *The Social Transformation of American Medicine.*

41 John Harvey Kellogg, "Oxygen Enemata as a Remedy in Certain Diseases of the Liver and Intestinal Tract," *Journal of the American Medical Association* 11, no. 8 (1888): 258–62.

42 Kellogg, "Relation of Public Health to Race Degeneracy," 649.

43 Ibid., 650.

44 Ibid.

45 Ibid., 658.

46 Ibid., 654.

47 Fishbein and Rose, *Your Weight and How to Control It*, vii.

48 Ibid., xiii.

49 Ibid., 27.

50 Ibid., 24.

51 Ibid., 23.

52 "John Harvey Kellogg," in *Dictionary of American Biography*, Supplement 3, *1941–1945*, 1973, American Council of Learned Societies, www.galenet.com, accessed Dec. 15, 2000.

CHAPTER 8. FAT, REVISITED

1 Fishbein and Rose, *Your Weight and How to Control It*, x.

2 Ibid., xi.

3 Starr, *The Social Transformation of American Medicine.*

4 Brumberg, *Fasting Girls.*

5 Ibid., 230.

6 Komaroff, "For Researchers on Obesity." The term "overweight" had existed since the seventeenth century in England. But beginning in 1917, it would be synonymous with "obesity," which is considered a disease. See *Collins English Dictionary*, 10th ed., s.v. "overweight," accessed Sept. 13, 2017, www.dictionary .com.

7 I. S. Falk, "Louis I. Dublin, November 1, 1882–March 7, 1969," *American Journal of Public Health and the Nations Health* 59, no. 7 (1969): 1083–85.

8 Brumberg, *Fasting Girls*, 231.

9 Björn Lantz, "The Large Sample Size Fallacy," *Scandinavian Journal of Caring Sciences* 27, no. 2 (2013): 487–92.

10 Fishbein and Rose, *Your Weight and How to Control It.*

11 Size 16 might have been about the size one would expect a sixteen-year-old to wear. Laura Stampler, "When—and Why—We Started Measuring Women's Clothing," *Time*, Oct. 23, 2014, time.com.

12 Fishbein and Rose, *Your Weight and How to Control It*, viii.

13 For the evolution of these tables and their centrality within the medical field, see Komaroff, "For Researchers on Obesity."

14 These data are based on my searches of the *JAMA* archive on Sept. 14, 2017. I limited my search only to articles in the main publishing venue, excluding articles in offshoots (e.g., *JAMA Dermatology*), each of which was created after 1883, and therefore would affect the standardization of the search.

15 Treon, "Medical Work among the Sioux Indians."

16 Ibid.

17 "The Female Athlete," *Journal of the American Medical Association* 35, no. 18 (Nov. 3, 1900): 1160.

18 Ibid.

19 "Food and Obesity," *Journal of the American Medical Association* 70, no. 10 (March 9, 1918): 694–95.

20 Peters, *Diet and Health*.

21 Ibid.

22 "Diet and Health with Key to the Calories," *Journal of the American Medical Association* 71, no. 12 (Sept. 21, 1918): 999.

23 William R. P. Emerson and Frank A. Manny, "Underweight and Overweight in Relation to Vitality," *Journal of the American Medical Association* 93, no. 6 (Aug. 10, 1929): 457.

24 Ibid.

25 Ibid.

26 This is what scientists today refer to as "confirmation bias," or the tendency to interpret data in ways that confirm preexisting hypotheses.

27 Elliott P. Joslin, "The Prevention of Diabetes Mellitus," *Journal of the American Medical Association* 76, no. 2 (Jan. 8, 1921): 79–84.

28 Ibid., 82.

29 John V. Gaff, "Obesity as a Cause of Sterility," *Journal of the American Medical Association* 28, no. 4 (Jan. 23, 1897): 166–68.

30 A. W. Sherman, "Thyroid Feeding in Obesity," *Journal of the American Medical Association* 34, no. 12 (March 24, 1900): 728–30.

31 Ibid.

32 Willard J. Stone, "Dietary Facts, Fads and Fancies," *Journal of the American Medical Association* 95, no. 10 (Sept. 6, 1930): 714.

33 Ibid.

34 Ehrenreich, *Complaints and Disorders*.

35 In this study, the average weights of women in 1885–1908 and 1955 were compared. While the weights of women in the intervening years were not presented, there is no evidence that weight jumped after 1908, only to fall by 1955. See

Milicent L. Hathaway, "Trends in Heights and Weights," in *Yearbook of Agriculture* (Washington DC: U.S. Government Printing Office, 1959), 53–58.

36 As it pertained to black people, the medical lacuna in terms of the etiology of illness among African Americans had been noted by W. E. B. Du Bois as early as 1899. By 1915, Booker T. Washington had begun a comprehensive campaign for public health among the black population, which was ultimately adopted by the U.S. Health Service in 1932 as part of its new Office of Negro Health. Thomas et al., "Historical and Current Policy Efforts."

37 Henry M. Friedman, "Muscular Development, the Causes for the Lack of It and the Value of Physical Exercise," *Journal of the American Medical Association* 58, no. 10 (March 9, 1912): 685–89.

38 Ibid.

39 Ibid.

40 Elliott P. Joslin, "The Diabetic Problem of Today," *Journal of the American Medical Association* 83, no. 10 (Sept. 6, 1924): 727–29.

41 Ibid.

42 Gilman, *Diets and Dieting*.

43 Joslin, "The Diabetic Problem of Today."

44 N. W. Winkelman and John L. Eckel, "Adiposis Dolorosa (Dercum's Disease): A Clinicopathologic Study," *Journal of the American Medical Association* 85, no. 25 (1925): 1935–39.

45 Bennett, Goldfinger, and Johnson, *Your Good Health*.

46 Brumberg, *Fasting Girls*.

47 "Ancel Keys," biographical sketch, Heart Attack Prevention, University of Minnesota, www.epi.umn.edu, accessed Sept. 25, 2017.

48 Henry Blackburn and David Jacobs, "Commentary: Origins and Evolution of Body Mass Index (BMI): Continuing Saga," *International Journal of Epidemiology* 43, no. 1 (April 1, 2014): 665–69.

49 Ibid.

50 Keys, "Coronary Heart Disease," 149–92; Blackburn and Jacobs, "Commentary."

51 Vanessa Heggie, "Body Mass Index: The Dieters' Bogeyman Discovered by a Belgian Astronomer-Mathematician," *Guardian*, last modified Jan. 16, 2014, www.theguardian.com.

52 Blackburn and Jacobs, "Commentary."

53 Ibid.

54 Chrisman and Maretzki, *Clinically Applied Anthropology*, 60.

55 Ibid., 160–61.

56 Komaroff, "For Researchers on Obesity."

57 Ibid.

58 Ibid.

59 Ibid., 7.

60 "U.S. to Widen Its Definition of Who Is Fat," *New York Times*, June 4, 1998, www.nytimes.com.

61 National Center for Health Statistics, "Health, United States, 1983; Prevention and Profile" (Washington, DC: U.S. Government Printing Office, 1983).

62 Thomas et al., "Historical and Current Policy Efforts."

63 Ibid., 326.

64 Ibid.

65 Boero, *Killer Fat*.

66 Ibid., 21.

67 Ibid.

68 Flegal et al., "Prevalence and Trends in Obesity among U.S. Adults."

69 Wagner and Heyward, "Measures of Body Composition in Blacks and Whites."

70 Fontaine et al., "Years of Life Lost Due to Obesity"; Campos, *The Obesity Myth*.

71 Sindya Bhanoo, "Study Suggests BMI Scale Is Weighted against African Americans," *Washington Post*, April 14, 2009, www.washingtonpost.com; Jessica Firger, "There's a Dangerous Racial Bias in the Body Mass Index," *Newsweek*, May 17, 2017, www.newsweek.com.

EPILOGUE

1 Rachel Auerbach, "Obesity Kills More Americans Than We Thought," CNN, Aug. 15, 2013, sec. The Chart, thechart.blogs.cnn.com; Ryan K. Masters, Eric N. Reither, Daniel A. Powers, Y. Claire Yang, Andrew E. Burger, and Bruce G. Link, "The Impact of Obesity on U.S. Mortality Levels: The Importance of Age and Cohort Factors in Population Estimates," *American Journal of Public Health* 103, no. 10 (2013): 1895–1901.

2 U.S. Department of Health and Human Services, Office of Minority Health, "Obesity and African Americans."

3 Kumanyika, "Obesity in Black Women"; Averett and Korenman, "Black-White Differences in Social and Economic Consequences of Obesity"; Fontaine et al., "Years of Life Lost Due to Obesity"; Campos, *The Obesity Myth*; Moreno et al., "Prevalence of Overweight and Obesity in Asian American Students."

4 See Auerbach, "Obesity Kills More Americans Than We Thought"; Maggie Fox, "Heavy Burden: Obesity May Be Even Deadlier Than Thought," NBCnews.com, Aug. 15, 2013; "Report: Obesity Kills More Americans Than Previously Thought," Fox News TV broadcast, Aug. 16, 2013.

5 Ibid.

6 Katherine M. Flegal, Brian K. Kit, Heather Orpana, and Barry I. Graubard, "Association of All-Cause Mortality with Overweight and Obesity Using Standard Body Mass Index Categories: A Systematic Review and Meta-Analysis," *Journal of the American Medical Association* 309, no. 1 (2013): 71–82.

7 Doehner, "Overweight, Obesity, and All-Cause Mortality."

8 Abhyankar and McDonald, "Overweight, Obesity, and All-Cause Mortality."

9 Allison Aubrey, "Research: A Little Extra Fat May Help You Live Longer," NPR, Jan. 2, 2013, www.npr.org.

10 Hughes, "The Big Fat Truth."

11 Ibid.

12 Ibid.

13 See Flegal's citation profile at scholar.google.com.

14 Lowe, *Immigrant Acts.*

15 Spelman, "Woman as Body"; Campos et al., "The Epidemiology of Overweight and Obesity."

16 Bourdieu, *Distinction*, 185.

17 Foucault, *Technologies of the Self.*

18 Ong, "Making the Biopolitical Subject."

19 Deborah Gray White, *Too Heavy a Load*; Hine and Thompson, *A Shining Thread of Hope.*

20 Maxine Leeds Craig, *Ain't I a Beauty Queen?*

21 Gilman, "Black Bodies, White Bodies"; hooks, *Black Looks*; Hobson, "The 'Batty' Politic"; Shaw, *The Embodiment of Disobedience.*

22 Further research is needed to establish the extent to which white immigrant women, demonized for their purported association to blackness, were aware of the fat phobia by which they had been interpellated.

23 Chernin, "The Tyranny of Slenderness"; Wolf, *The Beauty Myth*; Stearns, *Fat History.*

SELECTED BIBLIOGRAPHY

Abhyankar, S., and C. J. McDonald. "Overweight, Obesity, and All-Cause Mortality." *Journal of the American Medical Association* 309, no. 16 (April 24, 2013): 1680–81. doi.org/10.1001/jama.2013.3092.

Addison, Joseph, and Sir Richard Steele. *The Spectator: No. 170–251; Sept. 14, 1711–Dec. 18, 1711.* John C. Nimmo, 1898.

Alcott, William. *The Young Woman's Book of Health.* New York: Miller Orton and Mulligan, 1855.

Anderson, Benedict. *Imagined Communities: Reflections on the Origin and Spread of Nationalism.* Rev. ed. London: Verso, 1991.

Arendt, Hannah. *The Origins of Totalitarianism.* New ed. New York: Harcourt Brace Jovanovich, 1973.

Ashcroft, Bill, Gareth Griffiths, and Helen Tiffin. *Post-Colonial Studies: The Key Concepts.* New York: Routledge, 2003.

Averett, S., and S. Korenman. "Black-White Differences in Social and Economic Consequences of Obesity." *International Journal of Obesity* 23, no. 2 (Feb. 25, 1999): 166–73. doi.org/10.1038/sj.ijo.0800805.

Back, Les, and John Solomos, eds. *Theories of Race and Racism: A Reader.* London: Routledge, 2000.

Baddam. *Memoirs of the Royal Society, or A New Abridgment of the Philosophical Transactions from 1665 to 1740.* 1745.

Baker, John R. *Race.* New York: Oxford University Press, 1974.

Bancel, Nicolas, Thomas David, and Dominic Thomas, eds. *The Invention of Race: Scientific and Popular Representations.* New York: Routledge, 2014.

Banton, Michael P. *Racial Theories.* Cambridge: Cambridge University Press, 1987.

Bartky, Sandra Lee. "Foucault, Femininity, and the Modernization of Patriarchal Power." In *Writing on the Body: Female Embodiment and Feminist Theory,* edited by Katie Conboy, Nadia Medina, and Sarah Stanbury, 129–54. New York: Columbia University Press, 1997.

Beaumont, Sir Harry. *Crito, or A Dialogue on Beauty.* Edinburgh: E. and G. Goldsmid, 1885. http://hdl.handle.net.

Beliles, Mark A., and Jerry Newcombe. *Doubting Thomas: The Religious Life and Legacy of Thomas Jefferson.* New York: Morgan James, 2014.

Bennett, William, Stephen E. Goldfinger, and G. Timothy Johnson. *Your Good Health: How to Stay Well, and What to Do When You're Not.* Cambridge: Harvard University Press, 1987.

Bernier, François. "A New Division of the Earth." *History Workshop Journal*, no. 51 (April 1, 2001): 247–50. doi.org/10.2307/4289731.

———. *Travels in the Mogul Empire, A.D. 1656–1668*. Archibald Constable, 1916.

Bindman, David. *Ape to Apollo: Aesthetics and the Idea of Race in the 18th Century*. New York: Cornell University Press, 2002.

Bindman, David, Henry Louis Gates Jr., and Karen C. C. Dalton, eds. *The Image of the Black in Western Art*, vol. 3, *From the "Age of Discovery" to the Age of Abolition*, part 1, *Artists of the Renaissance and Baroque*. Cambridge: Belknap, 2010.

Black, Jeremy. *The Atlantic Slave Trade in World History*. New York: Routledge, 2015.

Blumin, Stuart M. *The Emergence of the Middle Class: Social Experience in the American City, 1760–1900*. Cambridge: Cambridge University Press, 1989.

Boemus, Johannes. *The Fardle of Facions*. Trans. William Waterman. New York: Da Capo, 1970. Originally published 1555.

Boero, Natalie. *Killer Fat: Media, Medicine, and Morals in the American "Obesity Epidemic."* New Brunswick: Rutgers University Press, 2012.

Bondeson, Jan. *The Two-Headed Boy, and Other Medical Marvels*. Ithaca: Cornell University Press, 2004.

Booth, Alison. *How to Make It as a Woman: Collective Biographical History from Victoria to the Present*. Chicago: University of Chicago Press, 2004.

Bordo, Susan. *Unbearable Weight: Feminism, Western Culture, and the Body*. Berkeley: University of California Press, 1995.

Boulle, Pierre H. "François Bernier and the Origins of the Modern Concept of Race." In *The Color of Liberty: Histories of Race in France*, edited by Sue Peabody and Tyler Stovall, 11–27. Durham: Duke University Press, 2003.

Bourdieu, Pierre. *Distinction: A Social Critique of the Judgement of Taste*. Cambridge: Harvard University Press, 1984.

———. "The Forms of Capital." In *Handbook of Theory and Research for the Sociology of Education*, edited by John G. Richardson. Westport, CT: Greenwood, 1986.

Brawley, Sean. *The White Peril: Foreign Relations and Asian Immigration to Australasia and North America, 1919–1978*. Sydney, Australia: UNSW Press, 1995.

Braziel, Jana Evans, and Kathleen LeBesco. *Bodies Out of Bounds: Fatness and Transgression*. Berkeley: University of California Press, 2001.

Brewer, D. S. "The Ideal of Feminine Beauty in Medieval Literature, Especially 'Harley Lyrics,' Chaucer, and Some Elizabethans." *Modern Language Review* 50, no. 3 (July 1, 1955): 257–69. doi.org/10.2307/3719759.

Brumberg, Joan Jacobs. *Fasting Girls: The Emergence of Anorexia Nervosa as a Modern Disease*. Cambridge: Harvard University Press, 1988.

Buffon, comte de (Georges Louis Leclerc). *Buffon's Natural History: Containing a Theory of the Earth, a General History of Man, of the Brute Creation, and of Vegetables, Minerals, &c. &c.* 1797.

Campos, Paul F. *The Obesity Myth: Why America's Obsession with Weight Is Hazardous to Your Health*. New York: Gotham Books, 2004.

Carlyle, Thomas. *Occasional Discourse on the Negro Question*. J. Fraser, 1849.

——. *The Sayings of Thomas Carlyle*. Edited by Brendan King. Lulu.com, 1993.

Castiglione, Baldassare. *The Book of the Courtier*. New York: Scribner's, 1903.

Chaudhri, S. K., and N. K. Jain. "History of Cosmetics." *Asian Journal of Pharmaceutics* 3, no. 3 (2009): 164–67.

Chernin, Kim. "The Tyranny of Slenderness." In *Race, Class, and Gender in the United States*, ed. Paula S. Rothenberg, 238–45. New York: Worth, 1981.

Cheyne, George. *The English Malady*. Edited by Roy Porter. New York: Routledge, 2013.

——. *The Letters of Dr. George Cheyne to the Countess of Huntingdon*. San Marino, CA: Huntington Library, 1940.

Chrisman, N., and T. Maretzki, eds. *Clinically Applied Anthropology: Anthropologists in Health Science Settings*. Dordrecht, Holland: Springer Science and Business Media, 2012.

Clark, Samuel. *State and Status: The Rise of the State and Aristocratic Power in Western Europe*. Kingston, Canada: McGill-Queen's University Press, 1995.

Clarke, Adele. "Women's Health: Life-Cycle Issues." In *Women, Health and Medicine in America: A Historical Handbook*, edited by Rima D. Apple, 3–40. New York: Garland, 1990.

Craig, Edward, ed. *Routledge Encyclopedia of Philosophy: Index*. New York: Taylor and Francis, 1998.

Craig, Maxine Leeds. *Ain't I a Beauty Queen? Black Women, Beauty, and the Politics of Race*. New York: Oxford University Press, 2002.

Crais, Clifton C., and Pamela Scully. *Sara Baartman and the Hottentot Venus: A Ghost Story and a Biography*. Princeton: Princeton University Press, 2009.

Crowe, J. A. *Titian: His Life and Times; With Some Account of His Family*. 2d ed. London, 1881. http://hdl.handle.net.

Curran, Andrew S. *The Anatomy of Blackness: Science and Slavery in an Age of Enlightenment*. Baltimore: Johns Hopkins University Press, 2011.

Cuvier, Georges. "Femme de race Boschismanne." In *Histoire naturelle des mammifères*, edited by Etienne Geoffroy Saint-Hillaire and Frederic Cuvier. Paris, 1824.

Dalton, Karen C. "The Black Emperor in the Drake Jewel and Elizabethan Imperial Imagery." In *Early Modern Visual Culture: Representation, Race and Empire in Renaissance England*, edited by Peter Erickson and Clark Hulse. Philadelphia: University of Pennsylvania Press, 2000.

Davenport, Charles Benedict. *Body Build and Its Inheritance*. Washington, DC: Carnegie Institute of Washington, 1923.

Derrida, Jacques. *Margins of Philosophy*. Chicago: University of Chicago Press, 1982.

Doehner, W. "Overweight, Obesity, and All-Cause Mortality." *Journal of the American Medical Association* 309, no. 16 (April 24, 2013): 1679–80. doi.org/10.1001/jama.2013.3083.

Donaldson, John William. *Varronianus: A Critical and Historical Introduction to the Ethnography of Ancient Italy and to the Philological Study of the Latin Language*. J. W. Parker and Son, 1860.

Dubois, Laurent. "Inscribing Race in the Revolutionary French Antilles." In *The Color of Liberty: Histories of Race in France*, edited by Sue Peabody and Tyler Stovall. Durham: Duke University Press, 2003.

Dürer, Albrecht. *The Writings of Albrecht Dürer*. New York: Philosophical Library, 1958.

Earle, T. F., and K. J. P. Lowe, eds. *Black Africans in Renaissance Europe*. Reissue ed. New York: Cambridge University Press, 2010.

Eco, Umberto, ed. *History of Beauty*. Translated by Alastair McEwen. New York: Rizzoli, 2010.

Ehrenreich, Barbara. *Complaints and Disorders: The Sexual Politics of Sickness*. Old Westbury, NY: Feminist Press, 1973.

Eliav-Feldon, Miriam, Benjamin Isaac, and Joseph Ziegler, eds. *The Origins of Racism in the West*. Cambridge: Cambridge University Press, 2009.

Emerson, Ralph Waldo. *English Traits: A Portrait of 19th Century England*. Boston: Phillips, Sampson, and Co., 1856.

———. *Journals and Miscellaneous Notebooks, 1832–1834*. Cambridge: Belknap, 1964.

Endres, Kathleen L., and Therese L. Lueck, eds. *Women's Periodicals in the United States: Consumer Magazines*. Westport, CT: Greenwood, 1995.

Erickson, Peter. "Representations of Blacks and Blackness in the Renaissance." *Criticism* 35, no. 4 (Oct. 1, 1993): 499–527.

Estill, Laura. "Proverbial Shakespeare: The Print and Manuscript Circulation of Extracts from *Love's Labour's Lost*." *Shakespeare* 7, no. 1 (April 1, 2011): 35–55.

Farrell, Amy Erdman. *Fat Shame: Stigma and the Fat Body in American Culture*. New York: New York University Press, 2011.

Fee, Elizabeth, and Theodore M. Brown. "John Harvey Kellogg, MD: Health Reformer and Antismoking Crusader." *American Journal of Public Health* 92, no. 6 (June 2002): 935.

Fields, Karen, and Barbara J. Fields. *Racecraft: The Soul of Inequality in American Life*. London: Verso, 2012.

Firenzuola, Agnolo. *On the Beauty of Women*. Translated by Konrad Eisenbichler and Jacqueline Murray. Philadelphia: University of Pennsylvania Press, 1992.

Fishbein, Morris, and Flora Rose, eds. *Your Weight and How to Control It: A Scientific Guide by Medical Specialists and Dieticians*. New York: George H. Doran, 1927.

Flegal, K. M., M. D. Carroll, C. L. Ogden, and C. L. Johnson. "Prevalence and Trends in Obesity among U.S. Adults, 1999–2000." *Journal of the American Medical Association* 288, no. 14 (Oct. 9, 2002): 1723–27. doi.org/10.1001/jama.288.14.1723.

Fletcher, Holly Berkley. *Gender and the American Temperance Movement of the Nineteenth Century*. New York: Routledge, 2007.

Fontaine, K. R., D. T. Redden, C. Wang, A. O. Westfall, and D. B. Allison. "Years of Life Lost Due to Obesity." *Journal of the American Medical Association* 289, no. 2 (Jan. 8, 2003): 187–93.

Foucault, Michel. *The Birth of the Clinic*. New York: Routledge, 2012.

———. *Discipline and Punish: The Birth of the Prison*. New York: Vintage, 1977.

———. *The Essential Foucault: Selections from Essential Works of Foucault, 1954–1984.* Edited by Paul Rabinow and Nikolas S Rose. New York: New Press, 2003.

———. *Technologies of the Self: A Seminar with Michel Foucault.* Amherst: University of Massachusetts Press, 1988.

Fowler, James. *New Essays on Diderot.* Cambridge: Cambridge University Press, 2011.

Fredrickson, George M. *Racism: A Short History.* Princeton: Princeton University Press, 2003.

French, Laurence Armand. *Frog Town: Portrait of a French Canadian Parish in New England.* Lanham, MD: University Press of America, 2014.

Fryer, Peter. *Staying Power: The History of Black People in Britain.* London: Pluto, 1984.

Galton, Francis. *Inquiries into Human Faculty and Its Development.* London: Macmillan, 1883.

Gikandi, Simon. *Slavery and the Culture of Taste.* Princeton: Princeton University Press, 2011.

Gilman, Sander L. "Black Bodies, White Bodies: Toward an Iconography of Female Sexuality in Late Nineteenth-Century Art, Medicine, and Literature." *Critical Inquiry* 12, no. 1 (Oct. 1, 1985): 204–42.

———. *Diets and Dieting: A Cultural Encyclopedia.* New York: Routledge, 2008.

———. *Difference and Pathology: Stereotypes of Sexuality, Race, and Madness.* Ithaca: Cornell University Press, 1985.

———. *Fat Boys: A Slim Book.* Lincoln: University of Nebraska Press, 2004.

———. *Obesity: The Biography.* Oxford: Oxford University Press, 2010.

Gobineau, Arthur. *The Inequality of Human Races.* New York: Putnam's, 1915.

Gossett, Thomas F. *Race: The History of an Idea in America.* New York: Oxford University Press, 1997.

Grant, Madison. *The Passing of the Great Race, or The Racial Basis of European History.* New York: Scribner's, 1922.

Griffith, R. Marie. *Born Again Bodies: Flesh and Spirit in American Christianity.* Berkeley: University of California Press, 2004.

Guerrini, Anita. "The Hungry Soul: George Cheyne and the Construction of Femininity." *Eighteenth-Century Studies* 32, no. 3 (1999): 279–91.

———. *Obesity and Depression in the Enlightenment: The Life and Times of George Cheyne.* Norman: University of Oklahoma Press, 2000.

Guglielmo, Thomas A. *White on Arrival: Italians, Race, Color, and Power in Chicago, 1890–1945.* New York: Oxford University Press, 2003.

Haddon, Alfred. *The Natural History of Man: Syllabus of a Course of Five Lectures on the Geographical Distribution of Man.* 1904.

Hale, Sarah Josepha Buell. *Ladies' Magazine.* Putnam and Hunt, 1828.

———. *The Ladies' Wreath: A Selection from the Female Poetic Writers of England and America, With Original Notices and Notes, Prepared Especially for Young Ladies; A Gift Book for All Seasons.* Marsh, Capen and Lyon, 1837.

Hall, Catherine, ed. *Cultures of Empire: Colonizers in Britain and the Empire in the Nineteenth and Twentieth Centuries; A Reader.* New York: Routledge, 2000.

Hall, Kim F. *Things of Darkness: Economies of Race and Gender in Early Modern England*. Ithaca: Cornell University Press, 1995.

Hannaford, Ivan. *Race: The History of an Idea in the West*. Washington, DC: Woodrow Wilson Center Press, 1996.

Hecht, Jennifer. *The End of the Soul: Scientific Modernity, Atheism, and Anthropology in France*. New York: Columbia University Press, 2012.

Hine, Darlene Clark, and Kathleen Thompson. *A Shining Thread of Hope*. New York: Crown Archetype Books, 2009.

Hobson, Janell. "The 'Batty' Politic: Toward an Aesthetic of the Black Female Body." *Hypatia* 18, no. 4 (2003): 87–105.

hooks, bell. *Black Looks: Race and Representation*. Boston: South End, 1992.

Hughes, Virginia. "The Big Fat Truth." *Nature* 497, no. 7450 (May 22, 2013): 428–30. doi.org/10.1038/497428a.

Iacobbo, Karen. "History of Vegetarianism—Rev. William Metcalfe (1788–1862)." 2000. International Vegetarian Union. https://ivu.org.

Ignatiev, Noel. *How the Irish Became White*. New York: Routledge, 1995.

Israel, Jonathan I. *The Dutch Republic: Its Rise, Greatness and Fall, 1477–1806*. Oxford: Clarendon, 1995.

Iyengar, Sujata. *Shades of Difference: Mythologies of Skin Color in Early Modern England*. Philadelphia: University of Pennsylvania Press, 2013.

Jiménez, Tomás Roberto. *Replenished Ethnicity: Mexican Americans, Immigration, and Identity*. Berkeley: University of California Press, 2010.

Jones, Robert W. *Gender and the Formation of Taste in Eighteenth-Century Britain: The Analysis of Beauty*. Cambridge: Cambridge University Press, 1998.

Kearns, Edward John. *Ideas in Seventeenth-Century France: The Most Important Thinkers and the Climate of Ideas in Which They Worked*. Manchester, UK: Manchester University Press, 1982.

Kellogg, John Harvey. *Ladies' Guide in Health and Disease: Girlhood, Maidenhood, Wifehood, Motherhood*. Battle Creek, MI: Good Health Publishing, 1891.

———. "Relation of Public Health to Race Degeneracy." *American Journal of Public Health* 4, no. 8 (1914): 649–63.

Kershner, Jim. "Jim Kershner's This Day in History." Aug. 21, 2012. www.spokesman.com.

Klein, Herbert S. *The Atlantic Slave Trade*. Cambridge: Cambridge University Press, 1999.

Klein, Richard. "Fat Beauty." In *Bodies Out of Bounds: Fatness and Transgression*, edited by Jana Evans Braziel and Kathleen LeBesco, 19–38. Berkeley: University of California Press, 2001.

Kline, Anthony S., trans. "Ovid's Metamorphoses." 2000. http://ovid.lib.virginia.edu.

Kolbert, Elizabeth. *The Sixth Extinction: An Unnatural History*. New York: Henry Holt, 2014.

Komaroff, Marina. "For Researchers on Obesity: Historical Review of Extra Body Weight Definitions." *Journal of Obesity*, 2016.

Kumanyika, S. "Obesity in Black Women." *Epidemiologic Reviews* 9 (1987): 31–50.

Lamont, Michele, and Annette Lareau. "Cultural Capital: Allusions, Gaps and Glissandos in Recent Theoretical Developments." *Sociological Theory* 6, no. 2 (Oct. 1, 1988): 153–68. doi.org/10.2307/202113.

Lamster, Mark. "The Art of Diplomacy." *Wall Street Journal*, Oct. 10, 2009, sec. Life and Style.

———. *Master of Shadows: The Secret Diplomatic Career of the Painter Peter Paul Rubens*. New York: Knopf Doubleday, 2009.

Lapouge, Georges Vacher de. "Old and New Aspects of the Aryan Question." *American Journal of Sociology* 5, no. 3 (Nov. 1, 1899): 329–46.

Larson, David. "Revisiting Ellen White on Masturbation." *Spectrum*, Aug. 6, 2008. https://spectrummagazine.org.

Lathers, Marie. *Bodies of Art: French Literary Realism and the Artist's Model*. Lincoln: University of Nebraska Press, 2001.

LeBesco, Kathleen. "Quest for a Cause: The Fat Gene, the Gay Gene, and the New Eugenics." In *The Fat Studies Reader*, edited by Esther Rothblum, 65–74. New York: New York University Press, 2009.

Lerner, Gerda. *The Creation of Feminist Consciousness: From the Middle Ages to Eighteen-Seventy*. Oxford: Oxford University Press, 1993.

———. *The Creation of Patriarchy*. New York: Oxford University Press, 1987.

Lindley, Susan Hill. *You Have Stept Out of Your Place: A History of Women and Religion in America*. Louisville, KY: Westminster John Knox Press, 1996.

Long, Edward. *The History of Jamaica, or General Survey of the Antient and Modern State of That Island*. London: T. Lowndes, 1774.

Lowe, Lisa. *Immigrant Acts: On Asian American Cultural Politics*. Durham: Duke University Press, 1996.

Lowenthal, Cynthia J. *Lady Mary Wortley Montagu and the Eighteenth-Century Familiar Letter*. Athens: University of Georgia Press, 2010.

Madsen, Axel. *Chanel: A Woman of Her Own*. New York: Open Road Media, 2015.

Manton, Catherine. *Fed Up: Women and Food in America*. Westport, CT: Praeger, 1999.

Mark, Peter. *Africans in European Eyes: The Portrayal of Black Africans in Fourteenth and Fifteenth Century Europe*. Syracuse, NY: Maxwell School of Citizenship and Public Affairs, Syracuse University, 1974.

Markel, Howard. *The Kelloggs: The Battling Brothers of Battle Creek*. New York: Knopf Doubleday, 2017.

Marshall, Wallace W. *Puritanism and Natural Theology*. Eugene, OR: Wipf and Stock, 2016.

Martin, Kirsty. *Modernism and the Rhythms of Sympathy: Vernon Lee, Virginia Woolf, D. H. Lawrence*. Oxford: Oxford University Press, 2013.

Marwick, Arthur. *It: A History of Human Beauty*. London: A. and C. Black, 2004.

McAteer, John. "Third Earl of Shaftesbury." In *Internet Encyclopedia of Philosophy*. www.iep.utm.edu. Accessed March 28, 2016.

McClintock, Anne. *Imperial Leather: Race, Gender, and Sexuality in the Colonial Contest*. New York: Routledge, 1995.

McCue, Margi Laird. *Domestic Violence: A Reference Handbook*. Santa Barbara, CA: ABC-CLIO, 2008.

Merians, Linda Evi. *Envisioning the Worst: Representations of "Hottentots" in Early-Modern England*. Newark: University of Delaware Press, 2001.

Moffet, Thomas, Robert James, and William Oldys. *Health's Improvement, or Rules Comprizing and Discovering the Nature, Method and Manner of Preparing All Sorts of Foods Used in This Nation*. T. Osborne, 1746.

Montagu, Mary Wortley. *Lady Mary Wortley Montagu: Select Passages from Her Letters*. Seeley, 1908.

———. *The Letters of Lady Mary Wortley Montagu*. Edited by Sarah Josepha Buell Hale. Mason Brothers, 1856.

Moreno, Jennette, Craig Johnston, Sarah Aimadeddine, and Deborah Whoeler. "Prevalence of Overweight and Obesity in Asian American Students Using Asian Specific Criteria to Determine Weight Classification." *International Journal of Exercise Science: Conference Proceedings* 2, no. 5 (Feb. 27, 2013). http://digital commons.wku.edu.

Morgan, Jennifer L. "'Some Could Suckle over Their Shoulder': Male Travelers, Female Bodies, and the Gendering of Racial Ideology, 1500–1770." *William and Mary Quarterly*, 3rd ser., 54, no. 1 (Jan. 1, 1997): 167–92.

Morrison, Toni. *Playing in the Dark*. New York: Knopf Doubleday, 2007.

Murray, Jacqueline. "Agnolo Firenzuola on Female Sexuality and Women's Equality." *Sixteenth Century Journal* 22, no. 2 (July 1, 1991): 199–213.

Ness, Immanuel, ed. *Encyclopedia of American Social Movements*. New York: Routledge, 2015.

Okker, Patricia. *Our Sister Editors: Sarah J. Hale and the Tradition of Nineteenth-Century American Women Editors*. Athens: University of Georgia Press, 2008.

Omi, Michael, and Howard Winant. *Racial Formation in the United States: From the 1960s to the 1990s*. New York: Psychology Press, 1994.

Ong, Aihwa. "Making the Biopolitical Subject: Cambodian Immigrants, Refugee Medicine and Cultural Citizenship in California." *Social Science and Medicine* 40, no. 9 (May 1995): 1243–57. doi.org/10.1016/0277-9536(94)00230-Q.

Orbach, Susie. *Hunger Strike: Anorexia as a Metaphor for Our Time*. New York: Norton, 1986.

Pagliaro, Harold, ed. *Racism in the Eighteenth Century*. Cleveland: Press of Case Western Reserve University, 1973.

Painter, Nell Irvin. *The History of White People*. New York: Norton, 2010.

Peabody, Sue. *"There Are No Slaves in France": The Political Culture of Race and Slavery in the Ancien Régime*. Oxford: Oxford University Press, 1996.

Peabody, Sue, and Tyler Stovall, eds. *The Color of Liberty: Histories of Race in France*. Durham: Duke University Press, 2003.

Perl, Jed. *Antoine's Alphabet*. New York: Knopf Doubleday, 2008.

Peters, Lulu Hunt. *Diet and Health: With Key to the Calories*. Chicago: Reilly and Britton, 1918.

Pinder, Sherrow O. *Whiteness and Racialized Ethnic Groups in the United States: The Politics of Remembering*. Lanham, MD: Lexington Books, 2012.

Porter, Roy. *Flesh in the Age of Reason: The Modern Foundations of Body and Soul*. New York: Norton, 2005.

Postle, Martin. *Thomas Gainsborough*. Mustang, OK: Tate, 2002.

Potter, Lois. *The Life of William Shakespeare: A Critical Biography*. Hoboken, NJ: John Wiley and Sons, 2012.

Pratt, Jamie. "'To Enliven Morality with Wit': *The Spectator*." *History Magazine*, Oct. 2001. www.history-magazine.com.

Prichard, James Cowles. *The Eastern Origin of the Celtic Nations Proved by a Comparison of Their Dialects with the Sanskrit, Greek, Latin and Teutonic Languages: Forming a Supplement to "Researches into the Physical History of Mankind."* 1857.

———. *Researches into the Physical History of Mankind: History of the European Nations*. 3d ed. London: Sherwood, Gilbert, and Piper, 1841.

Prince, Michael B. "The Eighteenth-Century Beauty Contest." *Modern Language Quarterly* 55, no. 3 (1994): 251–80.

Putnam, Ruth. *William the Silent, Prince of Orange: The Moderate Man of the Sixteenth Century; The Story of His Life as Told from His Own Letters, from Those of His Friends and Enemies and from Official Documents*. New York: Putnam, 1895.

Qureshi, Sadiah. "Displaying Sara Baartman, the 'Hottentot Venus.'" *History of Science* 42, no. 2 (2004): 233–57.

Radden, Jennifer. *The Nature of Melancholy: From Aristotle to Kristeva*. Oxford: Oxford University Press, 2002.

Ranchod-Nilsson, Sita, and Mary Ann Tétreault. *Women, States, and Nationalism: At Home in the Nation?* New York: Psychology Press, 2000.

Reilly, Kevin, Stephen Kaufman, and Angela Bodino, eds. *Racism: A Global Reader*. North Castle, NY: M. E. Sharpe, 2003.

Rivard, Christopher, Jeffrey Thomas, Miguel A. Lanaspa, and Richard J. Johnson. "Sack and Sugar, and the Aetiology of Gout in England between 1650 and 1900." *Rheumatology* 52, no. 3 (March 1, 2013): 421–26.

Roberts, Dorothy E. *Killing the Black Body: Race, Reproduction, and the Meaning of Liberty*. New York: Pantheon, 1997.

Roediger, David R. *The Wages of Whiteness: Race and the Making of the American Working Class*. Rev. ed. London: Verso, 2007.

Roger, Jacques. *Buffon: A Life in Natural History*. Ithaca: Cornell University Press, 1997.

Rosenthal, Lisa. *Gender, Politics, and Allegory in the Art of Rubens*. Cambridge: Cambridge University Press, 2005.

Rothblum, Esther, and Sondra Solovay, eds. *The Fat Studies Reader*. New York: New York University Press, 2009.

Rousseau, George Sebastian, and Roy Porter. *Exoticism in the Enlightenment*. Manchester, UK: Manchester University Press, 1990.

Royal Society Library. *Catalogue of the Scientific Books in the Library of the Royal Society*. R. and J. E. Taylor, 1839.

Rubens, Pierre-Paul. *Théorie de la figure humaine, considérée dans ses principes, soit en repos ou en mouvement*. Paris, 1773.

Rubies, Joan-Pau. "Race, Climate and Civilization in the Works of François Bernier." *Purusārtha* 31 (2013): 53–78.

Saguy, Abigail. *What's Wrong with Fat?* New York: Oxford University Press, 2013.

Sangster, Margaret Elizabeth Munson. *From My Youth Up: Personal Reminiscences; An Autobiography*. Chicago: Fleming H. Revell, 1909.

Sartwell, Crispin. "Beauty." In *The Stanford Encyclopedia of Philosophy*, edited by Edward N. Zalta. Spring 2014. http://plato.stanford.edu.

Scanlon, Jennifer, and Shaaron Cosner. *American Women Historians, 1700s–1990s: A Biographical Dictionary*. Santa Barbara, CA: Greenwood, 1996.

Schreuder, Esther, and Elmer Kolfin. *Black Is Beautiful: Rubens to Dumas*. Zwolle, Holland: Waanders, 2008.

Schwartz, Hillel. *Never Satisfied: A Cultural History of Diets, Fantasies, and Fat*. New York: Free Press, 1986.

Schwarz, Richard W. *John Harvey Kellogg, M.D.: Pioneering Health Reformer*. Hagerstown, MD: Review and Herald Publishing, 2006.

Seid, Roberta Pollack. *Never Too Thin: Why Women Are at War with Their Bodies*. New York: Prentice Hall, 1989.

Shaftesbury, 7th Earl of (Anthony Ashley Cooper). *Characteristics of Men, Manners, Opinions, Times*, 1790.

———. *Shaftesbury: Characteristics of Men, Manners, Opinions, Times*. Edited by Lawrence E. Klein. Cambridge: Cambridge University Press, 1999.

Shakespeare, William. *Julius Caesar*. London: Methuen, 1902.

———. *A Midsummer Night's Dream*. 1590. www.shakespeare-navigators.com.

Shapin, Steven. *The Scientific Revolution*. Chicago: University of Chicago Press, 1998.

Sharp, Gwen. "Fascinating Database about the Trans-Atlantic Slave Trade." *Sociological Images* (blog), Jan. 7, 2011. http://thesocietypages.org.

Shaw, Andrea Elizabeth. *The Embodiment of Disobedience: Fat Black Women's Unruly Political Bodies*. Lanham, MD: Lexington Books, 2006.

Shilling, Chris, "Educating the Body: Physical Capital and the Production of Social Inequalities." *Sociology* 25, no. 4 (1991): 653–72.

Silverblatt, Irene. *Modern Inquisitions: Peru and the Colonial Origins of the Civilized World*. Durham: Duke University Press, 2004.

Sloan, Phillip R. "The Buffon-Linnaeus Controversy." *Isis* 67, no. 3 (Sept. 1, 1976): 356–75.

Smedley, Audrey. *Race in North America: Origin and Evolution of a Worldview*. Boulder: Westview, 1993.

Smith, Ian. *Race and Rhetoric in the Renaissance: Barbarian Errors*. New York: Springer, 2009.

Smith, Samuel Stanhope. *An Essay on the Causes of the Variety of Complexion and Figure in the Human Species.* J. Simpson and Company, 1810.

Sparrman, Anders. "Account of the Hottentots." In *The New Annual Register, or General Repository of History, Politics, and Literature for the Year,* edited by Andrew Kippis. G. G. J. and J. Robinson, 1786.

Spelman, Elizabeth. "Woman as Body." *Feminist Studies* 8, no. 1 (1982): 109–31.

Spicer, Joaneath, ed. *Revealing the African Presence in Renaissance Europe.* Baltimore: Walters Art Museum, 2012.

Starr, Paul. *The Social Transformation of American Medicine: The Rise of a Sovereign Profession and the Making of a Vast Industry.* New York: Basic Books, 1982.

Stearns, Peter N. *Fat History: Bodies and Beauty in the Modern West.* New York: New York University Press, 1997.

Steele, Richard, and Joseph Addison, eds. *The Spectator,* vol. 1, 1711. www.gutenberg.org.

Stern, Alexandra. *Eugenic Nation: Faults and Frontiers of Better Breeding in Modern America.* Berkeley: University of California Press, 2005.

Stoler, Ann Laura. *Carnal Knowledge and Imperial Power: Race and the Intimate in Colonial Rule.* Berkeley: University of California Press, 2002.

———. *Race and the Education of Desire: Foucault's History of Sexuality and the Colonial Order of Things.* Durham: Duke University Press, 1995.

Strings, Sabrina. "Obese Black Women as 'Social Dead Weight': Reinventing the 'Diseased Black Woman.'" *Signs: Journal of Women in Culture and Society* 41, no. 1 (2015): 107–30.

Stuart, Tristram. *The Bloodless Revolution: A Cultural History of Vegetarianism from 1600 to Modern Times.* New York: Norton, 2006.

Stuurman, Siep. "François Bernier and the Invention of Racial Classification." *History Workshop Journal,* no. 50 (Oct. 1, 2000): 1–21.

Sydenham, Thomas, and George Wallis. *A Treatise of the Gout and Dropsy.* Philadelphia: Library of the College of Physicians of Philadelphia, 1788.

Tara, Sylvia. *The Secret Life of Fat: The Science behind the Body's Least Understood Organ and What It Means for You.* New York: Norton, 2016.

Thomas, Stephen B., Georges C. Benjamin, Donna Almario, and Monica J. Lathan. "Historical and Current Policy Efforts to Eliminate Racial and Ethnic Health Disparities in the United States: Future Opportunities for Public Health Education Research." *Health Promotion Practice* 7, no. 3 (2006): 324–30.

Tinagli, Paola. *Women in Italian Renaissance Art: Gender, Representation and Identity.* Manchester, UK: Manchester University Press, 1997.

Tompkins, Kyla Wazana. *Racial Indigestion: Eating Bodies in the 19th Century.* New York: New York University Press, 2012.

Treon, Frederick. "Medical Work among the Sioux Indians." *Journal of the American Medical Association* 10 (Feb. 25, 1888).

Tytler, Sarah. *The Countess of Huntingdon and Her Circle.* Sir I. Pitman and Sons, 1907.

U.S. Department of Health and Human Services, Office of Minority Health. "Obesity and African Americans." 2012. https://minorityhealth.hhs.gov.

Virey, Julien Joseph. *Histoire naturelle du genre humain*. Crochard, 1824.

———. *Natural History of the Negro Race*. D. J. Dowling, 1837.

Voogd, Peter Jan de. *Henry Fielding and William Hogarth: The Correspondences of the Arts*. Rodopi, 1981.

Vries, Jan de, and Ad van der Woude. *The First Modern Economy: Success, Failure, and Perseverance of the Dutch Economy, 1500–1815*. Cambridge: Cambridge University Press, 1997.

Wacquant, Loïc J. D. *Body and Soul: Notebooks of an Apprentice Boxer*. Oxford: Oxford University Press, 2004.

Wagner, Dale R., and Vivian H. Heyward. "Measures of Body Composition in Blacks and Whites: A Comparative Review." *American Journal of Clinical Nutrition* 71, no. 6 (June 1, 2000): 1392–1402.

Walpole, Horace. *The Letters of Horace Walpole*. Edited by J. Wright. 1840.

Warnke, Martin. *Peter Paul Rubens: Life and Work*. Hauppauge, NY: Barron's Educational Series, 1980.

Wedgwood, Cicely Veronica. *William the Silent: William of Nassau, Prince of Orange, 1533–1584*. Whitefish, MT: Literary Licensing, 2011.

White, Deborah Gray. *Too Heavy a Load: Black Women in Defense of Themselves, 1894–1994*. New York: Norton, 1999.

White, Ellen Gould Harmon. *The Southern Work*. Hagerstown, MD: Review and Herald Publishing, 1966.

Whorton, James C. *Crusaders for Fitness: The History of American Health Reformers*. Princeton: Princeton University Press, 1982.

Wiesner, Merry E. "Beyond Women and the Family: Towards a Gender Analysis of the Reformation." *Sixteenth Century Journal* 18, no. 3 (1987): 311–21. doi.org/10.2307/2540718.

Wild, Wayne. *Medicine-by-Post: The Changing Voice of Illness in Eighteenth-Century British Consultation Letters and Literature*. Amsterdam: Rodopi, 2006.

Willis, Deborah, ed. *Black Venus, 2010: They Called Her "Hottentot."* Philadelphia: Temple University Press, 2010.

Wilson, Brian C. *Dr. John Harvey Kellogg and the Religion of Biologic Living*. Bloomington: Indiana University Press, 2014.

Wolf, Naomi. *The Beauty Myth: How Images of Beauty Are Used against Women*. New York: William Morrow, 1991.

Wood, Christopher S. "Eine Nachricht von Raffael." In *Konturen im Fluss: Beiträge zur Geschichte der Zeichnung und des Diagramms*, edited by Friedrich Teja Bach and Wolfram Pichler. Munich: Fink, 2009.

INDEX

Note: Page numbers in italics indicate figures.

ABC News, "Is Being Overweight Really Bad for You?," 209
abolitionism, 175, 211
abstemiousness, 10, 61, 63
Académie Julian, 160
Actaeon, 34
Act of Uniformity, 114
actuarial tables, 11, 188, 192, 193, 195, 196–97, 199–200
Addison, Joseph, 108, 230n39
Admiralty Court of France, 94
Adult Weight Conference, 187, 189
aesthetics, 2, 4–5, 6, 9; African physique and, 19–21; Christianity and, 9; classical, 25; English philosophers and, 107–8; Enlightenment, 107–8; fat phobia and, 8; Flemish, 112; ideality and, 19; morality and, 107–8; neoclassical, 9; normativity and, 19; northern European seventeenth-century, 42–64; "obesity epidemic" and, 11; proportionality and, 16, 17, 21–24, 29, 30–32; Renaissance, 15–41; skin color and, 50–52; slave trade and, 16–18; of slenderness, 10; "standards of taste" and, 99–100; of voluptuousness, 9; whiteness and, 9, 220n27. *See also* art; ascetic aesthetic; beauty
Africa: in Diderot's *Encyclopédie*, 80–83; fatness in, 134. *See also specific countries*
African Americans, 200–201, 206; beauty contests for, 211; BMI and, 206; dearth of articles in *JAMA* on, 196; medicine and, 242n36; obesity and, 205–7, 208; public health and, 242n36. *See also* black people
African American women, 206; beauty contests for, 211; BMI and, 206; obesity and, 205–7, 208. *See also* black women
African heritage, southern Italian immigrants and, 195–96
"Africanity," weight and, 4–5
African physique, 19; aesthetics and, 19–21; Dürer on, 15
Africans, 29–30, 77, 85, 130–31; ascetic aesthetic and, 100; beauty and, 15–17, 112–13, 142, 143; body size and, 82–83; depicted as lazy and fat, 225–26n59; in Diderot's *Encyclopédie*, 80–83; in England, 42, 53; English view of, 221n42; exploitation of, 89–93, 98; facial features of, 17, 19–21, 36, 39–40; fashion and, 176; in France, 80; in Italian Renaissance art, 15–41; in Italy, 44; Kellogg's belief in eventual extinction of, 179–80, 182; in Low Countries, 42, 49–50; plumpness of, 77; portrayed as gluttonous, 81–83, 221n42; projected extinction of, 179–80, 182; purported inferiority of, 19; "savagery" of, 4, 5; as servants in Italy, 33–37, 35; as servants or slaves of Sephardic Jews, 54; in seventeenth-century northern European art, 46; shifting European views on, 51; stature and, 77, 83–84;

Sabrina Strings is Assistant Professor of Sociology at the University of California, Irvine. Her research examines how race, sex(uality), and class are inscribed on the body, such that the body itself can be marshaled to maintain social hierarchies. Strings is an award-winning author whose articles and essays are featured in venues including *Signs: Journal of Women in Culture and Society*, *Feminist Media Studies*, *Truthout*, and the *Feminist Wire*. A California native, Strings is also a 200-hour certified yoga teacher. Strings teaches donation-based yoga in community centers and community clinics. She has co-organized workshops and participated in conferences on yoga throughout the United States. This is her first book.